Date Due			

THE ORIGINAL

HAS THIS

SIGNATURE—

W. K. Kellogg

The Original Has This Signature—

K. Kellogg

BY Horace B. Powell

PRENTICE-HALL, INC. · ENGLEWOOD CLIFFS, N. J.

Contents

Foreword

NEARLY FIVE YEARS have elapsed since W. K. Kellogg died on October 6, 1951, in his ninety-first year. However, his famous signature continues familiar in the stores and homes of America and, because of his philanthropy, many people to whom he personally was only a name have had occasion to be grateful that he lived.

The achievement of material success by native intelligence, initiative and industry is a recurring theme in American history. But Mr. Kellogg was not content with building a world-wide company. He devoted the last decades of his life to a reinvestment of his fortune in the advancement of human welfare.

During the years since the death of W. K. Kellogg, there have been many suggestions for a biography of this industrialist-philanthropist who won a place of distinction among men. In February of this year, the Kellogg Company observed the fiftieth anniversary of its founding, and June will complete the W. K. Kellogg Foundation's twenty-fifth year as the vehicle for its founder's investment in people. As these milestones are reached, it appears appropriate to bring to the public the life-story of a man whose achievements do not lie buried in the past but "live on not only in the institutions which he helped to create but also in the countless men and women, boys and girls, whose lives are enhanced by his realized dream of helping others to help themselves."

A Man Who Lived Three Lives

ONLY IN A few instances is it true that "Life Begins at Forty." For most people the forties are the time when momentum begins to slow, when enthusiasms fade, when dreams are tossed one by one into the ashbin. But for a middle-aged bookkeeper of a health sanitarium in Michigan, the forties were not flagging years but the beginning of a "second life"— a quarter century in which, against all odds, he built a worldwide cereal industry and amassed one of the great fortunes of the twentieth century.

Even more amazing is the fact that this same man, when seventy, started a "third life." It was in this twenty-one year span that he reinvested his fortune in a philanthropic foundation designed to help people to help themselves.

But properly to describe the enigmatic, tradition-breaking W. K. Kellogg, much more needs to be told. So—

—this is the story of the Seventh-day Adventists whose ideas on health reform made Battle Creek the cereal food capital of the world. . . . It is the story of a naturally conservative man who was impelled to gamble his savings and credit in a highly competitive field. . . . It tells of his far-reaching decisions made instantly, instinctively, and yet with uncanny foresight. . . . It portrays a manufacturer who would play no role but "King of Corn Flakes," but who was humble in arenas outside of business. . . . It reveals that his "cold," impassive face was actually a mask to cover innate shyness. . . . It shows as deeply religious a man who seldom went to church. . . . And as the story of a rugged individualist, it also is a story of an age of personal initiative and free enterprise flowering to a great American period of creativeness and growth.

CHAPTER 1

"A Long Line of Stubborn Ancestors"

Frost had its teeth firmly fastened in the ground. One step into the weather and many of Battle Creek's six thousand citizens turned back into their homes to linger near glowing, pot-bellied stoves. But not young Will Kellogg! This was a very special day, cold spell or no.

As he hurried toward his father's broom factory, his impassive face showed no emotion. Deep down, however, the fourteen-year-old was warmed by a feeling of pride. Up to now he had merely held a job, that of apprentice broommaker. But on this wintry day of the year 1874 he had achieved a *position* —no less than that of salesman for J. P. Kellogg & Son!

As if in token of the lad's new eminence, the hostler in the stable adjoining the small factory had a sleigh ready for him. Hitched to it was a plug-horse which patiently occupied the time stomping its feet and breathing clouds of vapor toward the murky sky. Affectionately slapping the horse on a flank, the new salesman rushed into the factory. Soon he emerged with an armful of brooms and several armfuls later he had filled the

Will Kellogg at Age Fourteen.
From a tintype of 1874.

sleigh with kitchen and parlor brooms, the latter "the best and selling at $4 a dozen."

"Now if the merchants at Bellevue and the other villages will just buy," he muttered, "this will be a big day for me."

Certainly it proved an eventful day. Farm sleighs had broken through the heavy snow and their tracks marked the right-of-way leading toward Bellevue. However, his one-horse rig was not properly adjusted so that the horse could follow the course of one of a double team of horses while the sleigh runners would groove into the paths made by the two-horse sleds. Suddenly the cutter turned over. The cargo of brooms was pitched into the snow and the skinny, short-statured boy was confronted not only with a problem but also with some hard work. His gray eyes were serious and his brown hair wet with snow and perspiration as he righted the sleigh and reloaded the damp brooms. A few miles farther on the same thing happened again and it took quite a while to get things back into shape. A furlong or two and for the third time the brooms, the boy and the horse upset into a snowbank.

[2]

His Seventh-day Adventist rearing precluded profanity. Instead Will scratched his head ruefully, gazed at the chaos and then at the sky as if in beseeching prayer. Gritting his teeth, he upraised and reloaded the vehicle for yet another attempt at his destination.

"My pride wouldn't let me quit," he later recounted, "and, fortunately, my luck changed. The horse plugged along at the road center, the runners stayed in the grooves and I arrived safely at Bellevue."

And the business day recompensed the budding salesman for his earlier misadventures, for he not only sold his cargo but he also collected from one storekeeper an overdue account which his father had regarded as uncollectable.

Thus Will Kellogg displayed early the tenacity and the courage that were to stand him in good stead during catastrophes to come—those times when he stood in the embers of his year-old corn flakes factory, when he fought the Depression of the 1930s with a bold instruction to his staff, "Double our advertising," and the years when the lights went out for him one by one and with never a whimper he faced blindness forever.

2.

How and why did this nineteenth century youngster, after a latent period lasting to his middle age, amass one of the larger fortunes of his era and then concentrate on "aid to mankind, especially children"? Did his honesty, his urge for action, his ultimate practicality come from the Spartan environment of a Middlewestern town or from the credo of a conservative religious sect? Or did these traits stem from his Yankee ancestors and their forebears, the Puritans from England?

The chances are that the exceedingly modest W. K. Kellogg would never have discussed whether heredity or environment was responsible for his success. A faint smile did come to his serious countenance, however, when he recalled a witticism at his own expense. Always disposed toward the management of the affairs of relatives and friends, he had attempted to influence his granddaughter, Elizabeth Ann, to a certain course of action. When Elizabeth Ann adamantly refused his counsel, he wrote three letters to her mother (his daughter Beth, Mrs. Norman Williamson) explaining that the girl was being "stubborn." Mrs. Williamson had not wished to be caught in the crossfire but, forced to reply to his last letter, she wrote: "Well, after all, Elizabeth Ann gets her stubbornness honestly. It comes from a long line of stubborn ancestors." The grandfather saw the point and chuckled: "Do you suppose she could mean me?"

The long line of Kellogg ancestors can be traced back to the fifteenth century with public records showing a Nicholas Kellogg who lived from 1488 to 1558 in Debden, England, about forty miles north of London. Actually the name "Kellogg," not only in its present spelling, but also in many variant forms, can be found in English records dating back to the Middle Ages although the origin of the surname is lost in the mists of English and Scottish antiquity.

Because these names were first found in English towns settled by the Saxons, it is possible that the name derives from the German word *keilhau,* meaning "a miner's pickaxe." An old family tradition holds that the family originated in Scotland, and that the name was a combination of two Scottish words, *kill,* meaning cemetery and *loch,* meaning lake—"the family which had a cemetery on a lake."

W. K. Kellogg, however, always preferred the opinion of Dr. Emil G. Back of Chicago who said that the name Kellogg is derived from the Norse—"Kell" from *kelda,* a spring, and "log" from a word meaning brook. Hence the name would mean "a spring brook." By letter Mr. Kellogg advised his son J. L. of this version, commenting:

"This is really quite a romantic name, and as I wrote Dr. Karl (another son) this morning, this meaning is certainly more attractive than that given some years ago of 'Kill Hog'."

[4]

It seems probable that a Phillippe Kellogg, who lived in the village of Great Leighs, north of London, in the latter half of the sixteenth century, was a grandson of Nicholas Kellogg. From him a line of direct descent can be traced to the Kellogg family of Battle Creek, Michigan. One of Phillippe's sons was Martin Kellogg, a weaver who lived from 1595 to 1671. Martin's son Joseph, born in 1626, was the first of the family to migrate to the new colonies in the wilderness of North America. (Genealogies prepared for one branch of the Kellogg family purport to show that the lineage extends all the way back to William the Conqueror who stubbornly devoted fifteen years to the conquest of England.)

A century and a quarter before the American Revolution, Joseph lived for a few years in Farmington, Connecticut, and eventually came to reside at Hadley, Massachusetts. There he operated a ferry across the Connecticut River between Hadley and Northampton, served as town selectman for many years, and was a member, and later lieutenant, of a militia company. The militiamen sought to protect their lovely Connecticut Valley and its towns from raids by Indians who executed a massacre here, a scalping party there, and a kidnapping and looting operation both here and there.

For three generations members of the Kellogg family continued to operate the ferry. During this period a feminine member of the clan ran afoul of a puritanical taboo. Apparently intended to preclude the "keeping up with the Joneses," still prevalent in most places today, the regulation provided that people of limited financial means could not purchase and adorn themselves with expensive fabrics and ornaments. Violation meant prosecution and in 1665 officers from the Springfield Court took twenty-five valley women into custody.

Among these women was Mrs. Joseph Kellogg, who refused to plead guilty to a charge of dressing too smartly and wearing pretty colors and rich fabrics when it was suspected she could not qualify as to assets. Her attorney conceded her love of

[5]

fabrics (many years later W. K. Kellogg confessed to a predilection for clothing well-woven and tailored) but pleaded that in her dress she simply was living up to her station as the wife of a man with an annual income of two hundred pounds. The case was dismissed.

By this time, the Indian ravages of the valley had been stopped by the colonists and the Kellogg family seemed to be settling down to a permanent Yankee routine. Aside from the continued ferrying, some of the menfolk explored the source of the Connecticut River up Vermont way. Others took a look at eastern Canada. The Revolutionary War and its reconstruction period brought no particular tales of Kellogg valor although the war, as you well might suspect, did boom the sale of tobacco.

Tobacco, the commodity later and often referred to as "that vile weed" by W. K. Kellogg, soon superseded broomcorn as the staple product of the valley. Thus it was agricultural and economic change in the far-off New England of the 1830s that made Michigan, a lush green state with much soil untouched by plows, the twentieth-century backdrop for Kellogg family food experiments which literally changed the eating habits of much of the world. A Hadley broomcorn grower and close friend of the Kelloggs, Lansing Dickinson, decided to "Go West" and settle. Five other valley farmers soon joined him to establish "Dickinson's Settlement" near present-day Flint, Michigan. Word sent back about this "new land of opportunity" found willing ears insofar as John Preston Kellogg was concerned.

As if with some premonition of the fact that he eventually would have sixteen children to feed, he was discouraged by the impoverished soil of New England. Eagerly he listened to the lyrics of a current song which tantalizingly related that:

> "With little prudence any man
> Can soon get rich in Mich-i-gan."

Government agents, by the few promotional media of that

day, told of abundant lumber, minerals and fertile soil at $1.25 per acre. They grew lyrical about the pretty girls (no mention was made of the huge imbalance of males on the western frontier), the fishing, hunting, and the great forests.

Thus was fired the imagination of the man who was to be the father of W. K. Kellogg, John Harvey Kellogg, and twelve other children born in Michigan. In July of 1834, John Preston Kellogg gathered his little family, then consisting of his wife and two sons, and started West.

3.

The older of the two children (Merritt was a small child and his brother Smith Moses but a baby) later recounted the highlights of that rigorous journey in a privately published book, *Notes Concerning the Kelloggs:*

"I well remember how we traveled—first by horses and wagon to Albany, then by horse-drawn canal boat to Buffalo, and then by steam boat to Detroit. On the boats we had our own beds and my mother cooked for us."

The opening of the Erie Canal in 1825 and the daily lake boats between Buffalo and Detroit, made it possible for would-be settlers from New England and New York to get to Michigan, which in that day was a wilderness scarcely broached. Detroit was still little more than a fur trading post with a population of somewhat more than five thousand persons. By 1836 the state had been surveyed only as far north as Grand Rapids and, two years previous to this Tiffin survey, Michigan was very largely in the hands of the Indians who had a settlement at Saginaw and roamed afar in hunting expeditions. "The few white homesteaders were strung out along the eastern and southern borders of the lower peninsula."

But the members of the little pioneer family were undaunted by "a road walled on each side by high, dark woods." Their sole possessions in a wagon drawn by a pair of horses purchased in Detroit, they rode and walked down a wagon trail

A Painting of Early-Day Michigan.

Scenes as in this painting met the eyes of John Preston Kellogg when he brought his family from Massachusetts to Michigan in 1834.

toward Dickinson's Settlement, sixty miles to the northwest. The black soil must have looked good to the eyes of farmer John Preston Kellogg; in every direction he could see an almost unlimited supply of oak, hickory, ash and maple trees, many from three to five feet in diameter. Even more in evidence was the "inexhaustible supply" of white pine found along every trail and playing the leading part in getting early settlers out of shanties and into substantial log homes.

At the settlement came a joyous reunion with old friends from Hadley, Massachusetts, who were now comparative veterans of the wilderness. In the entire region around the tiny village of Flint were only fourteen white families, so that the newly arrived family was given a particular welcome. Among helpful suggestions as to the best tracts of land, John Preston Kellogg was offered, for $2,000, eighty acres where the business section of Flint now stands! "But there was no prospect of that mere hamlet ever becoming a thriving city" and John Preston, never too astute a farmer or businessman, decided to go two miles farther from the hamlet where he could get 320 acres of land "equally as good" for the sum of $400.

Even in this new country of fertile soil, the Kelloggs knew their life and destiny were to be hard. It took heroic hearts to endure the loneliness of this and other American frontiers. For neighbors, John Preston and Mrs. Kellogg (the former Mary Ann Call was far from her native Springfield, Massachusetts) had a handful of white settlers and many Chippewa Indians who insisted on camping in their tepees on the Kellogg property. The family temporarily lived in a rude shanty until there could be constructed an 18 by 24 foot log cabin, with parlor, sitting room, and dining room-kitchen below and two small bedrooms above.

"We had no cookstove or even an oven in which to bake," related the elder son, Merritt Kellogg. "A large open fireplace was the only means of cooking we had. Deer were plentiful as were wolves, foxes and other wild animals and these caused the settlers no little trouble. All the older children of the family grew up amid pioneer surroundings and were well acquainted with the hardships of frontier life. . . . I remember when the Indians attempted to steal wheat from the harvested sheaves, the fright mother had concerning the apparent loss of our food, and the method by which father drove the Indians away with a big stick. . . . Our food consisted chiefly of white corn, rye, barley, turnips, beans and potatoes, and provisions were sometimes short."

Further reminiscences of Merritt G. Kellogg relate that "Home-making on a frontier farm was a real business. Modern conveniences were wholly lacking and the work included many activities that are now conducted in factories. Weaving, dyeing, tailoring, dressmaking, even the tanning of skins into leather, shoemaking and harnessmaking were ordinary household operations which farmers' wives had to conduct or assist

in doing, in addition to buttermaking, cheesemaking, candle-
making, matchmaking, and a hundred other activities in which
self-dependent settlers had to engage."

Merritt recalls that two years after the arrival of the Kelloggs
his father attended a Baptist revival meeting in the growing
town of Flint and was baptized in the Flint River. Thereafter
family worship was held each day before a home altar. "Father
was ever an earnest Christian," Merritt Kellogg wrote. ". . . I
never knew of his telling an obscene story or using unbecom-
ing language. I never saw him angry or knew him to call any
of the children reproachful names."

John Preston Kellogg was ordinarily a thrifty and cautious
man but in 1837 he was lured into a get-rich-quick investment
that was to plague him for years. Urged by two neighbors and
against his own better judgment, John Preston gave his note
for $500 and signed as surety on the notes of the two neighbors
to aid in the establishment of the Bank of Genesee. The bank
collapsed within a year and the liability on the notes, provid-
ing 10 per cent interest, followed him like a horrible specter
for more than a decade.

This farmer-"banker" was to find that "Troubles come not
as single spies, but in battalions." He traded his 320-acre farm
for one of 160 acres, with some cash to boot. The cash went
to pay the mounting interest on the notes. Worry and her-
culean labor seriously impaired his health. Then his wife's
health began to fail!

Largely because of primitive living conditions, Mrs. Kellogg
had developed tuberculosis. Naturally, on the frontier there
was a scarcity of medical practitioners and those few relatively
unsuccessful physicians who ventured to the new West had
obvious shortcomings. The doctor summoned for the tuberculosis victim prescribed a treatment consisting of bleeding and
also the inhalation of resin fumes created by scattering the
substance upon a shovel of live coals. The family had no

choice but to look on sorrowfully as the ravages of the disease and the inadequacy of medical care led to the inevitable end.

(Previously a frontier physician with little or no formal training had applied a patch of sole leather to "draw out the soreness" from John Preston Kellogg's foot, severely cut in a tree-chopping accident. Another "doctor" subsequently treated this farmer for an inflammation of the eyes by putting a fly blister on the back of his neck! It was not strange, therefore, that two of the Kellogg sons sought later to master the skills of medical science through the *most thorough* preparation then available to them. Nor is it surprising that the Foundation created many years later by W. K. Kellogg has had a long-held interest in supporting many phases of medical education to implement the desires of the profession and the people for high quality medical care.)

Prior to her illness, Mrs. Kellogg had become acquainted with the daughter of a blacksmith who had brought his family from Geneseo, New York, to the frontier village of Threadville. This daughter, Ann Janette Stanley, was occasionally persuaded to come to the Kellogg farm to help during peak periods of farmwoman work. After the birth of the family's fifth child, Ann spent four months taking care of the household. Consequently, when Mrs. Kellogg suffered a severe hemorrhage in September of 1841, her first words to her husband were "Go to Ann Stanley, I want her and no one else." But Ann was twenty miles away, teaching school in a log schoolhouse, and could not be persuaded to relinquish that post. Feeling that she had only a few days to live, Mrs. Kellogg emphasized to her husband that Ann was the one person to care for the children when they became motherless. Mrs. Kellogg died September 27.

Although there were now thirty-six families living within a four-mile radius, in none of these was there a woman who could serve as foster mother to the five small Kelloggs. In October, Mr. Kellogg went to Threadville and again tried to hire Ann Stanley, but she again refused. With ten-year-old Merritt struggling through the housework and with the temporary assistance of the sixteen-year-old daughter of a neighboring farmer, the family somehow lasted the winter.

When the hired girl left in March, "Father seemed almost distracted for a day or so," Merritt Kellogg recalls, "but in a few days he saddled the horse and, after telling me to take good care of the baby and to be careful of the fire, he rode away and did not return until night drew on.

"A week later he did the same thing again. When he came back, he seemed much more cheerful. The next day or two were spent in cleaning up the house and fixing things in proper shape. A few days later, March 29, 1842, Father hitched up his team and drove away, saying 'I expect to bring someone home with me when I return. . . .' That night Smith Kellogg ran to the window and exclaimed, 'Father has come and he has a woman in the wagon with him.'

"The woman was Ann Janette, who that day had changed her last name from Stanley to Kellogg. After kissing the five children, she turned to the eldest, and said, 'Merritt, if you will build a fire, I will get some supper.'"

4.

A truly remarkable woman had become a member of the Kellogg family. Ann Janette Kellogg was generous, hard-working, self-sacrificing and uncomplaining. As the second wife of John Preston Kellogg, she early demonstrated her tremendous drive and efficiency. She became the motivation behind the more phlegmatic husband and many of the ideas which subsequently made him a comparatively prosperous farmer were her ideas. The day after her arrival at the farm, she told her husband that she was disappointed to find no sheep and no clover hay.

"From wool I could spin our own stocking yarn, and clover

is much better than marsh hay which barely gets stock through a winter."

Demurring at first, John Preston eventually took her advice as he was thereafter quite wont to do. Sheep and clover were added to the farm. Through the spinning wheel of a neighbor and the later purchase of a loom, Mrs. Kellogg had woolen cloth to make warm clothing for all the children. Within a few years, John Preston was able to sell his clover seed for $5 a bushel and, by plowing under some of his clover fields, he raised forty bushels of wheat to the acre where only ten bushels had been produced before. Merritt Kellogg recalled that "She wove our cloth every year for three years until the sheep and the clover paid the last cent of father's indebtedness, built a large addition to the house and paid for a two-seated light spring wagon."

One day while John Preston was away an Indian came to the farmhouse and demanded food. Ann Janette refused to let him in. He raised his tomahawk and threatened her, but not one inch did she retreat. "Brave squaw!" the Indian exclaimed and went away.

In December, 1842, John Preston Kellogg traded his farm for a 160-acre farm in Tyrone Township of Livingston County and the family moved there immediately, driving their sheep twenty-two miles over the snowpacked roads. Here they became community leaders, helping to establish a Congregational Church (John Preston served as its lay preacher and later was ordained) at nearby Hartland Center as well as the schoolhouse attended by their older children, Merritt, Smith and Albert.

Largely as a result of Ann's management, the Kelloggs now had four or five harvests every year: clover seed in February and March; wool and mutton sheep in July; wheat in autumn; and ten to twenty fat porkers in December. Once hard times were apparently over, Ann Janette gave up weaving and made a gift of her loom to a poor widow who had several children to support. When she learned that "Mr. Conklin's children are crying for milk" and her husband was unable to persuade his fellow churchmen to contribute toward a cow for the impoverished family, she persuaded John Preston to give one of his two cows so that "the children need not cry for milk!" Another instance of generosity on the part of the couple was the money given a neighbor, a Mr. Church, to forestall a sheriff's judgment and attachment on his farm. The $250 lent at a low rate of interest was never paid, for when the man told them he could pay neither principal nor interest the whole debt was forgiven.

These acts were but a few of the many instances of generosity on the part of John Preston and Ann Janette Kellogg. Their thought for others, if not an inheritable characteristic, was at least a precedent which, much later, must have influenced a philanthropic son in "the great and basic principle of his life: to help those who were eager to help themselves."

The couple's kindliness extended not only to their neighbors but also to fugitive slaves from the South. John Preston Kellogg became disgusted with William Henry Harrison's "hard cider" type of electioneering in 1840 and forsook the Whig Party to become an Abolitionist. After the passage of the Fugitive Slave Act in 1850, he became an agent on the underground railway and many a Negro slave was put up overnight in the Kellogg cabin while furtively escaping to Canada.

There was no more than the usual family excitement in 1852 when the fifth child was born to Ann Janette (actually John Preston's tenth child since he had five from his first marriage). There was no way for them to know that this child, John Harvey Kellogg, would some day be an eminent physician and surgeon whose program of "Biologic Living" and an "Aristocracy of Health" would circle the globe. However, even in early boyhood, this lad exhibited energy, inventiveness, and great self-confidence. These traits were later to characterize the famous Dr. John Harvey Kellogg who essayed to shepherd the

health of the nation with the calm assurance that he knew just
how everyone should eat and live.

5.

As a series of ever-widening rings spreads from a stone cast
into a still pond, so did a tragedy besetting the Kellogg family
eventually affect the medical and food theories of a nation.
The sad happening created a family interest in the medical
system of a religious sect. The family conversion to the new
faith eventually led John Harvey Kellogg to change the Adventist Western Health Reform Institute into the famous Battle
Creek Sanitarium. The sanitarium experiments with hydrotherapy and health foods had their effect on medicine, with the
food innovations proving the genesis of today's modern breakfast foods.

In late summer of 1849, the couple's two-year-old baby,
Emma Frances, became ill. Mrs. Kellogg was convinced the
child had an inflammation of the lungs but a physician from
Hartland Center insisted upon treating the baby for worms and
she died. A post-mortem examination revealed that Mrs. Kellogg's diagnosis had been correct.

The previously related and disillusioning contacts of the
Kelloggs with frontier doctors, and now the loss of their baby,
generated within the family a bitter disgust over the lack of
available medical skill. This made for their ready interest in a
water cure system advocated by a new religious sect, the Seventh-day Adventists. They subscribed to the *Water Cure Journal* for two years, but had no occasion to put the cure into
practice until Albert contracted measles. Subsequent treatment
of Albert by a Parshallville physician was ineffective, and when
all the Kellogg children except Merritt came down with the
disease, the resolute Ann Janette took matters in her own hands.

As Merritt Kellogg tells it, "Mother kept them warm in bed
until it was about time for the measles to come out. Then they
were put into cold wet-sheet packs, and kept there as long as

they felt comfortable. They were then taken out, and in every case the measles came out beautifully. The children were then put into bed, kept warm and with plenty of fresh air, and recovered rapidly with no after trouble."

Already a believer in Adventist hydrotherapy, John Preston Kellogg was preconditioned to the teachings of the Seventh-day Adventist movement which had spread to Michigan since its New England origin in 1818. James and Ellen White ("Elder White and Sister White") conducted a meeting at Battle Creek, Michigan, in 1850, and one M. E. Cornell, visiting Tyrone Township after the meeting, interrupted John Preston Kellogg's raking of hay to tell his extremely interested listener about the message given by the Whites. The date on which Mr. Kellogg joined the Adventists is not recorded but his sons Merritt and Smith joined the church while students at Oberlin College, which they entered in 1851.

By the time the Whites again visited Michigan to conduct meetings, the ordinarily phlegmatic John Preston was a fervent convert to the Adventist religion. M. E. Olsen in his *History of the Origins and Progress of the Seventh-day Adventists* records that in 1854 John Preston offered to lend the Adventists $200 they needed to buy a large meeting tent, the first ever used by the denomination and the precursor of annual tent meetings now held by the denomination in most states of this country and in other areas of the world.

In 1854, "in order to have money to spend for the cause he loved," John Preston Kellogg sold his prospering farm and moved to Jackson, Michigan, where memories of Connecticut Valley broomcorn contributed to his decision to take up the trade of broommaking. The following year he participated in a Battle Creek conference with three other votaries of the Adventist movement and each agreed to put up $300, without requesting interest on their money, to provide a Seventh-day Adventist publishing office. The establishment of this office was a strong factor in making Battle Creek the national headquarters of the Adventists (until a relocation to a suburb of Washington, D. C. in 1903). In 1856 the family made its last move, this time to Battle Creek where, in addition to devoting much time, effort, and money to the health and religious movement, John Preston Kellogg started the broom factory that was later to give W. K. Kellogg his first business experience.

6.

Thus came the Kellogg family to Battle Creek. This city, then a village of little more than a thousand people, was to be known over two hemispheres as "the Health City" and to become the world center of the breakfast food industry. Such renown came, not because of any superiority of resources, labor supply or geographic location, but primarily because the Seventh-day Adventists established their headquarters there.

(This photo taken in 1868 is from a collection of the W. R. French Studio.)

Early-Day Battle Creek.

During the boyhood of W. K. Kellogg, his home-town grew from a village of 2,000 population to a comparative "metropolis" of 6,000 people.

W. K. Kellogg

The food industry grew up in Battle Creek because the sanitarium was there. The sanitarium was there because Elder and Sister White and the Adventists established it there. The history of W. K. Kellogg and the corn flakes business is rooted in the history of the Seventh-day Adventist denomination.

In the course of American history, churches have often become expressions of cooperation to attain an end. In the case of the Adventists, their goal was to better the lives, physically and mentally, of the people, and this sect's contribution has not been little to the tremendous and dramatic advances made in modern public health and medicine.

Rooted also in the influence of this movement were the code of ethics and many personality attributes of the subject of this biography. While for most of his adult life W. K. Kellogg was estranged from the Adventists, he always spoke of them as "our people," and the injunctions of the church during his formative, impressionable years made indelible marks upon him. His aversion to alcohol and tobacco, his strict, almost rigid attitudes on mores and morals, his altruism and utter honesty, perhaps even much of his deep humility and loneliness, stemmed in considerable part from the teachings of this minority group. Any recounting of his "long line of ancestors" must include an abstract "ancestor," the Seventh-day Adventist Church, for to understand the somewhat enigmatic W. K. Kellogg, one must have acquaintance with the tenets of the Adventist movement.

This movement, which gets its name from belief in a Second Coming, or Advent, of Christ, originated with the teachings of William Miller, a New England Baptist. In 1818, after two years' study of the Bible, especially the prophecies in *Daniel* and in *Revelations* (see particularly *Daniel* 9:24) he concluded that Christ would return to earth, that the world would be consumed in flames and become a new earth in which the righteous would live forever, and that the bodies of the righteous dead would be raised.

From his studies, Mr. Miller calculated that the return of

[18]

Christ would occur during the Hebraic year between March 21, 1843, and March 21, 1844. He began to preach his message publicly in 1831. His teachings attracted a considerable following in New England and western New York, especially among members of the Baptist, Methodist, and Christian churches, which at first did not consider his views in conflict with their own.

In the spring of 1844 a group of Adventists in New Hampshire became acquainted with a doctrine of the Seventh-day Baptists, who held that the Fourth Commandment should be taken literally and that the Seventh Day, Saturday, should be observed as the Sabbath. Adopting this practice, they became known as Seventh-day Adventists.

When the expected Advent failed to materialize by March 21, 1844, the Adventists discovered a possible error in their computations and predicted that the Second Coming would occur on October 22 of that year. This resulted in a second disappointment, and many of Mr. Miller's fifty thousand followers became discouraged and left the movement. Among those who remained were differences of opinion over the exact interpretation of the prophecies and the "Millerites," as they were called, divided into several factions.

While some groups continued to recheck the prophecies and establish new dates, the larger proportion became convinced that the original calculations were correct and that some event, the nature of which they did not understand, had taken place in 1843–44. The "cleansing of the sanctuary" (Daniel 8:14) was reinterpreted to refer not to an earthly event, but to Christ's cleansing of the heavenly sanctuary before His return to earth. To these Adventists, the exact date was of minor importance; the core of their faith was the confident expectation of the Second Coming.

This was the view adopted by the Seventh-day Adventists who, under the spiritual leadership of Mrs. Ellen G. White, became by far the largest and most important of the Adventist groups. Mrs. White, born Ellen G. Harmon in Maine in 1827, suffered a childhood injury which made her something of a recluse and dreamer, deeply interested in religion. In 1840, when she was thirteen, she heard Mr. Miller preach in Portland and she joined the Adventist movement a few years later.

In 1844, during the period of uncertainty following the Adventists' second disappointment, Ellen, then seventeen, had a vision which became the basis of her religious teachings. Two years later she married an Adventist Elder, James White, and the two of them spent the rest of their lives spreading the gospel of the Seventh-day Adventists, at first throughout the United States and eventually throughout the world.

Sister White continued all during her life to have dreams and visions in which she received instructions not only on matters of religious belief, but also on every detail of the program and organization of the Seventh-day Adventist Church. Her testimonies, accepted by her followers as the revealed word of God, eventually filled nine volumes.

About 1844 an Adventist farmer who had stopped for a smoke while plowing his field suddenly concluded that he would not want the returning Christ to find him puffing on a smelly pipe. He threw down his pipe, plowed it under, and at the next meeting gave a testimony about his decision to stop smoking. By 1850, abstinence from tobacco had become a common part of the Adventist code. Very early in their history, the Adventists embraced the idea of "health reform," which embodied hydrotherapy or the "water cure," simple diet, and abstinence from tea, coffee, alcohol, tobacco, spices and eventually meat.

The water cure movement had originated early in the nineteenth century with Vincent Priessnitz, a Silesian peasant. When he sprained his wrist, he held it under a pump, then kept it wrapped in cold, wet bandages. The swelling went down and a rash broke out, leading the youth to conclude that the water had drawn out the inflammation.

Eventually Mr. Priessnitz invented a whole series of water treatments, including the sponge bath, wet sheet packing, sitz bath, foot and arm baths, the douche (a forced spray over the entire body), steam baths, dripping sheets, the plunge bath and others. These innovations led to the establishment of a water cure group in England in 1840, and the movement spread to America at about the same time.

It was in 1863 that Sister White was told in a vision that the Adventists must become "even more stubborn" advocates of health reform:

"We have a duty to speak, to come out against intemperance of every kind—intemperance in working, in eating, in drinking, in drugging, and then point to God's great medicine, water, pure soft water, for diseases, for health, for cleanliness, for luxury."

While in Rochester, New York, at Christmastime, she learned in a vision that the Adventists should set up their own sanatoria devoted to baths, diet, rest, exercise and fresh air. This led the General Conference of the church to establish the Western Health Reform Institute in Battle Creek. Eleven thousand dollars in stock were sold and the proceeds used to purchase a two-story farmhouse on eight acres of ground in the westernmost outskirts of the town. There on September 5, 1866, a staff of two physicians, two bath attendants, one untrained nurse and three or four helpers, opened the institution that was to play so large a part in the history of Battle Creek and in the saga of a new food industry for the nation. In 1867 the Institute was incorporated but some years later the stockholders relinquished their dividends and made it a non-profit institution.

Meanwhile the eldest Kellogg boy, Merritt (who in 1859 had used an ox team to cross the continent to California, there to establish the first Adventist congregation in San Francisco), became greatly interested in the articles on health living in denominational publications. He attained his M.D. degree in 1868 and that summer he returned to Battle Creek and served for several months on the sanatorium staff before returning to California in October.

To accommodate an increasing number of patients, the sanatorium had already built an addition to the farmhouse and taken over three or four nearby cottages. It was less than a decade later that Merritt's younger brother, John Harvey Kellogg, became physician-in-chief of the institution which was to evolve to the Battle Creek Sanitarium, famous throughout the world.

Of course, the health movement was only one of several facets of the Adventist movement which made it international in scope. In 1863, when the General Conference of the church was organized, it represented 3,500 members in states ranging from New England to as far west as Illinois. Thirty years later this number had enlarged to 42,763, and the church had started sending missionaries to all continents. Today there are 11,158 churches and a million members spread over forty-eight states of this nation and the six continents of the world. Approximately two thousand missionaries are now "laboring in overseas fields" including such remote places as Hong Kong, Formosa, Israel and Pitcairn Island. The interest in health reforms has also continued, with the denomination currently sponsoring a medical college, several schools of nursing and 114 hospitals and sanitariums over the world.

Regarded as ultraconservative in many of its beliefs, the church is as modern as the times in its communications system. The "Voice of Prophecy," founded by Adventist minister Dr. H. M. S. Richards, is a radio program beamed from Glendale, California to 842 radio stations in the United States and Canada. A large staff also aids radio broadcasting and Bible study correspondence in North, Central and South America, and in Europe, Asia, Australia and the Islands of the Seas.

Such is the church which was to be a mold for Will K. Kellogg in the formative years of his boyhood.

CHAPTER 2

"I Never Learned to Play"

I N 1860 EVEN the townspeople of remote Battle Creek knew that civil war was inevitable. Only a few months ahead were the usual heartaches of war, the loss of sons, the tears of women. However, as with all wars prior to the atomic age, its effects were severe but transitory. The one currently observable mark symbolizing the Civil War in the city is a weathered statue of two Union soldiers. They, with flag and rifle, mount guard over Monument Square and the heart of present-day Battle Creek.

A less dramatic and scarcely heeded event also occurred in 1860 which was to have a lasting effect upon the city. On April 7 a son was born* to John Preston Kellogg, struggling broom manufacturer and religious enthusiast, and to Ann Janette Kellogg, a country woman getting used to "town" after four years. They named the boy Willie Keith Kellogg. (Always hating the name "Willie" and not liking "William" much better, Mr. Kellogg waited until he was thirty-eight years old before having his name changed by court order to "Will Keith Kellogg.")

---

* Only a hundred miles away and approximately three years later, there was born another Michigander, Henry Ford, the innovator who did for the automotive industry what W. K. Kellogg did for the food industry.

W. K. Kellogg

"I was my father's seventh son, born on the seventh day of the week and the seventh day of the month. My father was a seventh child and the name 'Kellogg' has seven letters."

Throughout his life, Mr. Kellogg had almost the fervency of a numerologist in attaching significance to being the "seventh son of a seventh child" and, whenever possible, he secured rooms on the seventh floors of hotels and with room numbers ending in the "magic seven." For a number of years, Mr. Kellogg applied for his automobile licenses by specifying that the numbers should end in "seven" such as 7, 17 and 27.

This whimsy was one of the few indulgences permitted himself by the industrialist-philanthropist even in later years when he had the money and the time for leisure. He explained this by recalling that "as a boy I never learned to play." The cause was partly economic. "J. P. Kellogg & Son" (the "Son" was John Harvey Kellogg and not Will) was not a flourishing business and to aid at the factory as well as to earn money for his clothing, young Will from age seven worked after school and Sundays. Saturday, of course, was rigidly observed as the Sabbath Day by the SDA household.

Another restraining influence on the lad's spirit of play was his father's effort to meet the food needs of a large family. To do this the broommaker capitalized on the family labor supply and the then-cheap land in the village.

Will Kellogg recalled:

"Father had acquired quite a number of vacant lots in Battle Creek which he hoped would increase in value. These lots we cultivated and used for growing vegetables and small fruits. Before daylight in the summertime we boys were routed out of bed to weed berries and vegetables, or to root, bunch and wash onions and lettuce for the local market."

With the irony of understatement, this former "truck-gardener" commented that "I cannot say I enjoyed weeding the onions and other vegetable beds."

There were other reasons Will Kellogg "never learned to

play." Lingering from frontier days was some vestige of the
severe, fun-denying precepts of the Puritans. Life still meant to
most people, even children, hard work and long hours—the
harder and the longer the more praiseworthy. Further constrict-
ing the lad's play life was the shadow cast by a stern father
and mother who would not jeopardize by any frivolity the
treasures soon to be theirs in the next world. Perhaps this
shadow influenced the premise on which W. K. Kellogg established his Foundation sixty years later, when he stated that
"one of the most beneficial services that could be bestowed
upon civilization is to make the lives of little children happier,
healthier and more promising for their adult years."

The birthplace of W. K. Kellogg in Battle Creek, Michigan.

Undoubtedly the recollections of Mr. Kellogg overdrama-
tized some of the difficulties of his youth. Certainly he had his
boyhood friends including Frank and Charles Belden, George
and Fred Hall, Wilton Smith, and the Savage boys. Never compatible with his brother, John Harvey Kellogg, eight years

[25]

older—"I have vivid recollections of John Harvey warming his cold feet by placing same on my back, not conducive to my sleeping well"—Will was quite fond of his brother "Pet" (Preston S.) two years older, and his younger sisters Clara and "Het" (Hester).

Preston S. Kellogg wrote "Dear Brother Will" in adult years, recalling their boyhood as "happy days and we were pretty good chums. We had to improvise to amuse ourselves, oftentimes. Just now I am thinking of the caves and tunnels we dug in Dad's backyard, some of them ten or twelve feet below the surface. Old Mrs. Briggins, the cat, with her numerous and frequent progeny, was our only pet. I think we should have had a dog, for every boy loves a dog."

The family lot on West Main Street (later the name was changed to Michigan Avenue) was quite deep and extended about two city blocks to the narrow and slow-flowing Kalamazoo River. This afforded the children an occasionally taken opportunity for wading and water fights. On the lot nearer the house was a rather decrepit barn behind which Preston and Will experimentally smoked dried clover leaves. (Apparently the experiments were not too successful since Will came to adulthood with an aversion to smoking.) When the lad was about eight years old, John Preston Kellogg moved the family to the "Pearsall house" east of the old homestead. Will Kellogg later recalled that "It wasn't very homey and we children were all homesick for the old place." Another disadvantage was that the lot was much smaller so that the play antics of the children, close to the house, could be ended very abruptly by a call to chores from their mother.

A wish was a command when it came from the austere Ann Janette. Her black hair combed sternly back, the strong features, straight unrelenting mouth and snappy black eyes, gave authority to her quiet, firm voice. And overshadowed as husband John Preston Kellogg must have been, there nevertheless was something about his countenance which, like a chapter

Ann Janette Kellogg and John Preston Kellogg, W. K. Kellogg's parents.
(Photo by Doty.)

from *East Lynne*, called to mind a melodramatic picture of an adamant patriarch, a woebegone mother, a slammed door, and erasure of a daughter's name from the family Bible.

Severe parents they were, but just and of good will after their own fashion. Hence, in slack factory times and if his home chores were completed, Will was given permission now and then to go with the Belden boys to watch the Michigan Central trains roll into the station. Though the railroad had been a town pride since 1845, the trains with their wooden coaches still represented to the townspeople an exotic link with metropolitan Detroit as well as with the "Far West" of Illinois. With the smoke that poured from the boxlike chimney of the locomotive, the imaginations of the watching boys soared to the horizon and beyond to far-off places.

What a thrill was Will's first train ride; first times at anything are so important to youth! With his father, the eight-year-old lad took a forty-mile business trip to Allegan. He must have regarded the views from the train window as "among the sovereign sights of the world" for some eighty years later he was able to discuss this trip in detail, the people they talked with,

[27]

the towns through which they rode. Despite the numerous foreign travels of his adult life, his almost photographic memory indelibly retained a record of this momentous day of his boyhood.

When Frank Belden was made janitor of the little Seventh-day Adventist church, he appointed Will and Preston Kellogg as his assistants. They had a certain day to clean the church each week and seized the occasions to indulge in many boyish pranks. For instance, they would walk on the backs of the pews, propping themselves with long sticks to maintain their balance.

At one time there was a split in this Adventist church. Eventually, the factions got together again and those who came back signed a covenant that they would follow the church teachings as they had before. These covenants were placed in a covenant box which also contained the church Bible and the church rolls. One day the minister discovered that to the rolls had been added the names of a number of current infidels such as Robert Ingersoll, these forgeries purporting to show that Ingersoll and the others had joined the SDA church! In discussing this prank years afterward, neither Will Kellogg nor Frank Belden would acknowledge the caprice, but it was quite likely that one or both of them were responsible.

If Will Kellogg was the culprit, the prank can only be considered as boyish overzealousness rather than any irreverence for things religious. Many years later, W. K. Kellogg paid a visit to a warm friend of his boyhood. The friendship was ended that day, for the man, embittered by a failure in business, exhibited an irreligious attitude which alienated Mr. Kellogg. Such alienation was quite in character, for he never could tolerate either infidelism or profanity.

Infidelism, of course, had no place in the household of John Preston and Ann J. Kellogg. During the growing years of their large family, they were to offer many prayers to the severe, uncompromising Deity who is the Adventist God. In those days of little sanitation, no antibiotics, and slowly evolving medical care, their prayers were unavailing for daughter Emma Frances who died in 1849, and for the first Preston who died in 1855, and for Mary and Ella who were lost in 1858. Fate relented, however, in the case of young Will, very ill with malaria. Recounting his several months' illness as a boy, the grown-up W. K. Kellogg gave to the Lord commendation for his recovery but, with an ever characteristic practicality, gave equal credit to quinine:

"As I have already mentioned to you, many years ago, when a small boy, and when the entire State of Michigan was known for its malaria, I had several spells of the miserable disease. I would have a chill, then a high fever, and the next day I would skip the chill and fever and would occasionally feel fairly well. The use of quinine was known at that time in the form of a black substance that looked very much like stick licorice. Pellets were made from this product and the horrible bitter-tasting stuff was administered to me in applesauce. Capsules had not been devised. They did not administer this medicine until after several months of chills and fever. I lost much weight and also my ruddy complexion. My skin was a yellow, bilious color. My tongue was coated continuously and I had no appetite. However, the black nauseous medicine eventually cured the condition. Some years later the white quinine powder was developed from the crude form which had been administered to me."

As mentioned earlier, Will Kellogg did not have a dog during his boyhood, a strange fact in light of his adulthood affection for dogs. However, there was a focus of his love for animals. This was an old horse named Spot with which the Kellogg children became fast friends and playmates. He was ridden bareback, singly, and by twos and threes; astride, standing up, or sidesaddle. Sometimes the little folk hung onto Spot's tail and were dragged along without causing the horse any particular discomfort, for he never kicked or shook himself loose. The older children used to vary the routine by clutching the

The children of Ann Janette and John Preston Kellogg.

Preston S., Emma, W. K., Clara, John Harvey, and Laura. The picture pr
sumably was taken in 1866, just prior to the birth of Hester Ann Kellogg.

girth below and riding underside, upside down. A neighbor,
watching the latter performance and feeling sorry for the animal, asked the children:

"Don't you know that horse is an Arabian?"

His inference seemed to be that an Arabian horse should not
be treated in the way they played with Spot. Therefore, at the
supper table that night, the children informed their parents
that Spot was an Arab horse. This was news to the father, but
he did not discourage the idea. Whether or not the neighbor
was correct in ascribing Bedouin ancestry to the horse, young
Will was particularly impressed. Later when John Preston Kel-

logg sold the horse, the boy was brokenhearted and vowed
that someday he would own a whole stable of Arabian steeds.
A half century later, the vision of old Spot came loping through
the years and this memory contributed to the establishment of
the Kellogg Arabian Horse Ranch near Pomona, California.

2.

That Will Kellogg somehow gathered an education is obvious,
for in adulthood his keen gift of analysis, unusually retentive
memory, and an evidence of being well-read reflected the dis-
cipline of education. Yet it is just as obvious that he must have
gained such education informally, much as a chicken gathers
its breakfast, a grain here and a grain there. The boy had but
little formal schooling and that which he obtained was neither
remarkable in continuity nor in quality. Partly this was because his parents were little interested. Years later in a magazine interview, John Harvey Kellogg described his parents as
so firmly convinced of the imminent end of the world that
they considered it a waste of time for their children to learn
to read!

The school bells first rang for Will Kellogg at the Number
Three Ward School (which at a much later day he was to replace with the modern Ann J. Kellogg School named in honor

(Photo by W. R. French.)

School bells first rang for W. K.
Kellogg at No. 3 Ward School in
Battle Creek, Michigan.

of his mother) and his first three teachers impressed him sufficiently so that he was able to recall them and their names sixty-five years later.

"When I was a boy in school," Mr. Kellogg once related, "the teacher thought I was dim-witted because I had difficulty reading what was on the blackboard. I was twenty years old before I myself found out what was the matter: I was nearsighted. A proper medical examination would have settled that the day I entered school.

"Since then," he added, "I have often thought of what science can do for underprivileged children if they can be taken in hand at the proper time."

By the time Will was ten years of age, the Adventists had opened a sectarian "select school" in a building on Washington Avenue. (The school and the building were the genesis of the later Battle Creek College.) There Will, his elder brothers John Harvey and Preston S., and his sisters Clara and Hester, sat at the feet of a Professor Bell who believed that the Bible was the textbook needed for all his classes save arithmetic.

The headmaster was remembered by some of his students as a "terror." He was handy with beatings and quite intolerant of human weaknesses. Frank E. Kelsey recalled that Preston was once chastised with a stick of cordwood. However, Will Kellogg never received a beating from the professor, according to schoolmate Frank Belden:

"W. K. was into meanness just as much as the others but he had such a poker face that the teacher never blamed him for some of the pranks."

Will Kellogg used to enjoy telling of the day when Clara, his sister, then only four years old, happened to look up from her prayer, thus infuriating the professor. Clara later wondered, "How did he know I had my eyes open during the prayer?" Will never forgave the schoolman for, even when recounting the event many years later, he was divided between a chuckle over his sister's remark and a continuing fury over the injustice. Usually he would conclude the anecdote with the question "How far do you think that prayer went?"

In the late years of his life, W. K. Kellogg had the leisure to search back in his memory for facets of the schools he attended. Apparently in the Number Three Ward School he had been exposed to the famous *McGuffey Readers* or to some reading book of similar ability to stress moral values with considerable skill. He never forgot the many exhortative poems and used one of them sixty-five years later when he addressed the Michigan Beekeepers' Association (always in dread of making a speech, he consented to the ordeal because of enthusiasm over the use of honey as a sweetening substitute for sugar):

> The lark is up to meet the sun,
> The bee is on the wing;
> The ant her labor has begun,
> The woods with music ring.
>
> Shall birds and bees and ants be wise?
> And I my moments waste?
> Oh! let me with the morning rise,
> And to my duties haste!

Another poem, "It Was Night When the Lord Was Born," was a continuing source of comfort in times of sorrow during the later years of his life.

After he had reached the age of thirteen, Will's school days were almost over. Already related is his debut as a salesman at age fourteen when "my father was not as insistent upon my attending school as regularly as some fathers."

The young salesman's initial trip to Bellevue and other neighboring villages was so successful that John Preston Kellogg continued to use him to call on grocers and to take orders for brooms to be shipped by freight. Trips to nearby towns were made by horse and buggy or by sleigh, and Will Kellogg never felt too comfortable when twilight found him traveling through

the Berryton Hills or through a section called Whisky Run between Battle Creek and Hastings. However, only his boyhood
superlative "boss" (slang for the ultimate in perfection) was
an appropriate adjective for the romance of sales trips via the
train.

Along with the assumption of economic responsibility, he
was growing up in other ways. Memorable landmarks of his
adolescence, such as his first barbershop shave and the freedom to go about a bit with other lads, were recalled in a letter
which the eighty-four-year-old W. K. Kellogg wrote to his
boyhood friend, Frank Belden:

"I remember that when I was about fourteen I went into
Tom Weaver's barbershop where you were getting a shave,
and you insisted on paying for a shave for me, which I did
not need but I took it. This was my first barbershop shave.
Tom lived to be quite old; he died about ten years ago.

"I still recall that you were the first individual to pay for the
first oyster supper that I ever ate outside of my own home. If I
remember correctly, the place where you took several of us
boys for a treat was in the basement of a building on the corner of State and Canal, formerly occupied by Mayor Thompson
as a grocery and crockery store. I think the price charged at
that time was 20¢ and, as there was a crowd of us, you must
have spent at least a dollar of your hard-earned money. Dollars were hard to get in those days, but they went considerably
farther."

Train trips became more frequent as Will gained seasoning
as a salesman. One of these "far-off" journeys occurred on his
fifteenth birthday, April 7, 1875, when as commercial representative of the broom concern he alighted from a train at
St. Charles, near Saginaw, Michigan. At that time he acted
on an impulse by going to a photographer's and sitting for a
full-face portrait which shows a very thin, serious-appearing
boy with quite prominent ears. Shortly after this happening,

Dr. John Harvey Kellogg, who had completed his medical studies in New York that spring, convinced the family that Will should have more schooling. The boy attended school for a few weeks in the latter part of 1875 and in early 1876.

He was then put in charge of the family broom factory for a few months, while his father was incapacitated with a broken hip. In 1877–78, "I worked for a half-brother, Albert Kellogg, at Kalamazoo, in his broom factory. I was not an expert broommaker, but I preferred preparing the stock, ready for the broommakers to use."

Albert's company failed in the latter part of 1878 and he was unable to pay his employees. In retaliation, the men took hundreds of feet of broom wire and strung it all over the factory. Will Kellogg's solution was more practical. He moved his trunk onto the front porch of Albert Kellogg's home and announced that he was boarding with the family until his back salary was paid off. Albert paid the debt and Will returned to Battle Creek, again to work for his father.

Initiated into business at the early age of seven, Will Kellogg was a broom salesman by the time of his early 'teens.

Unknown to him he was on the eve of what he was to consider "a great adventure." The following year would find him
in a section of the nation strange to him, and faced with
"executive" responsibility as well as the incomprehensible
roistering habits of Southern factory hands. How well equipped
was he to meet this turn in his river of fate? What kind of
person was Will Kellogg at age nineteen?

3.

A tintype of Will Kellogg taken about the time when an
admixture of religion and brooms called him to Texas reveals a stripling perhaps 5′6″ tall and weighing about 120

Will Kellogg is shown at lower right, identifiable by boutonnière.
At the left, middle row, are Will's brother, Dr. Preston S. Kellogg,
and the physician's wife. The exact year of the picture is not known.

pounds. Presumably the photographer had furnished him with
a cutaway coat and this, coupled with a wing collar and bow
tie, formally complemented the face with its serious expression. Above slightly protruding eyes was a forehead somewhat
on the high side and straight, dark brown hair.

There was sensitivity in the face, particularly around the

thin mouth, and a shy, rather hurt look from out the eyes. One wonders if the slight mustache on the upper lip reflected a wish to hide the extreme self-consciousness which often in later years caused him to be thought "cold" or "harsh."

Only the most discerning of latter-day acquaintances would have disclaimed the appellation of "cold" for the adult W. K. Kellogg. Some, however, were able to divine that underneath his "mask," donned partially as a defense against predators of the rich but also to hide insecurely dammed emotions, was a person who longed to be understood and to be loved. Possessing these entirely natural desires, he was reluctant to form close relationships because of the fear of losing them. He moved cautiously among his fellow men, anticipating rebuffs and ready for the fight or the flight.

Mr. Kellogg realized he had this personality defect. In a 1941 letter to a psychiatrist concerning some emotional troubles of a grandson, he had this to say:

"I am not sure but what —— inherits some of his traits from his grandfather. I was very bashful and diffident as a youngster and I never got entirely over it. I don't like to meet new people now except on a business basis."

W. K. Kellogg grew up to be a silent man because in boyhood there was seldom anyone to whom he could confide his inner thoughts. The "long, long thoughts of youth" are rarely divulged to competitive and irreverent playmates. The Oedipus gap between father and son does not make for confidences. Who but a mother will listen and understand? Unfortunately for young Will, Ann Janette Kellogg was not a mother who wasted love. Adventist Elder Uriah Smith described her as ". . . a woman of remarkable vigor and endurance . . . possessed of an indomitable will . . . a glance from her piercing eyes was sufficient to bring the most rebellious child speedily to terms . . . some might have mistaken her reticence and dignity of character and bearing for coldness of disposition, but those who came near to her knew her to be an uncommonly generous and exceedingly tender-hearted person."

Much of this description of the mother could apply minutely to the son. The remarkable similarity could be traced in considerable detail for it is apparent that the character and personality of the son came largely through heritage from and conditioning by his mother. Will Kellogg often lamented his inability to smile or laugh. (He occasionally chuckled.) Many years earlier, one of John Preston Kellogg's children remarked concerning Ann Janette: "If we could just get Mother to laugh, we could get anything out of her, but it was not very easy to get her to laugh." Intent on her role as an efficient housewife making ends meet for a none-too-prosperous husband and their large family, Ann Janette had little time to laugh or to give attention to a small boy with a neurosis. A friend recalled that "it was a great big family, with everything so serious."

Among the mysterious forces which mold us into persons, those affecting Will Kellogg included a gloomy heritage from the Puritans, the "live not for this world" attitude of his parents and their religious community, the hard work during his boyhood, and later his twenty-five years in the shadow of the dominating John Harvey Kellogg for whom Will performed duties ranging from managerial to janitorial as a self-styled "flunkey" at the Battle Creek Sanitarium.

The four universal needs of any human being are to feel secure, to achieve status or recognition, to experience adventure and to receive affection. It is uncertain how many of these needs were satisfied for the young Will Kellogg, but apparently fate did stack the cards toward a certain rigidity of personality. Yet the very factors which circumscribed him by severe boundaries of conduct, ethics and mores, also gave him unusual virtues. Within limits similar to those of the characters in Grant Wood's "American Gothic" painting, he had commensurate strengths. His courage, his compulsion to put ideas into action, later were to make him a great executive, but it was the character traits unsensed by many contemporaries which made him a great man.

His mother was so busy that she could not demonstrate her love, but even as a boy he stifled the sadness of "not being loved," determined that he would not burden others with his sorrows. As a man, he dreamed of a "Shangri-La" which he never found in the course of his world travels. However, this failure did not dissuade him from his attempt to build model communities where good men could walk in dignity and in peace and where there were green places on which children could play. He did not wait to become rich before he became generous. As a middleaged man of modest means, his conscience compelled him to look after the welfare of friends and relatives. When rich, though his loneliness was as unalterable as one's eyes, he nevertheless dedicated his declining years to making life happier for many men, women and children on three continents.

One should not assume from the foregoing that the subject of this biography had no lighter moments. On the contrary, he occasionally exhibited a puckish sense of humor, he always had a gnawing curiosity about people and things and, as a teenager and young man, he was not immune to the charms of the opposite sex. It was in the spring of 1878 that this young man's fancy "lightly turned to thoughts of love." The object of his affection was a neighborhood girl by the name of Mary Aldrich. Possessing all the qualifications of a dream girl, including "golden, blonde curls," she was several years older than Will and the age gap plus his shyness apparently precluded anything but admiration from afar. However, his admiration for her must have been very strong because as a man in his seventies, W. K. Kellogg several times confessed to a lingering regard for this girl who long since had been in her grave.

Whether the tender reminiscences of an elderly man were of the girl *per se* or of an idealized memory of his bygone

The adolescent W. K. Kellogg.

From a tintype taken in Dallas,
Texas, in either 1878 or 1879.

youth, no one can say. It is possible that young Will Kellogg's
decision to go to Texas in December of that same year was
partly based on unrequited affection but, as a teenager will
do, he by this time had a new girl friend, a neighbor whom
he called "Puss" Davis. Actually, it was not romance but a
realistic business need and some "pull" through his Adventist
associations which were the chief factors soon to take him to
the Lone Star State for a stay of approximately a year.

4.

Elder James White, the Adventist leader, had joined with a
George H. King to set up a broom factory in Dallas. Mediocre
management and inexperienced, irresponsible help had contributed to a poor initial six months of operation and the
Elder advised King "to hire one of the Kellogg boys to show
you how to make brooms." After a visit to Battle Creek
during which King interviewed a number of applicants, including Preston Kellogg, he chose Will Kellogg and soon Will
was exposed to the utterly drab and dreary prospect of the
Texas plains in wintertime.

However, even to this somewhat phlegmatic youth, the journey represented high adventure:

"I left in December when the weather (in Michigan) was below zero and the ground covered with snow, and I had great expectations with reference to the wonderful climate of the South. The next day after my arrival, what was known as a 'Texas Norther' arrived and there were several inches of snow on the ground."

The Texans were having a hilarious time coasting in dry-goods boxes on runners, but their houses were not built for such freakish cold weather and, despite the thrill of a new locale, Will had nostalgia for Michigan and particularly for the warmth of glowing stoves in the Kellogg kitchen and the parlor.

His homesickness and his awe of metropolitan Dallas with its twenty thousand people evaporated under the passage of time and the stress of busy working days and surprisingly social nights. Throughout the year of 1879, Will Kellogg kept a diary, and a reading of the daily entries indicates that he then was not the extreme introvert that he later became but was a lad who took some time out for fun, even though he did work long hours, many nights, and some Sundays. Some of the diary references to chills and fever indicate that the climate, at least at the time, was not healthful, but this apparently did not impede a full schedule for the Michigander in Texas. The initial entry in the diary apparently was written shortly after his arrival in Dallas:

January 7, 1879—"Went to housekeeping today. Willson and I have a room all furnished. We will do our own cooking. I shall commence work tomorrow. Have not done any yet."

January 18—"Went to a singing school taught by Scott Kilgore (apparently an SDA preacher). After nine o'clock we went to a party up to a Mr. Roads. Had a fly time, all dutch." (*That slang of 1879!*)

January 21—"Got up at four, went to work at five. . . . Elder

White is very much pleased with my coming to Texas. He has written for me to come to Denison and start a shop there; will go in about two weeks." (EDITOR'S NOTE: *This shop did not eventuate, although in that year's travels about Texas to sell brooms, he did get to Denison.*)

January 25—"Got up at seven, ate breakfast at nine. King came up to have us go to Sabbath School. Went. He made me take a class of small boys to teach. Wrote to Frank. Went walking down to Trinity Bridge. Went to singing school. Got interduced (*sic*) to Miss Cole."

January 27—"Mr. King does not act much like a man of business. He is fearful slow and don't work any himself."

February 14—"I worked at sorting (brooms) this forenoon and bunched and cleaned up this afternoon and labeled. . . . Elder White and wife came from Denison this evening by team. Elder didn't know me. He didn't speak."

February 15—"Went to breakfast at seven and came home and got ready for church. Mrs. White preached this forenoon. She spoke to me after the meeting and so did the Elder. He didn't know me. He spoke *of* me in the meeting and so did Mrs. White." (*The entries of February 14 and 15 reveal the sensitivity strongly characteristic of Will Kellogg in his later years.*)

March 8—"Went to church, came home, wrote a letter to Pet and one to Het, posted them, went over on the flats and got a hatful of flowers. Wish I could send some to Puss D."

March 10—"Got a letter from Clara, also one from W. T. C. Wish it was from Puss." (*"Puss D." was Ella Davis who was to become his wife nineteen months later.*)

March 19—"Elder White called me out (of the shop) and then told King to get out to the farm and let me run the shop."

April 4—(At Denison, Texas) "The Elder called me in to talk. He wants me to take the business and run the whole thing. I don't want to."

April 26—"After breakfast I went to town, got shaved, went

to the P.O. and got a boss (*superlative*) letter from Puss. . . .
I was very glad to hear from her. It has been four months since
I have seen her."

May 13—"King wanted me to sign a note. I wouldn't."

June 10—(At Fort Worth) "Had lots of company last night.
Bedbugs and fleas. Got three bugs off myself this morning.
I like Fort Worth better than Dallas. It is higher."

June 16—"Got a letter from Mother. She is afraid I will get
killed or have the fever."

June 17—"I bought me an umberala (*sic*). . . . I received a
letter from Puss today with just the bossiest of pictures. It was
just splendid."

July 11—"I did not receive any letter from Puss today. I just
wish I could see her about this time."

July 25—"The sewers here in Dallas all run out in the open
air, some along the streets and some under the sidewalks.
Down by the central market, there is a fearful stench comes
up from under the sidewalks. I should think they would have
the fever if they don't clean up." Throughout his life, Will
Kellogg was ultrasanitary in his habits and fastidious with
reference to living conditions.

Will Kellogg and friend "Willson" at Dallas, Texas, about 1879.

W. K. Kellogg

The entries from late July through the month of August (with the exception of a cryptic July 31 statement that "I went up to Cole's with May Lamoreaux. . . . Had a very pleasant time. . . . Moonlight") concerned the fifty or sixty hands at work in the broom plant and illustrate one of several instances where the nineteen-year-old boy had to assume a man's estate, even to the extent of borrowing from this or that source to meet the payroll. Apparently Elder White was not much of a businessman, and perhaps this lack caused him greatly to appreciate the quality in young Will. Even at that early age, the lad showed business judgment and tenacity.

In an early August entry he related "There has been a whole posse in after their pay. . . . Sent to the Elder after some money last Monday but it didn't come." Apparently, however, that crisis was successfully bridged, for on August 11 he wrote: "It has been a very busy day. Nearly all the broomcorn cutters have been in. I have paid them all off. Paid out about $250. One of the fellows named Smith got in the jug last Friday night."

Perhaps it was in this period that there occurred the birth of Mr. Kellogg's distaste for liquor. The fruit-of-the-vine not only created disturbances among the factory workmen but also brought him a reprimand from the Adventist Church, as will be seen from the following entries:

August 27—"We worked until ten o'clock. We intend to start for the Arbor meetings in the morning. Had a fearful time with Thom Alison. He was drunker than a fool. Came near having some trouble. Had to take some beer with him."

September 10—"Has been warm all day. They had a meeting at the church today. Had my name up for treating some of the hands to beer. Also Bates for drinking it."

However, before he left Texas, things went smoother and he had time for some recreation. For instance, on October 24: "Willson and I went to the opera; Mrs. Oatts in 'Pinafore'." Then on October 26: "At the show we saw the electric light and a few animals and a poor circus." Two days later, the entry relates: "Don't feel very well today. We had a fearful time last night. I am going to swear off and am not going around any more."

The novelty of the Texas scene had begun to pall, and that nostalgic pull which reaches most persons away from home eventually caused Will to return to the community life of his native Battle Creek. Intuitively he had come to this homeward decision which proved an important factor in his later achievement. When the time arrived to form his own business, his Battle Creek friends and acquaintances proved resources upon which he was able to draw.

By November 29, he was home again and the entry for that day comments on "I hardly knew the girls, they had grown so. Folks were all glad to see me and I to see them. I saw Puss and she made me go home with her."

5.

The remainder of the 1879 diary chiefly concerns Puss, a continual round of activity with her including "boss" dinners, going to fires, supping at oyster bars, attending instrumental concerts and singing schools. Many of these likings were sustained by Mr. Kellogg throughout his life, for he would even get up in the middle of the night to view a large fire and he could hardly wait for months having the letter *r* so that oysters would be in season. On December 25, there was a fore-omen of his philanthropic attitude of later years:

"Merry Christmas it has been all day. I gave about $18 worth to make the folks happy."

The concluding entry was on December 31:

"Happy New Year is coming and the old one is going as fast as it can. Goodbye to 1879, also to this diary."

Several additional diaries written by Will Kellogg have been found, the next a chronicle of five years later, in 1884, when he was a young married man. That is fortunate because he usually was laconic in his speaking and writing and the diary served as a practical vehicle for his thoughts. Mr. Kellogg's addiction to brevity caused some of his acquaintances to opine that it must be one of his ancestors who is buried in an ancient English cemetery under a headstone bearing only the succinct epitaph: "I WAS."

Be that as it may, the year of 1879 had been an eventful one for the subject of this biography. The year ahead was to include a compressed "higher education," a romance, his marriage, and the start of a 25-year affiliation with his brother, John Harvey Kellogg, and with the Battle Creek Sanitarium.

Even in 1880, Will Kellogg was a person in a hurry. During his year in Texas he had formed a strong opinion that he needed more formal education and his purposeful impatience relative to obtaining such training was representative of a lifelong characteristic. After a short time at a business college in Battle Creek, which proved too slow-gaited for him, he in-

A certificate given Mr. Kellogg in 1880 by the Parson's Business College.

vestigated the possibilities for acceleration at the Parson's Business College in nearby Kalamazoo. Forthrightly, "He told the big, red-headed Irishman who ran the college that he wanted a business education but he did not propose to spend years in acquiring it. He was willing to work long and hard hours if there was some way to speed up the educational process. Thereupon the Irishman said, 'You take this seat right next to my desk, work like hell, and any time you want to know something or to have more lessons piled upon you, just say the word.'"

By following through on this suggestion, the impatient student had his certificate as a qualified bookkeeper and "accountant" at the end of three months. (This certificate in Mr. Kellogg's personal files avers instruction in "Single and Double Entry, Wholesale and Retail, Manufacturing, Banking, Commercial Calculations, Business Correspondence, Deeds and Mortgages"!) He had speedily conquered a course that took most students at least an academic year to complete, this in spite of the fact that he once in a while referred to himself as a "slow learner."

Will took more time in another project of the year—that of the wooing of Ella Osborn Davis (the "Puss D." of his diary) who was the daughter of Obadiah Davis, a grocer and erstwhile clock repairer. Perhaps his was the usual reluctance of the young male to submit to the fetters of marriage.

The springtime of his twentieth year went by and Puss, though acknowledgedly his best girl, nightly parted company with him at the parental front door. Then came the long twilights of June when the elders rocked on wide front porches and enjoyed the cool summer breezes typical of Michigan. The younger set played croquet under huge shade trees that gave a bit of privacy from inquisitive adult eyes. And after darkness, several couples often would go into the parlor to have fun singing oldtime songs.

Oh, those were "boss" nights, and no wonder the lad weakened in his resistance to the thought of marriage. The sky became filled with stars and violins, the days danced by like a ballerina, and even the neighbors' teasing over his infatuation with "the Davis girl" was titillating to a quiet and ultra-conservative suitor.

From a more prosaic angle, he was a young man with means enough for marriage and the start of a home. Through his part-time work since early boyhood, his "sorting and preparing" broom contracts and the years as a salesman, he had accumulated savings of more than $1,000, and the Texas adventure added an additional $500 to his nest egg. Then, since April, he had held a new job. His position at the Battle Creek Sanitarium initially paid only $6 a week and room and board but a pay increase elevated this to $9, and with one's elder brother at the helm of the growing institution, an expectation of additional advances in pay and position seemed logical.

Quickly weighing all the factors, as was ever his custom when confronted with a momentous problem, Will Kellogg decided that marriage between him and Ella Davis was desirable. The date of the marriage was November 3, 1880, but there is no record of the details of the ceremony. What was left of the bridegroom's nest egg of $1,500 (after his commercial course expenses) "was expended in paying for the furnishing of the three rooms we first used in housekeeping, and the balance on a little home located at No. 319 on the south side of Champion Street, between Cass and Kendall."

Young Will Kellogg had left boyhood behind him. Now he had the prestige and the responsibilities of a married man. Ahead was a quarter century which mistakenly might be regarded as primarily a period of frustration and stalemate, but which actually was a period of preparation for a "second life" destined to affect not only his own future but that of Battle Creek and the food habits of the nation.

CHAPTER 3

"Am Afraid I'll Always Be a Poor Man"

————THE MIDDLE YEARS

W. K. KELLOGG'S DIARY for the year 1884 reveals him as a "Mr. Average Man." He is now twenty-four years old and a married person with all the connotations of joys and worries contained in the word "marriage." He is an affectionate but very firm father of two sons and apparently any walking of the floor at night with the young ones is his lot since "Puss has lost all her teeth and is ailing." Also, he is a man who likes to work and gets plenty of it in his fifth year as a sanitarium employee of his brother, Dr. John Harvey Kellogg.

From the daily jottings there does not emerge the introvert that Will Kellogg later became. Young Will seems quite a social fellow. The diary tells of his frequent shaking of dice with Spicer (the Doctor's secretary) for lemonades or ice cream, visits to the opera house when Mrs. Kellogg felt up to it, periodical excursions by horse and buggy to Gull Lake and his following of every nocturnal fire in Battle Creek, whatever the time of night.

Many of the entries show a lively interest in the town happenings and particularly in vital statistics concerning acquaintances and friends. They present a picture of an average, middle-class, salaried worker, at this time not too discontented with his fate. Other data and tintypes reveal him as a slim man, about 5' 7½" tall, who twice daily (at noon and at night) rides "an old, tall-type high-wheeler bicycle" the short distance between his home and the Battle Creek Sanitarium.

In the diary he makes much use of the word "considering" to express some reservations in a kind of mental shorthand: "I have spent this day quite pleasantly *considering*." The same conservatism is evidenced in his entry of September 27:

"I feel kind of blue. Am afraid that I will always be a poor man the way things look now."

That was poor prophecy from a man who was to build a $100,000,000 business! It is more understandable, however, in the light of other diary disclosures, such as "Puss wanted to go to church but I had no decent shoes to wear" and "I could not go to church as it was too warm to wear my black winter suit and my summer clothes are getting rather seedy."

In recalling early, impecunious times, Mr. Kellogg once commented that "After my marriage, my pay was $9 a week, and continued at the same rate for three and one-half years. This was not a very large sum of money with which to rear a family. My first raise, after three and one-half years, was $1 a week, but prior to this, I had secured a job of taking care of a horse, at $3 a week."

Just when most of us think we will be able to make both ends meet, somebody moves one end. Through sheer determination, Will Kellogg met the payment schedule for a thirteen-year mortgage on his home, but the obstacles were many. The death of his father, John Preston Kellogg, on May 10, 1881, necessitated Will's giving of some aid to his widowed mother,

Ann Janette, so that she could maintain her home. The ill health which plagued his wife Ella through the years was beginning to create doctors' bills and, of course, there were costs involved in the births of Karl and John.

The arrival of Will Keith Kellogg, Jr., in 1885 (his death four years afterward was a great blow to the father) and the addition to the family of the only daughter, Elizabeth ("Beth") a few years later, also added to the young married man's financial burdens:

"I was doing so poorly financially that I became somewhat discouraged and thought perhaps I should sell out what I had, take the money and go West. . . . I made partial arrangement to emigrate, but at last decided to stick to my job. . . .

"I found it impossible to meet the expenses of the growing family with the rather meager income and had acquired considerable indebtedness. About 1893 or 1894, Dr. J. H. (John Harvey Kellogg) told me that if I could succeed in finding some agents to sell his subscription books, he would give me 25 per cent of the net profits on sales made on any I might secure. Although at the time I was working fifteen or more hours a day, I was fortunate in securing the services of several first-class book men, with the result that at the end of thirteen and one-half years, I was free from debt and felt very happy to have my last mortgage paid."

Even though there was not much money to be made at the nonprofit Battle Creek Sanitarium, there was a whirl of activity and while a man might wear out, he would never rust out from disuse. Serving as a self-styled "bookkeeper, cashier, packing and shipping clerk, errand boy, and general utility man," Will in his more bitter moments referred to himself as "J. H.'s flunkey," and alleged that he even shaved the doctor and blacked his shoes.

For a quarter of a century, he lived in the deep shadow of his elder and brilliant brother, Dr. John Harvey Kellogg. "The Doctor," as Will usually called him, had always assumed

authority over his brother, even in boyhood. From the eminence
of his eight years of greater age, John had given Will occasional whippings, and the younger never forgave the elder for
these indignities. After the elder had become Physician-in-
Chief of a sanitarium growing by leaps and bounds, his zeal
knew no curbs. Brilliant innovator that John Harvey proved
to be (in surgical operations; in the evolution of health theories including "Biologic Living"; in the discovery and promotion of health foods) he possessed and cultivated an ability to
concentrate almost ruthlessly on certain intellectual and scientific pursuits. Hence he had a manner of being calloused to the
needs and wants of his close associates, including those of his
younger brother Will, in whom resentment began to smolder.

2.

It was a sanatorium, not a sanitarium, when the twenty-
four-year-old John Harvey Kellogg became Physician-in-Chief
(superintendent) of the Seventh-day Adventist institution in
Battle Creek. Crusader for the entire sixty-seven years in
which he headed the "San," he was not discouraged that only
twelve patients were on hand when he arrived, fresh from
Bellevue Hospital, New York, in 1876.

Zealot that he was, this 5′ 3″ dynamo was to find a perfect
environment in the enthusiasms of the Seventh-day Adventist
Church for its health reform program. It would be difficult to
overemphasize the tremendous force upon the history of this
nation exerted by the several denominational churches. Such
organizations, banded together for social or health reform—
the Lutherans and their establishment of hospitals; the Congre-
gationalists and their concern for the abolition of slavery; the
Methodists and their espousal of temperance; the many sects
which sponsored denominational colleges; the Seventh-day
Adventists with their tenets of the simple restorative methods
of nature, and the use of hydrotherapy and vegetarianism—
have made an indelible mark upon our country.

To the Adventists' zeal for a vegetarian diet, Dr. Kellogg added the latest discoveries in diagnostic medicine. During his studies in Europe, the Doctor had observed many institutions of healing, each representing some new therapeutic agent which, regarded as a panacea for human ills, was exploited to the neglect of other measures equally valuable. According to the *Calhoun County History* by Washington Gardner, the new Physician-in-Chief was determined to reorganize the establishment "so that patients could have the advantage of many methods of treatment, scientific feeding, massage, application of electricity, baths and other like measures." The idea was to add to the advantages of the ordinary hospital all the recently developed resources of physiological medicine, plus optimum diets and scientific nutrition. The aim also was to stress "the principle of healing through Nature's simple restorative methods: water treatments, proper rest, exercise, correct mental hygiene, and simple food. Restoration of health without the use of drugs was the goal. The diet excluded tea, coffee, meats, condiments, highly seasoned foods, and alcoholic drinks."

The changes proposed by John Harvey Kellogg actually added a new word to the English language. When Dr. Kellogg prepared literature for the institution in the early '80s, the name was printed as "Battle Creek Sanitarium." Soon letters began to arrive pointing out that evidently an error had been made, for while the word "sanatorium" could be found in the dictionary, "sanitarium" could not. Unabashed, the Doctor replied that it would quickly find its way into the dictionary, and it did.

"The new policies demanded a new name," Dr. Kellogg wrote. "The word 'sanatorium' was then defined by Webster's dictionary as a term used in England to designate a health resort for invalid soldiers. A change of two letters transformed 'sanatorium' into 'sanitarium'."

The rechristened sanitarium immediately began a phenomenal growth. Within two years it had outgrown the four or

Dr. John Harvey Kellogg.

The eminent health reform advocate who was the employer of his younger brother, W. K. Kellogg, for a quarter-century at the Battle Creek Sanitarium.

(Photo by W. R. French.)

five two-story cottages which had supplemented the original farmhouse. With $10,000 in profits, $5,000 in contributions, and a $115,000 loan, a five-story building capable of housing two hundred patients was built in 1878.

The *Calhoun County History* records an almost constant building program:

"The unique character of the sanitarium, its recognition by physicians in every part of the world, soon caused patients from every state in the union to throng to Battle Creek. Addition after addition was constructed, doubling the capacity of the institution but this still was not sufficient. A six-story addition on the south end of the main building was followed by the building of a hospital structure north of the main structure and another six-story addition to the north end of the main building. The latter was completed in 1884. In 1897 a chapel was added which would seat one thousand persons."

A biographer cannot hope to analyze the comparative merits of hydrotherapy and those of vegetarianism as espoused by the sanitarium, any more than it would be possible today for him to give definitive appraisals of psychiatry or of psychosomatic medicine. Water cures, spas, mineral baths were among the

[54]

health vogues of the late '90s and even beyond World War I, and to a sizeable number of people vegetarianism seemed one answer to the problems which resulted when Americans changed from pioneering physical work to more sedentary pursuits. Countless people have agreed that while not all the enthusiasms of Dr. John Harvey Kellogg have stood the test of years, in many ideas he was two generations ahead of his time. A former secretary relates:

"Some of the things that John Harvey Kellogg talked about fifty years ago are again being seriously considered today. For instance, he discussed lung cancer from smoking more than half a century ago and later went to the expense of having a film made concerning the harmful effects of tobacco. Before the turn of the century, the 'San' commanded its patients to follow a practice which again has become fashionable: the counting of calories. The dining room menu listed opposite each dish the number of units of proteins, fats, or carbohydrates therein. I can remember Dr. John begging employees to drink yogurt buttermilk and to use molasses—things that have had subsequent and considerable vogue. Another memory is of sitting in at a dinner party and hearing Dr. Kellogg tell his guests that the day would come when there would be so many people mentally ill that there would not be half enough facilities to take care of them. It looks as if this is a prediction coming true."

Another former associate, looking back through the years, recalled that the Doctor in 1898 or 1899 wrote an article on "Fresh Air and Sunshine in the Treatment of Tuberculosis" which was branded as "heresy" by the Boston Medical Society.

Though the Doctor may have seemed revolutionary to his more conservative colleagues, he actually was restating and implementing basic health ideas which had been in the minds of men for several centuries. Long years before, men had pulled slightly aside the veil which partially obscures learning

[55]

and truth—very early, men of medicine had voiced a belief that light and fresh air and optimum diet might prevent or cure many bodily ills—but John Harvey Kellogg was a man interested not merely in the shadow of the truth but in the full substance. So he threw the entire and surprisingly great power of his diminutive body into what became, for him, a seventy-year crusade.

To be discussed later is the fire of February 18, 1902, which completely destroyed the main building, the hospital and the annex (the original building). A new building dedicated on May 31, 1903, brought congratulations to the management from President Theodore Roosevelt, Secretary of State Elihu Root and scores of other high governmental officials. Six stories high, the structure was 550 feet long and was built in a modified Renaissance style, the front elevation being marked by a series of six Ionic pillars superimposed upon massive arches. The north and south elevations of the building bore similar porticoes with four columns each, and at the rear of the sanitarium was a semicircular space containing a "palm garden" of tropical plants.

Radiating from the palm garden like the spokes of a wheel were three wings containing separate treatment rooms for women and men, and to the center was a large gymnasium. In the treatment rooms "are to be found every facility and device known to modern therapeutics for the cure of disease." Chief among the treatments was the system of hydrotherapeutic application comprising more than two hundred kinds of baths, douches and fomentations. "Hot and cold water accomplish a wide variety of results, in single or in a large number of complications—effects both stimulating and quieting, not only upon the skin but upon every organ and function of the body," according to sanitarium literature. Light treatments (the electric light bath was an invention of the Doctor) and the use of electric current in "diathermy" or "thermo-penetration" were also widely used, as were extensive facilities for the application of vibration and for mechanical massage. Radium and X-ray departments had increasing use and the sanitarium laboratory was claimed to do analytical and chemical work which compared with the best of the era.

3.

For a man dedicated to a cause, the time and energies of himself and others are expendable commodities. John Harvey Kellogg, intent on making the sanitarium the greatest in the world and on spreading "Biologic Living" to all corners of the globe, drove himself and all others around him, including his brother Will. A typical day of the Doctor, as described by Albert Edward Wiggam in a December, 1925, *American Magazine* article, showed Dr. Kellogg "omitting breakfast because he had an emergency operation at 4:00 A.M. Operated again in forenoon at 11 o'clock. Then he had a board meeting until late afternoon. Followed conferences with patients and work on books—'I can eat some other time'." According to author Wiggam, John Harvey's secretary had four assistants to do correspondence work and to aid the Doctor in experiments with gastric juices from a dog subject. His commands to them were rapidfire:

"Make the bearing in that new machine two millimeters smaller. Get the French and German excerpts ready for my Ann Arbor speech next week. Wire that girl's parents that their daughter is doing fine work and will make a good dietitian."

The Doctor's day didn't end with sundown. He might work most of the night to translate a foreign book on hydrotherapy or to write one of the scores of books from his pen. An attendant massaged his head occasionally or applied ice bags to keep him awake. His record for uninterrupted dictation was a twenty-hour stretch. Eight hours of continuous dictation was nothing for one of his secretaries.

With their employer setting such a pace, the employees at the growing institution found plenty to occupy their working

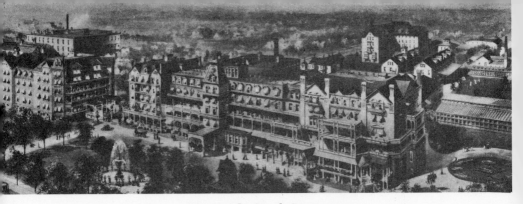

The Battle Creek Sanitarium.

Long a Mecca for the health pilgrimages of Americans, including many celebrities, the Battle Creek Sanitarium by 1897 was the sprawling, multi-building institution shown in the top photograph. After the fire of 1902, a new structure 550 feet long and 6 stories in height was erected and in 1928 a 15-story addition was completed, both shown in the middle picture. The bottom picture is a front view of the sanitarium, showing its front porch and lawn, and taken about 1929.

(Top photo courtesy W. R. French Studio. Bottom ph
Battle Creek Sanitarium Photographic Departme

day, which in this period was about twelve hours long. Any conclusion that the younger brother of the headman might have special privileges would be quite erroneous. In some memoirs which W. K. Kellogg wrote during his late years, he mentions that "Dr. Kellogg was a prodigious worker. He worked long hours and was not only willing but insisted that others work with him. . . . One year I kept a record of the number of hours I was on duty for the sanitarium. This record shows that one week I was on duty 120 hours. . . . Saturday was the rest day at the sanitarium. However, I was expected to open the heavy mail on that day as on other days in order to have the porter meet the trains on which patients might be arriving, since some of them might require an ambulance."

Mr. Kellogg also recalled that it was about seven and one-half years before he was awarded his first vacation of two weeks, and that Dr. Kellogg did not believe in holidays. "For many years we worked on Christmas and New Year's Day and were also on duty the Fourth of July."

However, even long days seem short if the pace is hectic enough. Will's duties at first largely concerned the shipping of the Doctor's books as published by the affiliate Good Health Publishing Company. But only for a few months were his talents largely confined to the purchasing and the sawing of lumber to make book crates. The efficiency and the coordinative ability of the younger Kellogg brother were soon recognized and gradually Will became "Mr. Fix-it" around the sanitarium. Whatever came up, people looked to him to take care of things. Whether it was he or others who conceived the ideas, Will was the one who shouldered the responsibility to see that the ideas were carried through. He became a man great on details, a careful observer, and a shrewd bargainer. "Even at that early date," recollected a longtime Battle Creek attorney, "he had a far vision and would take a calculated chance. He was more than a mathematician. He liked to see things grow and progress."

W. K. Kellogg

A doctor formerly at the sanitarium recalls:

"The helpers around the San held this united opinion: If you want anything done, go to W. K. He will listen to your story and he will give you an answer and the answer will be perfectly fair, and it will be accomplished as he says!"

Besides working for the sanitarium, Will Kellogg soon was "putting in nights and mornings to look after the Doctor's personal affairs." The younger brother's financial genius was particularly helpful in these "personal affairs," which were largely connected with Dr. Kellogg's many auxiliary businesses. The Doctor established more than thirty companies and publications in a span of fifty years, including the Michigan Sanitarium & Benevolent Association, Sanitary Supply Company, Sanitarium Health Food Company, Battle Creek Health Food Company, Sanitarium Food Company, *Health & Temperance Beacon, Modern Medicine Journal, Bacteriological World, Modern Medicine & Bacteriological World, Health Reformer,* American Health & Temperance Association, Good Health Publishing Company, Good Health Publishing Association, Sanitas Nut Food Company, Ltd., Sanitas Food Company, Modern Medicine Publishing Company, Modern Medicine Company, Race Betterment Foundation, Social Purity Association, Battle Creek Food Company, Kellogg Food Company, Noko Company, Electric Light Bath Company, the Rice Flake and Biscuit Company. In addition he founded three educational institutions: the School of Home Economics, the Sanitarium Training School for Nurses and the Battle Creek Sanitarium School of Physical Culture. Later these were merged into one organization, Battle Creek College. Two other John Harvey Kellogg institutions were the Haskell Orphan Home and the James White Memorial Home.

Before a decade had elapsed, W. K. Kellogg was responsible for all correspondence received by the sanitarium and the auxiliary companies. By 1890 some sixty to a hundred letters required replies each day and as the correspondence increased with the growing reputation of the sanitarium, Will Kellogg eventually was dictating to three or four stenographers daily:

"First I answered all inquiries concerning rates. Then I saw to it that Dr. Kellogg answered the purely medical inquiries. I was indirectly responsible for the Good Health Publishing Company as well as for Modern Medicine Publishing Company and Sanitas Food. I was a member of the labor committee and chairman of the committee in charge of the Sanitarium Food Company. I acted as unofficial credit manager and also was in charge of the issuing of cards and making prices for all operations. I was responsible for investigating and issuing cards to charity patients and was always called on in cases of death to go with friends and relatives to the undertaker and to assist in the selection of a casket. I was always notified when insane patients succeeded in getting away." With characteristic self-deprecation, W. K. Kellogg concluded these work reminiscences with the observation:

"I was so overloaded with work that I am conscious that very little, if any of it, was performed satisfactorily."

It was not until 1890 that Will Kellogg was to have an office, a small room on the first floor of the hospital building, with its one window darkened by a veranda. Drama in various degrees was to use this room as a stage as indigent clients sought free or low rates, as the well-to-do clamored for special services, and as employees with a grievance put their case in the hands of a man acknowledged to be a just man and an efficient straw boss. "I kept account of the people who called on me one evening after 5:00 and they numbered thirty-three."

Here, as well as in the daily rounds he made of the growing sanitarium property, he was to show the quick, almost intuitive thinking that later took him to the top of the business world. In an instant he would decide that here was a person meriting the attention of sanitarium doctors regardless of his lack of funds, or that the next appeal for low rates was a "phony" one. His decisions were as quick and nearly always right whatever the

field of interest, whether it was in the purchase of newsprint
for the medical publications, the sampling of a health food to
ex-patients of the sanitarium, or the salvage or the firing of the
irresponsible among the scores of "call boys" (messengers).

The job he dreaded most came in the early afternoons. Then
he interviewed people who needed medical or surgical aid but
did not have the funds to pay for it. If the sanitarium were to
remain solvent, it could care for only a fraction of those desiring
free treatment. Sometimes Will Kellogg, his heart torn by the
pity of a case, "could work miracles" through appeal to Dr.
Kellogg or to the Board. At other times, from his own meager
funds he could dredge enough for the care of a little child.

The faces of the crippled—the blind or the deaf—faces which
reflected a belief that he had the answer to their pitiful problems, kept crowding his mind. However, because of the ava-
lanche of such appeals, he could not always have the answer
and this unofficial sanitarium manager was to spend many
sleepless nights trying to solve this major problem. "Some day,"
he occasionally would muse, "I'll be in a position to help people
to help themselves."

Dr. Kellogg made a number of trips to Europe to study the
latest medical devices and methods and, during these periods,
left no one officially in charge of the sanitarium. Hence, Will
Kellogg was called upon very frequently to assume executive
responsibility. However, "when the Sanitarium Board voted to
make me business manager (during the absence of Dr. Kellogg)
and to print my name on the letterhead, I declined the offer."
Mr. Kellogg once told his friend, Arch Shaw, that "I never had
a title while I was at the San."

If the approach was right and no attempt was made to fool
those keen eyes which steadily appraised you, then one could
always expect justice and, oftentimes, mercy from Will Kellogg.
One instance of his altruism proved many years later to be
"bread cast upon waters."

An early motor car pioneer, Mr. Kellogg, together with his

chauffeur Henry Johnson, essayed the hazards of an automobile trip to San Francisco in 1915. (You will recall that road travel in those days meant dust or mud, getting lost because of the lack of road signs, or running out of gasoline because of the many miles between garage-service stations.) Somewhere west of Omaha, Nebraska, Will's Franklin roadster became hopelessly stuck in gumbo mud. A farmboy seeing the plight of the two men tried to pull the car out of the hole with a team of horses. Later the boy's father came along and with the aid of two teams was able to get the car out of the mudhole and into a comparatively safe rut of the road.

Mr. Kellogg gratefully turned to the rescuing farmer and said, "What do I owe you?" The farmer merely looked at him and said nothing. The food manufacturer then repeated his question, "What do I owe you?" The farmer said nothing. Puzzled, Will Kellogg turned to the farmer's son and asked, "Doesn't your father hear well?"

"Oh, I hear all right," the farmer explained, "but what I am trying to do is to recall where I have seen you before. . . . Now, I remember. About twenty-five years ago, my wife was very ill and our local doctor advised me to take her to the Battle Creek Sanitarium. She was there quite a while, and I began to run out of money. In desperation I went up to your office and you assured me that my wife would not lack for treatment simply because I had run out of money. That's why, Mr. Will Kellogg of Battle Creek, you don't owe me a penny."

An eighty-year-old Los Angeles woman physician recollected her eight years at the sanitarium and her observation of the growth of W. K. Kellogg during that period:

"He was an austere man—just like he had swallowed a ramrod. But back of that austerity, you knew he could and would help you."

Was this austerity from shyness or had Will Kellogg begun to look far down the road of life? Was his "differentness" of a neurotic origin or did it result from a call to conscience out of his puritanical background? Thoreau once said: "If a man doesn't keep pace with his companions, perhaps it is because he hears a different drummer."

In his life, a man may wear many hats. Will Kellogg wore the cap of a broommaker and the felt of an unofficial business manager. The time was to come when he would wear the fedora of a captain of industry, the rakish deck cap of a world traveler. But it was a sweatstained hat that he wore in his sanitarium days. One reason for this was that as John Harvey Kellogg's fame grew as a surgeon and health reform advocate, he was in great demand for speeches, and extrovert and showman as was the Doctor, he gladly made many public addresses. In the '80s and '90s, John Harvey's magic lantern was put to great use in illustrating his lectures.

You can guess that it was his younger brother Will who operated the magic lantern. Several hours were sometimes necessary to generate the gas for the lantern and to erect the projection screen for one of these showings, and a long drawn-out meeting might mean that the subsequent "tear-down" would require Will's time until the wee hours of the morning. Perhaps late work grew to be a habit with Will Kellogg and had something to do with the discord that showed up in a later family relationship. A February 6, 1884, diary entry tells of a long afternoon and night conference that the Doctor had with a Mr. Condit. Will was peremptorily commanded to stay around so that he could drive the guest to the railroad station. It was almost morning before the conference broke up and Will's diary relates that "Puss came up to the office about half past seven to see why I didn't come home. She was so scairt (*sic*) that she cried."

W. K. Kellogg recalled in later years that during the period when his children were small, there were many days at a time that he left home in the morning before the children were up and then he returned home late at night after they had gone to bed. "Most men lead lives of quiet desperation," according to Thoreau, and at least during this period, Will Kellogg was no exception.

Likely it was in this period that the subject of this biography became a "poor sleeper," a curse to him for the balance of his life. Hard, intense work and an overstimulated mind often kept his eyes open during the long hours of the night. During W. K. Kellogg's greatest activity as head of the Kellogg Company, his associates always knew when he had endured a sleepless night, for the nocturnal scribblings in a notebook always at his bedside produced countless memoranda. One such memorandum contained more than forty advertising, sales and production ideas. Another wakeful night might produce a sheaf of memoranda on what he wanted each of the family, children, grandchildren, even great-grandchildren, to do.

Whatever the cost to sanitarium personnel, the sanitarium grew and grew—almost within reaching distance of John Harvey Kellogg's dream of building an internationally famous institution. By the late '90s, the institution was caring for approximately five hundred patients annually and the years ahead were to see this number reach more than five thousand. Much of this success was due to the Doctor's enthusiasms. To use modern terminology, he was definitely an idea man. He not only had the imagination to dream up the ideas, but he also had the enthusiasm and intelligence to get them over to the other fellow. Thus, any lack of follow-through which the Doctor may have had was compensated for in his ability to get other people to follow through for him.

Dr. Kellogg made friends easily and was a chief reason for the use made of the sanitarium by many celebrities. Another secret of the success of the institution was its appeal to the well-to-do as a place where they could secure the most constant and deluxe services—"where they were catered to, entertained, massaged, babied." Of more lasting importance, however, was the excellence of the medical and nursing services. An ingredient in the financial success of the sanitarium, while it was under

W. K. Kellogg

Seventh-day Adventist auspices, was that the religious connection made available a labor supply of people who worked not so much for money as for the love of the cause. There was enough Yankee in the Doctor to enable him to rationalize the low salaries paid to personnel in this nonprofit enterprise. One of John L. Kellogg's recollections was of the time his uncle called the sanitarium staff together to tell them that "We have decided to reduce the wages of everyone because all of us are doing the Lord's work."

Yet another reason for the success of the "San" was W. K. Kellogg, who in those days made an unglamorous figure beside his famous and dashing older brother. In an unspectacular way, he was "a man always on the job, a real executive" and "the works" insofar as follow-through was necessary for the welfare of either patient or employee. While his fifteen-hour days took a toll from him and his family, they paid dividends to the Battle Creek Sanitarium. It is, therefore, understandable that in those days nothing infuriated W. K. so much as when, during increasingly frequent quarrels, the elder brother called the younger a "loafer."

CHAPTER | 4

"Like Two Fellows on the Same Ladder"

O<small>F</small> IMMEASURABLE BENEFIT have been the contributions of the genius and the near-genius to social progress, but their trail often is flecked with the "blood" of their families. Persons with tremendous drive, with single-track concentration toward a goal, are obviously departures from the norm. Because of myriad things to do and the tension draining their physical and mental resources, they have neither the time, energy nor perhaps the inclination to be good family men. They are fanatics and as such cannot and should not be judged by standards which apply to so-called "normal men." Theirs is a lonely obsession which puts blinkers upon them, permitting them to look straight ahead but preventing their seeing very intimately the phenomena (their families, their homes, their friends) alongside the road. Madame Grundy may or may not praise the genius but invariably she pities his family.

Neither John Harvey Kellogg, the idea man and topnotch promoter, nor Will Keith Kellogg, whose spark of genius was to affect industrial and philanthropic fields, was a good family man. Both were men who loved their families, but chiefly *in absentia*. They were too busy to be good husbands or fathers in the closest sense.

Over a gap of years, W. K. Kellogg's daughter Beth recalled the gradual change of her father from the gregarious young fellow of his early diaries to the weary breadwinner who might squelch the conversation at the family dinner table by saying, "I don't want to talk. I've had a long, hard day."

She elaborated by calling to mind:

"Particularly after the fire of 1902, there were several long hard years for Father at the sanitarium—eighteen to twenty hours a day trying to get the San back on its feet again, soliciting Adventists and other people for funds to rebuild. He was a man who dedicated himself to this project, in spite of the fact that the Doctor left the burden of refinancing almost entirely on his shoulders. . . . Father even would lend his only horse to the construction foreman so he could go out and gather up his workmen. There were funerals at the sanitarium which took literally hours to arrange. When a mental patient escaped, it was, of course, Will Kellogg who had to go after him and Father might be out most of the night. All this at times made him a stranger to his family. Maybe we would see him once a week. . . . In later years, subsequent to the sanitarium period, he was opening food factories in different countries of the world so that just now and then he had opportunities to be with us."

Although the demands of his employment did increasingly build a wall of silence between him and his family, Will Kellogg treasured his spouse and their children after his own fashion. He always had great pride of family and, firm though he was with the children, he was willing to fight and sacrifice for their future. And through the thirty years in which the heroine of his adolescent diary, "Puss" Davis, was his wife, he retained much of his love for her, though he seldom expressed this love in either word or flamboyant deed.

A friend who lived in the home for several years recalls:

"I have seen Mrs. Kellogg hurt but never angry. She was a tiny, sweet woman whose horizon did not reach beyond her home. She did not like to be annoyed with business and ofttimes remarked to me, 'I am so happy Mr. Kellogg has you to talk with. I dislike anything about business and I have no aptitude for it.' However, she was far from inane on subjects that caught her interest. She was a lovely conversationalist and was never blue or depressed, even when she was so ill. She kept that family on an even keel, which was a much more wonderful attribute for a wife than that of being able to discuss business. She admired her husband very much. She was secure in his love and did not have to be fondled or told. She knew it was there."

A relative who lived in the home for a period—Will Kellogg always kept open house for his relatives and anyone who needed a meal or lodging came and got it—remembers Mrs. Kellogg:

"She was about 5'4" tall, of average build, a quiet woman and not so much shy as absorbed in her work and thoughts. She was a good churchwoman (Seventh-day Adventist), a good housekeeper and her home and family meant everything to her. With W. K. the kind of man he was, she had to be ready to take in one or many guests most any time. . . . She wasn't the kind who came and put her arms around you, but she did the necessary things for your comfort."

That Kellogg did have concern for his wife was evidenced by his resentful impression that Mrs. Kellogg was overworking in soliciting funds for the SDA Church. (Of course, some of this resentfulness may have been actuated by his now lukewarm feeling toward the church.) Later when his personal finances made it possible, Will purchased a team of Kentucky bay horses and urged his wife to make use of them. A woman companion of "Mrs. K." remembers that "We were expected to exercise them, and both Mrs. Kellogg and I loved the job. We

(Photo by H. A. Edelman.)

Forty-year-old Will Kellogg was preoccupied by
eighteen-hour workdays at the sanitarium.

always went together, for it took both of us to hold the horses
as neither of us weighed a hundred pounds. It was a familiar
sight to see us dashing through the streets driving these spirited
horses."

Long before he was a wealthy man, W. K. Kellogg made a
magnanimous gesture to some of his relatives. The Pan American Exposition at Buffalo in the early 1900's kindled excitement even in the Midwest and he took from his small store of
money enough to send his daughter Beth and two of his half-
nieces (daughters of his half-brother Albert) to the glamorous
event.

Apparently the sanitarium jack-of-all-trades was able to get
away from work for an occasional evening at home for "During
those early days of 1899, on some of the evenings Uncle Will
would join the family (Mrs. Kellogg didn't sing) in singing

(*Photo by Doty.*)

W. K. Kellogg's wife, the former Ella "Puss" Davis,
whom he married after his return from Texas.

around the piano. I would play the instrument and we would
sing the good old songs, mostly old hymns or 'Marching
Through Georgia,' 'America,' etc. Uncle Will's voice was not
particularly strong or outstanding; he just sang the air like the
rest of the folks. He seemed to enjoy the singing as well as
being with his children."

Once in a great while, W. K. was free to take his family to a
concert or vaudeville show. His love for the theatre perhaps
answered some deep need, and he was willing to risk the displeasure of the "San" where the SDA personnel frowned on
the stage as too worldly. These few evenings, plus visits from
relatives, made up most of the social life of the Kelloggs, for
even years later when W. K. Kellogg became wealthy, the family seldom mixed with other people of the town. Perhaps this
was. because Mrs. Kellogg was an Adventist, Will's parents had

been Adventist, and the SDA made up a minority of the people of Battle Creek, then as now. The followers of the religion, as are many devout people, were branded as "different," a devastating appellation by the provincial to anyone with ideas foreign to their own.

As the turn of the century came near, the Kellogg children, Karl, John Leonard, and Beth, were in or approaching adolescence. These were the three children who lived into adulthood, Will Keith, Jr.'s death having been chronicled previously.

As if to take away some of the pain of the death of Ann Janette Kellogg in March of 1893 (his mother was ever a proud memory of Will Kellogg) Irvin Hadley, the only redhead of the family, was born in 1894 and—

"My Uncle Will was so proud of Hadley. Busy as the father was, he managed to take time to play with the baby every morning for awhile in uncle's own bed, a folding bed which could be tipped up on end and stood against the wall when not in use. One morning, the baby was overlooked by uncle amongst the bedding and the bed was folded against the wall. Sometime later, the baby was missed by my aunt and finally located in the bed, but neither smothered by bedclothes nor damaged by his head-down position.. . . Uncle Will liked, also, to have Hadley in the hammock with him, and once the baby fell out of the hammock, this time bumping his head. Uncle Will, it seemed, did not make a very good baby-sitter in spite of his fondness for his little redhaired son."

A great joy faded out of Will Kellogg's life when Hadley died from a contagious disease in August of the following year. It was in this year that Mrs. Kellogg "was threatened with nervous prostration and stayed at the sanitarium for three or four weeks." Her health thereafter was never robust.

Another glimpse of W. K. as a father is afforded by a recollection of a Kellogg family visit with Will's half-brother Albert in nearby Kalamazoo:

"Lenn (John Leonard), then about eight years old, was along

and as youngsters will do, became quite boisterous in play and several times interrupted the talk of his elders. W. K. simply turned toward Lenn and snapped his fingers and the boy quieted at once."

Autocrat in his own home as were most husbands and fathers of that day, when W. K. Kellogg issued an edict the boys and Beth gave a prompt "Yes, sir." That quiet influence was somehow communicated even to grownups and secured an almost similar reaction. This stern man, who smiled only rarely and laughed never, had strength of personality.

The children, from preadolescence into adulthood, had their battles of will with the father. Rarely, however, did Karl and Lenn dare open rebellion to his iron will, while only the most discerning would have noted the flash of resentment in the eyes of Beth. She was a quiet girl, relatively content with her studies and with her pony and cart, which equipage was unique in Battle Creek. One day she left the cart at the barn and, after saddling the pony, rode it into the country. Some pigs ran across the road, causing the pony to shy and to throw Beth off. Relieved of his load, the little horse bolted to a nearby oats field. An infuriated farmer chased the pony out of the oats and, almost fifty years later, the then wealthy W. K. Kellogg received a belated letter from this farmer to the effect that "I saved your daughter's life and never did get a reward. When will I get it?"

Although family affairs were not going so happily for Will Kellogg and he was increasingly irritated by the foibles of his employer-brother, financially he was "getting out of the woods." Never to make more than $87 a month salary during his quarter-century with the sanitarium, his 25 per cent commission on the sale of the Doctor's books made possible an occasional luxury denied to a man dependent upon salary alone. So in 1898:

"I purchased forty acres of land on the bank of Mill Lake, twelve miles west and north of Battle Creek, for $800, making a down payment of $100. From then until about 1906 the family lived at the place in the summers, and I would go there for a day on each week end."

The large summer cottage of white siding, a low roofline and spacious screened porches, was atop an elevation resembling an Indian mound. The main room of the house was in the shape of a Greek cross and about forty-five feet square, and there were sleeping accommodations for twenty-two people. With an interior of Georgia pine, a combination billiard and pool table in the main room, a windmill, an ice house and also a hydrant for watering the lawn, the place was quite de luxe and the Kelloggs made the most of their bargain.

The eight summers at Mill Lake (in 1906 the place was sold to John Harvey Kellogg) were happy ones, particularly for the children. Will himself grew quite fond of the house and lake and occasionally brought guests there from the sanitarium. On one particularly elite occasion, he hired a horse-drawn English tallyho, complete with a manually operated horn, to bring guests to the place. In an impish mood which struck him once in awhile, the host and several of his acquaintances startled farmers by touring the countryside on the tallyho, making the distinctive horn sound loudly and often.

A caustic wit once observed that "W. K. did not really approve of strong feelings of any kind unless pets were concerned." Too severe an indictment, it did point up his ever-strong affection for animals of all kinds. This was demonstrated by an occurrence at the Mill Lake summer home. Arriving at the home one Friday night, he was met by ten-year-old Beth who told him that she believed their beloved old cat had given birth to kittens in the unfinished attic of the house. Afraid that the kittens might fall down through the partitions, Will went upstairs and squirmed down into a very narrow space between the attic floor joists. Handing the kittens one by one to his daughter, he then tried to boost himself to the floor level only to find that insufficient leverage prevented this. Eventually he had to send Beth to the barn to bring back a saw with which he sawed out part of the floor and joists and thus effected his escape.

John Harvey Kellogg's home on Manchester Street was the scene of another peril for brother Will. The tall, many-windowed house which, with large grounds, a deer-yard and barns, occupied more than a city block, also had a huge vegetable garden worthy of this chief exponent of vegetarianism. On a walk one Sabbath morning with two young relatives, W. K. strolled the garden now abandoned to autumn and then started to cut through the adjacent deer yard. The trio was charged by a buck deer. Having a cane, Will fended the buck off but the enraged animal was able to reach one boy and tossed him a distance. He then turned again on Mr. Kellogg, got him down and trampled him. Only his heavy clothing saved the bookkeeper from death, and as it was, he was laid up for a number of days.

2.

"John Harvey Kellogg and W. K. Kellogg were like two fellows trying to climb up the same ladder at the same time."

This observation by a physician formerly at the sanitarium suggests competition and rivalry. At first thought, it might have seemed ridiculous at the time to compare the adulated Dr. Kellogg—a friend of many celebrities, the author of more than fifty books, a man who performed thousands of major operations during his career as a surgeon—with his younger brother, always in the shadow of the elder and until after 1906 practically unknown outside of the sanitarium even in his native Battle Creek.

Yet there was a rivalry, seldom overt until their association was ended, but always in the consciousness of the two men. Each recognized the strengths and the weaknesses of the other and was wary of the strong points and contemptuous of the weak ones. It was a case of two near-geniuses, coming from the same father and mother but whose actual heredity must have stemmed from widely different genes. The result was an extreme extrovert, who had a flair for the dramatic, in conflict with an introvertic personality who leaned backward to be different from his exhibitionistic brother.

"The two men did not seem like brothers at all," further recalled the physician. "They resembled each other but slightly and John Harvey was envious of Will's larger physical proportions. The Doctor was a man not more than 5'2" or 5'3" tall whereas Will was of average height, 5'7½", and looked taller. One thing that rankled in the younger brother's heart was that John Harvey never recognized him as business manager of the sanitarium though he was that in actuality. I believe the elder deliberately kept the younger down. As a matter of fact, he never encouraged any Kellogg to study medicine because he did not want more than one doctor in the family."

Many persons have remarked that the incompatibility of the two Kellogg brothers represented a distinct loss to the world. Their talents complemented each other's and, as a team, even their large contributions to society might have been greater. John Harvey was an inventive genius, a man overflowing with ideas, but he was one of the poorest of financiers; in many instances he was lacking in follow-through, and, in contrasting the two brothers, one scientist recalls "irresponsible emotionalism" on the part of the elder:

"W. K. Kellogg actually had much more of the scientific attitude than his doctor-brother. He would not make an extreme statement or take an extreme position until he had controlled and corroborated evidence. Characteristically, he first wanted to try things, to get a corroboration of ideas and then to validate his evidence. In financing, through his Foundation, various studies on health, his was the attitude of the scientist as contrasted with a remembered less valid approach to many subjects on the part of his brother."

While Dr. Kellogg was an eminent figure in the scientific

world, sometimes his enthusiasms led him to exaggerated flights of speech beyond objectively tested facts. This led to an embarrassing situation at the University of Michigan where he addressed a society of the inner circle of scientists at the university. The Doctor had been cautioned not to exaggerate before these scientists but when he warmed to his task of speaking, his dramatics got the better of his scientific learning and he made a number of unvalidated statements regarding the amount of nicotine in tobacco, the hazardous effects of its use, etc. He had gone on in this vein for a few minutes when his audience walked out in a body, leaving only the chairman of the meeting and Dr. Kellogg in the room.

A scintillating personality, an eminent surgeon, a skilled writer, Dr. Kellogg, on the other hand, "was gouged right and left, could be appealed to by the most obvious of overtures, and was often defrauded." The financial aptitude, prodigious memory, and developed judgment of Will Kellogg could have saved the Doctor from many predators—but neither brother was often willing to take counsel from the other.

An eminent figure in the public health field who knew both the Kelloggs summarized his impressions:

"Temperamentally the two brothers had totally different senses of responsibility. W. K. always felt keenly responsible for the entire solidarity of any position that he took. John Harvey had an idea and he ran with it until there was nothing left of it. . . . One was a systematic business executive, the other, although also possessing a keen mind, was an emotional person always playing to the public. He had found that personal advertising pays and he advertised himself and his ideas in ways that would have been unnatural to his younger brother. . . . While one might conjecture that Will's contempt for this side of John Harvey caused him to lean over backward from extrovertism, his good judgment and cautious, conservative approach likely were integral and innate parts of his character."

However, if Will Kellogg had contempt for the weaknesses

of his older brother, it is equally obvious that he admired him for the greatness which he shared with other members of the medical and surgical profession. A grandson of Will recalls that "Grandfather really was a frustrated M.D. I am sure that if he could have had his choice of professions, he would have chosen medicine. Most of his closest friends throughout his long life were from that profession. And never in talking to us grandchildren would he speak of a person having a 'cold' but instead would say 'He is suffering from rhinitis' or make some similar use of a medical term."

It was his introvertism that caused W. K. Kellogg to be less forgiving than his extroversive brother. The younger believed that he had much to do with the success of the sanitarium (at one time the San had a gross annual business of $4,000,000) and resented the fact that the Doctor was unwilling to share the limelight. Only now and then did this smoldering resentment break into flame. "I think we only had three eruptions," wrote Mr. Kellogg to a sanitarium friend on February 3, 1944. "The major one was between 2:00 and 3:00 in the morning and over a seventy-five-cent item."

But if the eruptions were few, the fire deep down was a latent volcano in the younger brother. Relative to an occasion when Dr. Kellogg countermanded an order from Will Kellogg which prohibited employees parking their bicycles near the business offices of the sanitarium, the latter had this to say:

"It was somewhat humiliating for one who was acting as business manager of the sanitarium to have a reasonable order countermanded by the superintendent. However, this circumstance was only a sample of the medical superintendent's manner of handling of affairs. He was a czar and a law unto himself, ignoring his associates and subordinates."

After the irritations of the sanitarium days had deepened from lawsuits into a feud which lasted a lifetime, it was John Harvey Kellogg "(who) could be arrogant and inconsiderate but (who) did have sentimental moments when he wrote letters which, in essence, were conciliatory. But incidents apparently had been burned very deeply into the consciousness of Will Kellogg, so much so that he never forgot nor forgave."

The above observation from a Chicago psychiatrist, related to the subject of this biography by marriage, keys in with the recollection of a financier associated for a number of years with Will Kellogg. This person believed that "One of the great stimulants for Mr. Kellogg to achieve business success was his resolve to become a peer of his brother. His experiences were on a very inferior basis, as a distinct subordinate of John Harvey Kellogg, and for twenty-five years he was dominated by an elder brother whose attitude was that the elder should be the sun, and the brother and all others only very small satellites revolving around this sun."

There can be no argument but that Dr. John Harvey Kellogg was a very brilliant sun in the sphere of the sanitarium and a figure of considerable prominence in the greater outside world. The Doctor was an experimenter, a man not afraid to venture into unexplored areas, and while his exploitation of some of his ideas may have earned him derision, the ideas themselves gained him wide respect. During all his career, he preached the gospel of fresh air and sunshine, and he was the inventor of several devices to administer ultraviolet and infrared light. As a surgeon he gained the interest of leading doctors and surgeons of two generations, and after he performed the first known operation for a lygated stomach, Dr. Will Thornton and Dr. Will Mayo of the famous Mayo Clinic visited him at the sanitarium to secure details. Most important to the thread of this biography is the fact that his experimentation with health foods was the genesis for the flaked cereal industry which currently is supplying an important part of the nation's food. (That portion of his work, alongside his assistant who was his younger brother, is detailed in the next chapter.)

The Doctor's advocacy of "Biologic Living" and the "Aristocracy of Health"—his way of labeling Nature's simple restorative

methods of simple food, mental hygiene, exercise and rest—
brought him into contact with leaders in many other fields besides those of medicine. Theodore Roosevelt, William Jennings
Bryan and William H. Taft, for instance, were familiar with
the teachings of the Battle Creek Sanitarium. John Harvey had
more than a nodding acquaintance with such diverse persons
as George Bernard Shaw, Dr. Alexis Carrel and Dr. Wilfred
Grenfell. Dr. Allan Dafoe, who brought the famous Dionne
quintuplets into the world, was very appreciative of Dr. Kellogg's suggestion and gift of soy acidophilus milk which cor-
rected a severe health trouble of the five girls.

John Harvey Kellogg was a Fellow of the American College
of Surgeons, as well as the American Association for the Advancement of Science, the Royal Society of Medicine (England)
and of the American Medical Association. He made a number of
trips abroad to study surgery under the world's greatest surgeons in Vienna, London, Paris and Berlin, and was acquainted
with Pasteur through studies at the Pasteur Institute.

A celebrity-acquaintance from a quite different field was
neighbor Henry Ford of Dearborn, Michigan, whose first view
of the sanitarium was during a visit to a patient, the famous
naturalist John Burroughs. Mr. Ford came back occasionally,
for he was intrigued by the personality and some of the experiments of Dr. Kellogg. They had a common interest in the development of soybeans for food and plastic values, and later
the automobile manufacturer exploited a hobby by bringing
to the sanitarium his square dance orchestra which played for
several dances in the Union Building of the block-long sanitarium plant. (No Adventist taboo was violated since the
dances occurred a number of years after a split between the
church and Dr. Kellogg because the church wished to move
the sanitarium to the suburbs of Washington, D.C.)

Until the grim years of the 1930s, the Battle Creek Sanitarium combined the features of a diversified clinic, the Chau-
tauqua lecture circuit and White Sulphur Springs.

With proper diet and exercise the keynote, the efforts of a large staff of physicians, many of them specialists, were aided by hundreds of nurses and bath attendants. Dr. Kellogg gave frequent lectures on food chemistry and dietetics. He exhibited strange plant foods he had collected on his voyages. Health booklets were distributed. The famous health foods not only were served on the sanitarium tables but also were sold by the box at a counter set up in the lobby.

There were the glamour, the de luxe atmosphere, the meticulous attention to the many details of care, comfort and luxury which, as charmingly sketched by Cleveland Amory in his *The Last Resorts,* made rest-health-play institutions "the place to go" for the comparatively prosperous in the late nineties and also the first three decades of the twentieth century. The San's professional staff saw to it that there were few dull moments for those not seriously ill. The national and even worldwide reputation of the Battle Creek Sanitarium was built upon its health facilities, but its word-of-mouth advertising from clients usually included the happy postscript that "you'll have a great time there, too."

The Monday Night Question Box.

A weekly Sanitarium feature, which became almost an "institution" in itself, was the "Question Box" conducted by Dr. John Harvey Kellogg and consisting of questions and answers relative to health.

Picnics and outings vied with Shakespearean plays, gymnasium classes and cooking schools as vehicles to keep the patients entertained. Every evening was chock-full of activity. A high spot was the Grand March, an intricate pattern of drills to music, including a serpentine pattern. Often there were demonstrations and wide participation in the use of Indian clubs. Rating high in attendance were the aforementioned lectures for, with the varied and wide-flung clientele, colorful personalities were easily obtainable for the rostrum. Dr. Kellogg's Monday night "Question Box" sessions in the parlor always drew a full house while musicales, including some personages famous in instrumental and vocal music, attracted the more aesthetic.

According to a long-time employee, an underlying reason for the sanitarium's heyday was that it was "before the days when a man could go into his club for a massage, electrical appliances for reducing, special diets, etc. Many people from the East and South came to the sanitarium for vacations combined with a health program and perhaps a clinical stay. Some were ill, some came to get away from everything, others came for a rest."

The clientele was largely (but not exclusively) that of wealthy people. Fifty years ago the rates of $35 to $40 per week for room, board and treatment represented a considerable sum of money. Of course, most of the patients were from the United States but beturbaned visitors from India, swarthy patients from Turkey and from Egypt, crisp-speaking Englishmen, even Chinese in their mandarin coats, were so common that their presence evoked little curiosity. Well-dressed, even famous persons, lolling in the ornate palm gardens or dining to orchestral music in a room then called "the largest dining room in the world without supporting pillars"—all this was a background much appreciated by John Harvey Kellogg and one which helped to build him into a figure of much eminence.

But if the great popularity of the sanitarium played a part in Dr. Kellogg's growing recognition, the advantages were mutual. The Doctor's personal charm, his gift of showmanship, and his ability to "sell" the institution were prime factors in the flow of celebrities to Battle Creek. As a result, "The railroad traffic to the San was so heavy at one time that the Michigan Central ticket office sold more tickets than any other station of its size in the country." A listing of famous persons who have visited the sanitarium through the years would take many pages of this book. They were from all strata of American life and from many corners of the world. From the sphere of business came C. W. Barron, John D. Rockefeller, Jr., Henry L. Doherty, Harvey Firestone, Harry Sinclair, economist Irving Fisher, S. S. Kresge, J. C. Penney, J. H. Patterson and many others. Billy Sunday, Evangeline Booth, and, of course, many Adventist missionaries (who rated cut prices until the sanitarium and the Church parted ways in 1904) represented the religious contingent. From the world of the arts were such persons as Will Durant, Mrs. Sidney Porter, Temple Bailey, John Burroughs, Lowell Thomas, Winfield Sheehan, A. E. Wiggam, Ruth St. Denis, Eddie Cantor, Richard Halliburton, Madame Lotta Lehmann, Sir Carl Busch, Percy Grainger, David Rubinoff and Iturbi.

Men of action, sportsmen like Johnnie Weismuller and William "Big Bill" Tilden and explorers such as Captain Roald Amundsen and Commander Richard Byrd came to learn more about "Biologic Living." Many state governors, United States Senators, and Cabinet Members have been guests at the San. The sanitarium, while much smaller than in its heyday, is still very much of a going institution with several thousand patients annually and about 350 employees. In recent years, a number of governmental dignitaries and prominent business persons have come to the institution for rest and treatment.

Battle Creek itself has claimed as citizens for varying lengths of time persons who have been in the public gaze—Adlai Stevenson, Perle Mesta, Gene Markey, Betty Hutton, Bernarr Macfadden—but none has been more colorful than John Harvey

Kellogg. After a visit to the sanitarium by a rich importer and lecturer on nutrition, Horace Fletcher (the innovator of "Fletcherism" which prescribed that each morsel of food be chewed many times before swallowing), Dr. Kellogg adopted that person's mode of dress. Thus the Doctor started wearing white clothing from hat to shoes, rationalizing the idea by proclaiming that white clothing admits more sunlight to the body. An exotic sight in Battle Creek was that of this short, plumpish man, completely attired in white, riding a bicycle, and with an all-white cockatoo perched on a shoulder. On the Doctor's frequent trips to New York, many heads would turn to wonder at this man dressed all in white in the middle of winter.

As another bit of showmanship, Dr. Kellogg quite frequently would have one of his secretaries telephone the Michigan Central railroad station to "hold the train; the Doctor will be there in a minute or two." Passengers wondering about the delay would crane their heads out of the windows to see a dramatic arrival, but the drama did not cease at that moment. The Doctor took a secretary on most of these trips and the two were no sooner seated in the parlor car than the secretary began to write letters, causing the other occupants of the car to ask: "Who is that distinguished man wearing the white suit and dictating letters so assiduously?"

But those were the palmy days and when the building of a several million dollar, fifteen-story addition to the sanitarium in 1928 (Henry Ford was the first guest to sign the register in the new building) practically coincided with the disastrous Depression of the 1930s, both the sanitarium and the Doctor were in trouble.

CHAPTER 5

"The Twenty-five Years Were Not Waste Years"

——FOOD EXPERIMENTATION BUILDS A BUSINESS

O<small>UR</small> <small>MORNING</small> <small>BREAKFAST</small> was almost invariably hot pancakes with bacon fat and molasses and our dinner was of pork, fried or boiled."

Merritt G. Kellogg, the elder half-brother of John and Will Kellogg, often pondered the possible connection of the ill health in his father's family with the type and quantity of food consumed. Until just a few years before World War I, a common practice in this country was to have a breakfast which consisted of meat and/or fried eggs, fried potatoes, lots of boiled coffee and bread topped with molasses, with perhaps a dish of fried mush or corn meal, and a triangle of pie for dessert. A load like that required twelve or more hours of sledgehammer labor to utilize it.

Very active people could handle such generous rations without too ill an effect. However, by the late nineteenth century, the struggle for existence had advanced beyond the pioneering and physical state. More and more people were engaged in sedentary pursuits. Machinery was taking some of the sinew-grinding characteristics out of labor. Yet eating habits, much like those of the pioneer who plowed and cultivated and chopped and reaped from before dawn until sunset, continued.

Here and there in the nation farseeing individuals or organizations were taking stock of the harm resulting from improper diet. Sister White, as has been related, had made proper diet a tenet of the Seventh-day Adventist religion and a studious follower of that faith had decided by the time he was sixteen that his was to be a career in diet reform.

Influenced by Dr. Sylvester Graham (inventor of Graham bread and the Graham cracker) the young student, John Harvey Kellogg, continued his food experiments after enrolling in the Bellevue Hospital medical school in 1874. Into his rented room he lugged a barrel of apples and a barrel of Graham crackers and these constituted the bulk of his diet. Breakfast, for example, consisted of seven crackers and two apples. One coconut a week and an occasional side dish of potatoes or oatmeal completed the menu. After a year of this regimen he had gained seventeen pounds and was feeling fine.

Nearly seventy years later, the ninety-one-year-old Dr. John Harvey Kellogg was to give the Associated Press an interview in which he asserted he had "done pretty well for a grass eater." The apostle of "Biologic Living" then reiterated his life-long belief that "man was intended to eat the plants and fruits and not the animals. . . . I haven't touched meat for more than seventy-five years. . . . I don't take patients at my sanitarium unless they agree to abstain from eating flesh foods and from smoking and drinking, at least as long as they want me to help them."

During the last quarter of the nineteenth century and continuing to the present days, the menu at the Battle Creek Sanitarium has been vegetarian. It has included several meat or butter substitutes made mostly of nuts and grains and served under such names as Protose, Nuttose and Nuttolene. The meat substitutes are made up as roasts and even as vegetarian steaks. Coffee and tea are taboo, a vestige of the old proscription by the Adventists, and currently caffeineless Sanka coffee and Minute Brew are served along with milk. Not very much pie or cake and no alcoholic beverages are allowed. Neither Dr. Kellogg nor Will Kellogg ever smoked (if one excepts Will's boyhood smoking of dried clover leaves) and there has always been a sincere enforcement of a "No Smoking" rule, although it is, of course, occasionally violated.

"After being at the San, people modified their food habits substantially. Certainly a stay there made them quite conscious of eating for health. People did not object to being vegetarian for a time, particularly since if they worried too much about it, they could sneak off to town and eat meat."

There was even a "meat speakeasy" called the "Red Onion," a small shantylike eating place conveniently located across the street. Only a block away from this "illicit" restaurant was another off-bounds place known as the "Sinners Club," mentioned in the Battle Creek *Enquirer and News* when it commented on October 24, 1954, regarding the death of Edward H. "Boss" Crump of Memphis:

"We knew him here as a quiet, modest gentleman who smiled pleasantly when asked if it were true that he had joined the 'Sinners Club'—Dr. John Harvey Kellogg's designation for those who sometimes gathered at the nearby fire station and there broke sanitarium training by lighting up cigars."

Duke, a St. Bernard dog proudly owned by Dr. Kellogg, proved that the flouting of disciplinary measures is not peculiarly a human trait. The Doctor, possessing this dog at a time when vegetarianism loomed large as a way of life, bragged that Duke was a vegetarian dog who ate and thrived on greenstuff alone. Many persons in Battle Creek, however, chuckled over this assertion since they knew that on the side Duke was getting meat bones and meat trimmings from a friendly butcher in a shop just a few blocks from the Kellogg home.

Many circumstances impelled Dr. Kellogg to intensify the food experiments which were to occupy a large part of his time for the next forty years. He found himself in charge of a number of invalids, many of them suffering from digestive disturbances. He was committed to a medical program built around proper diet rather than drugs. Since many of the patients were complaining about the monotonous fare at the sanitarium, and some were leaving before their treatments were completed, the Doctor set out to devise vegetarian foods which would be more attractive and more digestible.

The menu in the dining room included "Granula," leftover bread which had been dried in an oven and then ground up, and zwieback, a raised bread which is sliced and then oven-baked. There also was a cereal coffee substitute made of burned bread crusts, bran and molasses and labeled "Caramel Coffee" (later "Caramel Cereal"). The breads were used by the Doctor for a study of the effect of oven heat upon starchy foods. This heat, acting with the diastase in the cereal grain, converts the starch into dextrin. Since saliva must convert raw starch into dextrin as the first step in the human digestive process, a starchy food which is dextrinized in an oven is partly predigested.

There was dissatisfaction with Granula because it was not thoroughly dextrinized. Zwieback was more completely modified but its hardness was a disadvantage. One sanitarium patient broke her false teeth on the hard bread and demanded that the institution replace them.

In his efforts to evolve better foods, Dr. Kellogg in 1876 or 1877 tried mixing wheat, which contains practically no fat, with oatmeal and cornmeal which have a higher fat content. The grains were formed into biscuits and baked until the starch was thoroughly dextrinized and then ground into granular form. Patients found the product much tastier than zwieback, and eventually the new food was named "Granola."

(The Doctor also attempted to improve the coffee cereal substitute and eventually so improved it with the addition of malt that it found several imitators.)

Granola and Caramel Cereal, along with various kinds of crackers and wafers, were made in the sanitarium's own kitchen, primarily for patients. Then persons who had left the institution began writing back for the foods, and they were sent to them by mail. As the demand gradually developed, improved roller mills were devised for the grinding of Granola, and additional employees were added to the sanitarium food department. The food business was carried on merely as one department of the sanitarium. About 1880, an experimental kitchen was set up to investigate the effects of cooking upon various foods.

As Dr. Kellogg became more and more interested in the invention of new foods, he decided to go into business for himself and established the Sanitas Food Company. The sanitarium food department continued to handle the older line of sanitarium foods, doing business under the name "Battle Creek Sanitarium Health Food Company." The profits from the earlier line went to the sanitarium. However, those from Dr. Kellogg's food company went personally to the Doctor since "the Sanitarium Board of Directors did not think it best to incur the expense of the necessary experimental work." This change of direction was to have an important effect upon Will Kellogg, to whose many duties was added the managership of the new Sanitas Food Company. Instead of a salary, he now received one-fourth of the profits of the new company as well as of the Modern Medicine Publishing Company. Despite Dr. Kellogg's opposition to more than a modicum of advertising and sales promotion, Will succeeded in building the companies into rather substantial enterprises.

2.

When the Kellogg brothers produced the first precooked flaked cereal in 1894, they had no idea they were inventing a breakfast food. The phrase itself was unknown. What was being sought was a more digestible substitute for bread.

A sanitarium patient brought to Dr. Kellogg one day a sample of a new health food, a shredded wheat, which had been sent to her by a friend in Denver. The food appeared to promote the flow of saliva in the mouth and gastric juices in the stomach and thus was more readily digestible than bread. So interested was the doctor in the product that he made a special trip to Denver to see the innovator, one Henry D. Perky, a lawyer. The two compared notes on food experiments and Perky promised to send one of his shredding machines to Battle Creek. However, this machine never arrived and its lack, plus an evolving conclusion that a shredded food was not the solution to his problems, caused the Doctor to announce: "We'll invent a better food."

This was an inventor who could call his shot. In an interview years later, he said that the idea of flaking wheat by compressing it came to him in a dream. Dream or not, his first efforts in the kitchen of his own home proved a failure. He did not succeed in producing individualized flakes and he turned to Will Kellogg for assistance in the experiments.

"He sent over a sample of boiled wheat," Mr. Kellogg later related, "and wanted me to make something like it, but he did not know just the length of time to boil it. My instructions from him were to boil a quantity for fifteen minutes, another for twenty, twenty-five, and thirty, and up to one hour.

"These experiments I did in the kitchen of the sanitarium, on the range, at night, when I had finished my other work. After it was boiled, the Doctor took it to another part of the basement where there was a set of smooth rollers which had been used to grind Granola."

With the ingenuity of his Yankee forebears, W. K. Kellogg contrived a roller-knife arrangement which made possible the first wheat flake, the ancestor of all flaked cereals. Seeking a more digestible substitute for bread, the brothers Kellogg had no idea they were inventing a breakfast food.

These rolls, as Mr. Kellogg recalled them, were eight inches in diameter and about twenty-four inches long. Dr. Kellogg fed the wheat into the hopper at the top and it was Will Kellogg's duty to squat down underneath the rolls and scrape the sticky and gummy dough off the rolls with a chisel. After one or two nights of this, Mr. Kellogg suggested that the scraping could be done better by a large knife, such as those used in book binderies and printing offices. He obtained a pair of worn-out knives and, with some aid, fastened them to the lower side of the rollers, weighting them so that they pressed firmly against the rolls and scraped off the dough.

The experiments continued for some time without success. Then on a Thursday or Friday, a batch of wheat was cooked for some additional tests to be run that day. Other duties intervened, however, and nothing was done until Saturday night. Although by then, the cooked wheat had become decidedly moldy, the two brothers decided to run it through the rollers to see what would happen. Much to their surprise, it came out in the form of large, thin flakes, each individual wheat berry forming one flake!

There happened to be a fire in the kitchen range. The flakes were baked and came out crisp and tasty, if one overlooked the slight moldiness. It was some time before the Kellogg brothers unearthed the reason for their accidental success. They had inadvertently stumbled upon the principle of "tempering." To equalize the moisture throughout the wheat, the Kelloggs after considerable experimenting learned to temper the cooked wheat by letting it stand for several hours in a tin-lined bin. This eliminated the moldiness.

"For some reason," Mr. Kellogg later summarized, "the Doctor thought best to take the flakes after they had been nicely formed, put a sieve over a barrel and break the flakes up and rub them to pieces. It was my own suggestion that the flakes be allowed to remain whole and be served in that way." Mr. Kellogg prevailed and flaked foods were born.

Even though these early Granose flakes had little in common with the light, delicate flakes produced in the Kellogg plant today, for they were tough and rather tasteless since salt was the only flavoring, they were immediately popular with the sanitarium patients and showed a steady growth in sales until they were crowded out of the market by more aggressive imitators.

On May 31, 1894, Dr. Kellogg filed an application for a patent on "flaked cereals and process of preparing same." The patent covered flakes made from "wheat, barley, oats, corn, and other grains." At first the new food was supplied only to patients, but as the mail orders began to come in from former sanitarium visitors, Granose was put up in ten-ounce packages selling retail at fifteen cents a package.

During the closing years of the nineteenth century, Dr. Kellogg's food business expanded almost in spite of itself. Because of medical ethics, the Doctor refused to allow his name to be associated with the foods. Ultraliberal in many of his attitudes, the Doctor was a conservative in business matters and was opposed to large-scale national advertising, permitting the new flakes and other goods to be advertised only in the *Good Health* magazine, in the Battle Creek *Idea* and by direct mail to former patients. These restrictions chafed at the innate and developing business talents of Will Kellogg:

"About 1898 the health food business, without advertising or promotion of any sort, was continuing to grow. Orders were coming in so rapidly with so little effort on the part of any-one that it seemed to me there was a great future for the food business if it could be conducted as a company and separately from the sanitarium. *Dr. Kellogg and others did not seem to believe at the time that the business was susceptible of being developed.* (Italics ours) On my own I spent two or three days presenting the idea for a factory to several out-of-town members of the Board. The Board finally decided to accept a location on Aldrich Street, and a two-story building with a basement was erected. Real ovens were ordered and the business continued to grow under rather mediocre management.

"When talking to Elders Fargo and Starr and other members of the Board, I recall having offered a suggestion that, in my opinion, if given the opportunity, the food company would develop in such a manner that the sanitarium would be only a side show as to the magnitude of the food business. I confess at the time I little realized the extent to which the food business might develop in Battle Creek."

3.

At first the food sales were handled entirely by mail. Later a few department stores, food jobbers, and restaurants began to purchase the more popular of the foods. The Sanitas Company opened a small office at 72 Washington Street, and the foods were packed and shipped from there. Food products were being shipped to SDA sanitaria all over the world for, even at this early day, such institutions were as far away as England and Australia.

For W. K. Kellogg these were indeed busy days. An employee who was with the Sanitas Food Company in the '90s recalls that it was a habit of Kellogg to come into the office every morning about 9:00 to inspect food samples from the Sanitas Food factory. She further remembered that "Mr. Kellogg, always a man of quick and usually unerring judgment, would sample new products and make an instantaneous decision, a firm 'yes' or 'no'." Now past thirty, the sanitarium "jack-of-all-trades" was not only serving as business manager for the sanitarium but also managing the Sanitas Food Company, the Modern Medicine Publishing Company, the *Good Health* magazine and a half dozen smaller companies Dr. Kellogg had set up to sell surgical apparatus, medicines, exercisers, and other products of his inventive mind.

Busy with medical duties, surgical operations and the propagation of his dietary theories, John Harvey devoted little of his time to his business enterprises. He performed some of the experimental work himself, but usually he merely jotted his suggestions on memos and sent them to his brother. Will Kellogg initiated many of the food experiments himself.

Most of the one hundred odd health foods that eventually found their way onto the sanitarium tables were developed in the period from 1895 to about 1905. Dr. Kellogg had become interested in nut foods and another company, the Sanitas Nut Food Company, was created to market them. One of the food products invented was peanut butter. Actually, as Dr. Kellogg discovered some years later on a trip to Europe, the Egyptians had been making a similar product called "sesame" for many years, but the sanitarium developed it independently in this country.

"Dr. Kellogg asked me one day," Mr. Kellogg recalled, "to secure a quantity of peanuts, remove the hulls, and put them through the Granose rolls. I bought ten pounds of peanuts, roasted them in the oven a little while, put them in a pillow case to remove the hulls, winnowed out the husks, put the material through the rolls and made the first peanut butter. I took it to Dr. Kellogg and he named it. . . . A quantity of peanut butter was made up, and it was sold almost entirely to Seventh-day Adventists. After awhile the doctor had an idea that roasted peanuts were not wholesome. They were then cooked by steam instead of being roasted, and the little trade that was developed was lost."

No effort was made to promote the sale of peanut butter and others reaped the benefit of the sanitarium research. Other nut products, however, were produced including Nuttose, Protose, Nuttolene, and other substitutes for meat or for butter or shortening. Nuttolene was individually the discovery of Will Kellogg but "the Doctor did not compliment me very highly on the product. A week later he introduced the identical same thing, and called it Nuttolene, and said it was a very fine article."

Will Kellogg, it seems, was doing most of the actual shirt-sleeve work and the Doctor was getting most of the recognition as a food inventor. Testifying in the suit filed by his brother in 1916, Mr. Kellogg remarked, "I did the work as business manager of the sanitarium and got no glory and very little money. . . . In our food business the Doctor and I were doing business together. Some of the formulae he worked out, some I did, and he made suggestions and I made suggestions, and I think he took most of the credit for the work I did. I wrote a great many hundreds of notes for experiments to be conducted, and I have never claimed any glory—the Doctor has claimed that."

In a slightly different vein, W. K. Kellogg wrote a letter on January 17, 1939, to the J. Walter Thompson Company of Chicago, reminding this advertising agency that "the advertising should not imply that I claimed full credit for the invention for, if it does, I am afraid Dr. Kellogg's feelings would be injured. As a matter of fact, we worked together in the matter of inventing the wheat flakes. The corn flakes were developed later by a process somewhat similar."

W. K. Kellogg

Early in 1899, the growing health food business was incorporated and Will Kellogg received a formal contract as general manager of the new corporation, his payment to be one-fourth of the net profits. Because the Sanitas Nut Food Company, Ltd. (a merger of the food company and the nut food company) was selling much of its output to the sanitarium, Mr. Kellogg a year later voluntarily relinquished his salary from that institution in order to avoid any criticism. He continued to look after the San's business affairs without charge.

Dr. John Harvey Kellogg used a bicycle as his mode of transportation between his home and the Sanitarium. It was not unusual to see the Doctor pedaling his bike from his home while younger brother, Will, jogged alongside to discuss forthcoming activities of the San day.

Business conferences between the Doctor and his manager-assistant, Will Kellogg, became more frequent and to combine exercise with these conferences, it was John Harvey's custom to ride his bicycle around a circle in front of the sanitarium while Will trotted along at his side. It was not unusual to see the Doctor bicycling between his home and the sanitarium, with his younger brother jogging along beside him to discuss the day's business.

The factory constructed on Aldrich Street just behind the sanitarium bakery on White Street utilized one of the earliest known of "traveling ovens" for toasting the wheat flakes, as well as especially designed flaking rolls. While the building was under construction, special precautions were taken to prevent competitors from seeing any of the equipment. A doorman barred unauthorized visitors, and machinery repairmen had to obtain special passes to get into the plant.

These precautions did not represent melodramatics but were quite necessary. Every American is a potential businessman and the more affluent and venturesome are constantly alert to the possibilities of riding the coattails of pioneers who start an industry on the basis of a new food, a new gadget, or any new convenience of particular appeal to the public. And despite employees' affidavits, night watchmen, and other efforts toward secrecy, the method of making wheat flakes soon leaked out. The period from 1900 to 1905 saw the formation of dozens of competing wheat flake companies in Battle Creek.

The Kelloggs were to become concerned about this health food boom in Battle Creek, but before it reached its crescendo and for many an ultimate decrescendo, there was excitement right at the doorstep of the brothers. When the factory building was completed at a total cost of $50,000, Dr. Kellogg said he had not authorized the expenditure and insisted that Will Kellogg would have to pay for the building!

In a triumph of understatement, John L. Kellogg testified some years later, "I guess my father did not like that very well." Actually, this was a crisis which was ever to remain a memory to Will Kellogg. Much as he disliked borrowing from friends and relatives, this was the only alternative to personal bankruptcy. It was at this point in his life that his evident integrity and quiet efficiency paid dividends, for people who knew him were confident that he not only would be willing but also able to repay their loans.

A half-niece of Mr. Kellogg recalls the day he came to her and asked if she would co-sign a note with him. Such was her trust in her uncle that she signed the note without looking at the amount, but she remembers his saying:

"If I don't pay this and my other debts within three months, I will lose everything I have in the world."

The sequel was a happy one. Sanitas Food Company sales continued to rise and Will's one-quarter share of the profits allowed him to reduce his large indebtedness. Then the sales system he had previously set up for the Doctor's books, with subagents working the year round on commission and some thirty college students selling in the West during summer vacations, began to bring increasing returns "which were sufficient in 1903 to pay up all of my indebtedness including the mortgage on my home."

But if Will had thankfulness to Providence for rescue from a nervewracking emergency, he had no thanks to give to brother John Harvey Kellogg. Abruptly he told Doctor Kellogg that he could not work for him any longer. (The break did not affect the Sanitas Company arrangement since Will, as manager, was agent for the corporation rather than an employee of his brother.) The squeeze play relative to the Sanitas building was, of course, a major cause for his decision.

Another culminating difference between the brothers was the Doctor's refusal to postpone the moving of the business office from a previous location to the college building although the move interfered with the coming marriage of a valued employee. The ensuing quarrel resulted in Will's clearing up his desk and leaving the sanitarium. However, in breaking a connection which had lasted for twenty-two and one-half years, the younger brother "told the doctor that I would continue looking after his personal interests until his debts, then amounting to about $63,000, were paid, and then I was going out for myself."

Fate intervened for Dr. Kellogg, however, for as Mr. Kellogg later related: "The sanitarium fire of February 18, 1902, occurred six months to the day after I had discontinued working for the institution. Since Dr. Kellogg was not in town and since the sanitarium seemed part of my life work, I met with the members of the Board and offered to come back to work for nothing and board myself as long as my services were needed. The doctor returned late the day of the fire or the following day, and my offer was accepted. . . . During the building of the new sanitarium building, I was given the job, in addition to my other work, of securing money with which to pay the bills. It frequently happened that on Thursday or Friday the treasury was without funds but in one way or another I secured the funds so that the payroll was never defaulted. These two and one-half years which completed my work of twenty-five years with the San were the hardest years of my life, and no amount of money would tempt me to repeat those years."

4.

Even though he had somewhat cleared the atmosphere by telling off his older brother, Will Kellogg's summary of his last two and one-half years with the sanitarium was not exaggerated. This man, now about forty, divided his fifteen-hour days between bookkeeping, troubleshooting, the selling of bonds to finance the new building, and solution of the intricacies of food manufacturing and sales for the Sanitas Company. Imitations of sanitarium products had begun to spring up on every hand. In some instances, formulae and processes were deliberately stolen and renamed, packaged and then put on the market.

Other would-be rivals learned about basic food production processes by a method which later was to become commonplace, the hiring of Kellogg employees. Former Sanitas employees set up food companies of their own. From 1902 through

Between 1902 and 1904, forty-two companies were organized in Calhoun County, Michigan, to manufacture cereal foods and beverages. Shown is the ultra-competitive Battle Creek food boom as seen by famous cartoonist, James T. McCutcheon, and as carried in a Chicago newspaper.

> 1904 Battle Creek was in the midst of a wheat flake boom
> comparable to a Texas oil strike or the Florida real estate
> boom of the 1920s. In a city of less than thirty thousand popu-

lation, there were approximately thirty wheat flake companies in addition to Sanitas!

Families invested their life savings in cereal manufacturing machines and set up plants in sheds or even in tents. New companies mushroomed overnight. Many of them never got into production at all, having been formed primarily as stock-selling schemes. The reputation of the sanitarium had made the Battle Creek name so highly prized that one company which manufactured wheat flakes in Quincy, Illinois, called itself the "Battle Creek Breakfast Food Company."

The New York *World,* in its issue of September 7, 1902, waxed eloquent concerning the boom:

"There is not a pauper in Battle Creek, not a hovel home in the town. Every worker, however humble, lives in a pretty house surrounded by grass and flowers. One street of the town is called Bride's Row because every time a clerk marries he builds a home in the row for his bride. . . . As for the factories, most of them are running by night and on Sundays in order to keep pace with the demand for their goods. . . . Battle Creek is the greatest cereal food producing city in the world. It has thirty-two plants devoted entirely to the scientific preparation of cooked grain for the breakfast table."

Records at the Court House of Calhoun County, Michigan, reveal that actually forty-two companies were organized in the county to manufacture cereal foods and drinks. However, as quickly as it came up, the boom died down, with only the strongest half-dozen companies to survive. "Bankers and investors began to turn thumbs down on food companies as investments. The industry had earned for itself a very bad reputation."

Of all the early Battle Creek competitors, only one besides Sanitas produced a corn flake and this firm was bankrupt within a few years. As health foods evolved to breakfast foods, history records that only Will Kellogg spotted the one that was capable of becoming the most popular ready-to-serve cereal: toasted corn flakes. He was certain that a more satisfactory product would come from what some skeptics still termed a "horse food."

The exact date on which the first corn flake was produced is unknown. Dr. Kellogg's patent application for "flaked foods," prepared in 1894, specifically mentions the possibility of using the process for flaking barley, oats and corn in addition to wheat:

"Within three or four years after the invention of Granose flakes," Will Kellogg testified in 1917, "I took some raw corn and had it boiled in an open boiler and dried out and put through the mills and flaked. The Doctor looked the product over and may have made some suggestions, I don't recall.

"The corn flake business was not a success from the first. The formula was changed and it was not made twice alike; the machinery was not satisfactory. It was some time after the first experiments before the product was really marketable."

Corn flakes, which proved an overnight success when Mr Kellogg started his company in 1906, lay virtually unnoticed from 1898 to 1903. The key to this obscurity was in the fact that the earliest corn flakes were made from *whole* corn instead of from corn grits, and were unflavored.

Will Kellogg began to experiment with hominy grits and found corn much harder to deal with than wheat. Ingeniously he discovered that a long blade from a paper cutting machine would cause the moist flakes to peel off readily and that, toasted, the flakes became crisp and golden brown in color. A source in Indianapolis was found for hominy grits in the bulk but the Indiana concern, learning the use made of the grits by Sanitas, started making corn flakes in direct competition with their best customer for the basic material. It took Mr. Kellogg several months to find another source for the grits.

Later malt flavor and other improvements were to be added and an aggressive advertising campaign launched, as will be told in the next chapter.

The thick and comparatively flavorless corn flakes made experimentally by the Sanitas Company in the early 1900's apparently found no imitators but the competition in wheat flakes proved disastrous to Granose and the Toasted Wheat Flakes produced by the company. The handsome $24,542 net profit of 1901 vanished, and for the year of 1902 the company took a net loss of $6,428. What this did to Will Kellogg does not have to be imagined:

"As I was at the time working long hours at the sanitarium without compensation, I was not in very good shape financially to take any loss and was not obliged to do so, but I instructed the bookkeeper to charge to my account a sum in excess of $3,000."

Despite the heavy inroads made by competition, Dr. Kellogg still clung to a merchandising policy based on timidity rather than aggressiveness. He frequently told his brother: "Let's be content with a small business. As soon as we start advertising and attracting attention, one of the big companies will come along and take the business away from us."

Will Kellogg, who was to become a plunger insofar as advertising was concerned and whose company was to become one of the nation's largest users of promotional media, could not go along with this idea but was unable to sway the doctor. Doubtless the scintillating rise of a comparative newcomer to Battle Creek, C. W. Post, was an influence in his thoughts that "Some day. . ."

5.

One of the patients who arrived at the sanitarium in 1891 was a thirty-seven-year-old businessman who, in a greatly emaciated condition, was conveyed about the premises in a wheelchair by his wife. He had suffered reverses as a salesman, agricultural implement dealer and hardware retailer and was at a low ebb of his career.

However, after some months away from his business worries and under good medical care, his health improved and he regained forty or fifty pounds. During C. W. Post's stay at the sanitarium, one of the principal health foods manufactured there was a cereal coffee substitute, *Caramel Cereal*. The formula was no secret and there was no apparent effort to cloak the method of its production from the public.

Following his departure from the sanitarium and his subsequent establishment of the La Vita Inn near Battle Creek, Mr. Post late in 1894 began making a cereal coffee* which he at first called "Monk's Brew." This beverage did not have immediate success, for Post lost $800 on it in 1895 and broke even in 1896. He changed the product name to Postum Cereal and established the Postum Cereal Company, Limited.

With the aid of a Chicago advertising agency, Post then launched a vigorous advertising campaign. Postum packages carried the phrase MAKES RED BLOOD. Advertising copy extolled Postum as a builder of nerves, red blood, and all-around health. With some financial aid from the Fuller Company, Mr. Post was able to bridge the early, lean years and by 1900 was said to be netting $3,000,000 a year! The success of Postum inspired imitations of cereal coffee and helped to launch the aforementioned Battle Creek food boom.

In 1898 Post produced a product, Grape-Nuts, which bore some resemblance to Granola, a granulated cereal food which the San had been making for nearly twenty years. The Post product was promoted with the same hard-hitting advertising policies that had proved successful with Postum, and it proved a big success.

Meanwhile Will K. Kellogg, working day and night for the sanitarium and the Doctor's hodgepodge of food and publishing companies, was itching to take one of their more popular health foods and to promote it in a vigorous way.

---

* C. W. Post's original equipment consisted of a secondhand, two-burner gasoline stove for roasting bran and a small hand-operated peanut roaster for roasting wheat, a coffee grinder and several mixers. His supplies included two bushels of wheat, two hundred pounds of bran, ten jugs of molasses, fifty packing cases and two thousand cartons. His initial investment was approximately $69.

6.

Bankers who grew increasingly skeptical of the breakfast cereal business as the Battle Creek boom began to collapse were not the only cynics. The whole idea of prepared, ready-to-eat cereals had been ridiculed from the start. "Businessmen had called the idea foolish and housewives, not yet emancipated from their kitchen stoves, felt that mere man could not possibly cook cereals in a factory as well as they could cook them at home. Besides, the idea of eating a cereal *cold* was too revolutionary."

Too revolutionary—except for the handful of men who rode through the boom and its collapse and who had the capacity to look far into the future. Among these men were Will Kellogg and a young-man-with-an-idea, Arch Shaw, who was to be a close friend and advisor of W. K. Kellogg for more than a half-century. A lost cuff link was the genesis of their long association.

Shaw, while a Jackson, Michigan, student tutoring for admission to West Point, conceived the idea of a card filing system for businesses similar to the records used by libraries. While in the industry of this period a common phrase was "My business is different," he believed there were functions common to all businesses and devised systems to perform these functions. Dismissing the thought of West Point, he began to travel in an effort to sell the systems.

Mr. Shaw, who was later to become an economic advisor to President Herbert Hoover and who was to have close contacts with such personages as William Howard Taft, Theodore Roosevelt, Thomas A. Edison, Bernard Baruch and Robert A. Taft, recently recalled the story of the lost cuff link:

"The fourth city in which I sold recording and indexing systems happened to be Battle Creek. While in that city for the first time, I lost one of my cuff links and went to a small jewelry store on the west side of town. After buying another pair of links, I naturally began to try to sell the man a ledger system.

In the course of our conversation, he asked me, 'Have you ever been to the San?' I said to him, 'What is the San?'

" 'The sanitarium,' the jeweler explained, 'is just about the biggest thing in town. You go up there and ask for a man named Will Kellogg. Maybe he can use your system.' "

Shaw took the tip and went to the San:

"This was in 1897. I found Mr. Kellogg was doing the buying for the sanitarium and I sold him a buyer's outfit for keeping quotations from his suppliers. We set up a sort of friendship that day and I went there a number of times, subsequently doing business with the Good Health Publishing Company and others of the companies they were promoting. Gradually a mutual liking developed and W. K. and I many times afterward agreed that 'Fate makes the wisest decisions.' Had I not lost a cuff link, I would not have gained contact with Mr. Kellogg and we would not have become unofficial partners through the years."

As a memento of his first visit with Kellogg, Shaw still wears a duplicate of the set of cuff links he bought in Battle Creek that morning in 1897. Two years after the happening, Arch Shaw and L. C. Walker established the Shaw-Walker Company. Its house organ, *System*, eventually became the nucleus of a publishing business (Shaw's assistant editors for several years were the yet-to-be-famous Carl Sandburg and Edgar Rice Burroughs) which was a pioneer in the field of general business magazines and books. Because Shaw's business brought him into close contact with many different industries and for the reason that he was especially interested in advertising and sales problems, he proved a valuable friend and counselor to the Sanitas and Kellogg companies. As a director, he of course participated in many of the decisions of the company.

Both Will Kellogg and Arch Shaw were at an opposite pole from Dr. Kellogg insofar as was concerned his conservative attitude toward advertising and sales. Mr. Shaw recalls that "I think it was I who suggested that at least there ought to be

sales of these good foods to patients who had become familiar
with them while in the sanitarium. When W. K. and I followed
through on this, I recall that the Doctor was not very enthusiastic about the circularization of former patients, or the advertising by which the mail order business was built up. Apparently
he was impressed by the assertions of some of the physicians
in the San that such advertising was hurting their professional
reputations and making a medical enterprise a business."

Will Kellogg was now at a point of "middle-aged revolt"
where he was no longer disposed to follow the conservative
dicta of his elder brother. Seeing far down the road, he was en-
visioning a national food business of hitherto undreamed of
proportions. This was evidenced by his reaction in an incident
described by Roy O. Eastman, who worked for Sanitas and
later was advertising manager for the Kellogg Company:

"One day," Mr. Eastman recalls, "I came to work and found
that my desk in the Sanitas warehouse was completely surrounded with cases of some new food. I thought that was splendid because it gave me a little privacy. I knew from past
experience that such a large supply of a Sanitas food would be
on hand for months. But a few days later the packages were
gone. I asked what had been in them and learned it was corn
flakes.

"Everybody was excited about the possibilities of selling
corn flakes by mail—everybody except Mr. Kellogg, that is. He
said, 'I'm not interested in a mail order business. I want to sell
those corn flakes by the carload.' Everybody laughed at him at
the time, but it wasn't long before he was doing just that."

Neither Will Kellogg nor Arch Shaw could see why Sanitas
should sit idly by while others made millions by copying Sanitas products and renaming them. Consequently, they planned a
new Sanitas advertising campaign. Instead of appealing only
to former sanitarium patients through *Good Health* and the
Battle Creek *Idea*, they decided to offer the foods to the general public through a wider list of publications and to stress the

appetite appeal, although some advertisements were to mention the medicinal value of the foods.

Mr. Shaw subsequently wrote an ad that was headed: WILL YOU LIVE THE BATTLE CREEK LIFE FOR THIRTY DAYS? It offered a $4.50 assortment of Sanitas foods which readers could purchase by direct mail in order to try the sanitarium diet in their own homes.

At about the same time, Shaw helped prepare a booklet in which the newly developed four-color process was used to picture the foods in an appetizing manner, a technique which has since become standard in food advertising. According to a company historian: "Will Kellogg reasoned that there were more well people than sick people. Hence the product should be sold as something good to eat rather than as a health food. Today there is no arguing with the soundness of his bold reasoning, but at the time it took daring for Mr. Kellogg to turn his back on the supposedly surefire health appeal. Had he been wrong that single decision would have been enough to have wrecked the new business. Characteristically, after weighing the probabilities, he took that chance."

Although this campaign was successful, Dr. Kellogg was not happy about it because of the thought that he was endangering his professional standing by promoting a generalized food business. He was, therefore, determined that his name should not be identified with the foods.

The exact reason for placing W. K. Kellogg's signature on the cartons is not clear. However, it safely can be assumed that Will was endeavoring to guard against the host of imitations beginning to flood the market. Dr. Kellogg, in the bill of complaint he filed against his brother in 1916, alleged that Will Kellogg "suggested and urged and finally interwove the name Kellogg as a distinguishing mark on the goods manufactured and sold by them (Sanitas), and adopted the phrase 'None genuine without the signature of W. K. Kellogg,' this phrase appearing conspicuously and thereby identifying many of the products manufactured by Sanitas."

At another point, the Doctor testified that the signature was put on the packages "at his request, and not mine, and rather against my wishes. I knew it went on, but I raised the question as to whether he needed to have it on. He convinced me that it was necessary for our protection, and I permitted it to be used. . . ."

A letter Mr. Kellogg wrote to Mr. Shaw on March 8, 1906, further bears on the well-known signature:

"The following is a matter I would like you to especially consider: What would you think of calling these flakes 'Kellogg Corn Flakes' instead of Sanitas Corn Flakes, and then using a signature somewhere on the package similar to the attached? In thinking of this matter, don't take into consideration for a moment that I am ambitious to have my name appear in this way. The only thing I am interested in is the business that will result. I have not spoken to Dr. J. H. about the matter, but I am sure he would object to the plan and he would suggest that the inference would be that it is his corn flakes, but the signature on the package ought to take away this objection. I am exceedingly anxious to do this just right and want the benefit of all the help I can get in making the decision."

Perhaps, as a Canadian Justice suggested in a later lawsuit, Dr. Kellogg felt that the use of his brother's name on the cartons would enable the Doctor to reap the profits from the foods while at the same time avoiding any professional stigma. Whatever the exact reasons that led to the step, early in 1903 red-inked words: "Beware of imitations. None genuine without this signature. W. K. Kellogg" appeared on many of the sanitarium products, although not on the corn flakes packages of the new company until three years later.

7.

Meanwhile the advertising campaign became faster paced now that a proven product was on hand: corn flakes. The 1903 ads, now prepared by an agency, concentrated on one food: corn flakes. The copy stressed taste as well as dietary properties: A BREAKFAST TREAT—THAT MAKES YOU EAT. Newspaper space was taken in a number of cities and door-to-door sampling campaigns delivered corn flakes packages to nearly every house in a city. (The introduction of such an ambitious house-to-house sampling program was probably one of W. K. Kellogg's most significant contributions to the packaged food industry. It enlisted the powerful salesmanship of taste.) In addition, the Sanitas Company was using street car signs, window displays and billboard advertising and several salesmen were calling on institutions, department stores and food jobbers.

Late in 1905 Sanitas increased its production to 150 cases of corn flakes a day but still was unable to keep up with the orders. However, the gross sales volume of $100,000 a year was a niggling sum in comparison with C. W. Post's three plants and his multimillion dollar business.

Another incident in contravention to the Doctor's wishes was to make bigger business possible for Kellogg-manufactured products. John Harvey Kellogg had refused to permit the use of cane sugar in any Sanitas product because of its possible harmful effect upon diabetics. However, while the Doctor was in Europe that winter, W. K. Kellogg disregarded his wishes and added sugar to the flakes. He found that the sugar not only sweetened them, but also enhanced the "nutty" flavor of the malt-and-corn combination. The improved flake was a truly delicious breakfast cereal.

"The Doctor came back from Europe and had a fit," John L. Kellogg, son of Will, related. "He was going to fire Mr. Butler, the superintendent, because he made the flakes with sugar, but he did not make much headway. He got after my father, and

Mr. W. K. and the Doctor had a row about it, but Mr. W. K. kept on making the flakes with malt, sugar and salt as the flavoring."

Mr. Kellogg realized that he now had a breakfast food superior to anything yet developed. He had seen competitors walk off with what could have been a sanitarium monopoly on cereal coffee, a granulated cereal and wheat flakes. Unless bold steps were taken to capitalize on this new opportunity, the same thing could happen to corn flakes. He was about ready to take these bold steps.

8.

Several conversations with Charles D. Bolin, a St. Louis insurance man who came as a patient to the sanitarium in 1905, revealed that both he and W. K. Kellogg had confidence in the future of corn flakes. In addition, Bolin could raise enough capital in St. Louis to launch a new company devoted solely to the manufacture and sale of corn flakes. There remained the hard task of securing an option on the rights which belonged to Dr. Kellogg.

"It took me nearly six months to secure that option," Mr. Kellogg later related. "The patent on flaked cereal foods had been declared invalid (in a case lost by the Sanitas Company against the Voight Cereal Company of Grand Rapids in 1903) and all I needed to do, if I wanted, was to start making corn flakes myself. But I wanted to play the game fair and square."

Dr. Kellogg was willing to sell some of his food interests, especially since some of the notes which the sanitarium had given to finance its rebuilding were about to mature. He apparently did not believe the new company would be very profitable, however, and insisted that it be capitalized at $200,000 so he could get a large sum for his rights. Will Kellogg was not in favor of such a large stock issue, but eventually he gave in on that point and on January 22, 1906, an option was signed.

Later, confusion and controversy arose from the fact that

W. K. Kellogg in 1910, at age fifty—

—as he looked during the early years when his
company was young and struggling for existence.

Dr. Kellogg gave two completely different options, both of which were accepted. The first one transferred to the new company the right to sell corn flakes anywhere in the world; the second was limited to the United States.

Five days after the new Battle Creek Toasted Corn Flake Company was incorporated on February 19, 1906, Dr. Kellogg decided that he had not intended to sell the worldwide rights (the first option, known as the Bolin option) after all. Instead the Doctor submitted a new proposition of sale, conveying only the right to manufacture and sell within the United States. In return he was to receive $170,000—$22,440 in cash and $147,560 in stock. Mr. Kellogg did not think the Doctor had any right to limit the new company's sales after signing the Bolin option, but Dr. Kellogg insisted upon the limitation and Will Kellogg reluctantly yielded.

It will be recalled that W. K. Kellogg's contract with the Doctor's Sanitas Company allowed him one-quarter of the profits. He therefore asked for one-fourth of the $170,000 proceeds of the sale. After considerable haggling, Dr. Kellogg paid him $42,500 in stock.

W. K. also asked that his brother take over the Sanitas factory building, according to prior agreement, paying for it in stock and finally the Doctor gave his younger brother $30,000 in corn flake company stock for this building.

Thus from the launching of the new company, Will Kellogg received approximately $70,000 in stock. Of this he gave $1,000 in stock to Judge Jesse Arthur, who had drawn up the incorporation papers, and $10,000 in stock to various officers and trustees of the new company to heighten their interest in the business. He had $60,000 in stock remaining and this figure is corroborated by the corporation stock book which lists Mr. Kellogg's holdings in December, 1906, as 5,921 shares.

Will Kellogg also was to receive a $250 per month salary as president of the company. Dr. Kellogg insisted, however, that his brother was still his employee and was therefore entitled to only one-fourth of this payment. For nearly a year, Will Kellogg was required to endorse his pay checks over to his brother, who gave back to Mr. Kellogg one-fourth of the amount and kept the rest for himself. This unusual arrangement did nothing to improve the relationship between the two brothers!

Meanwhile Charles Bolin was having his troubles in disposing of the stock of the company but by early spring several St. Louisans had made purchases and on April 2, Dr. Kellogg received the remaining shares due him. Apparently the Missourians did not trust Dr. Kellogg's business judgment, however, for they stipulated that he should not dominate the business. For initial working capital the new company had the $35,000 raised in St. Louis, plus $60 in qualifying shares.

One wonders if the Biblically-minded W. K. Kellogg did not liken the opportunity to "deliverance from Egypt and into the land of Canaan." A quarter century of virtual bondage had ended and ahead was a breathtaking vista. What mattered it that he was forty-six years old and "middle-aged"? His was not the psychic turmoil of a man in his middle years casting about frantically for wealth, but there was a need to prove to himself, to his brother, and to the world that he could scale the heights.

The Battle Creek boom had collapsed and perhaps there were certain portents that a national financial panic might not be far away. With a quiet confidence, however, Will Kellogg surveyed the future, and this attitude and his integrity inculcated a similar confidence in his backers. He had concluded that the odds were not too long. Perhaps, as Arch Shaw believed, "the quarter century did not represent waste years at all for W. K. Kellogg" but a period of preparation for a belated blooming. At last his maturing executive abilities were to have freedom to function without the handicap of an ultraconservative board.

No easy years were in prospect for this white-collar employee, finally turned manager. This little known man was to play an important role in a highly competitive era of American enterprise and to astound an industry with his vision, aggressiveness and courage. His life outside the business arena was to be very important, but particularly valuable at this stage of his biography is an appraisal of W. K. Kellogg, *the businessman,* by his old friend and counselor, Arch Shaw:

"The essence of W. K. Kellogg as a businessman was simplicity, for Mr. Kellogg, along with his business genius, had also some of the traits of the artist—certain intuitions and sensitivity through which he could get 'the feel' of a matter. He did not clutter his mind with details or engage in unnecessary mental cerebration. He had the ability to sense a change in the factors which entered into a problem and, therefore, could get directly to its core.

"He had intuition which told him when to act and how to act. He arrived at his best decisions through such intuition. Business, then, was an art to him and he achieved rich satisfaction out of his work over and above the money he made from it. In a tactical victory, he gained a confirmation of his imagination and his instincts—great satisfactions to a creative man. He could be involved in a situation and at the same time sit back to watch himself as well as the other businessmen across the bargaining table. Business was almost a game to him—a fascinating opportunity to move pawns to reach the king row— and he was a master player who knew it by a surging of power and a confidence that the goal ahead would be swiftly reached."

W. K. Kellogg's original factory.

CHAPTER 6

"I Sort of Feel It in My Bones"

—THE COMPANY GROWS AND MATURES

F<small>IRE!"</small>
The clanging of alarm bells and the clomp of horses' hoofs made for a noisy start to Battle Creek's Fourth of July of 1907. As the town's newest pride, an up-to-the-minute pumper fire truck, clattered down cobblestoned Bartlett Street, a number of the slumbering citizens awoke to dress and run toward a rosy glow in the east.

Even eyes still dim from sleep could see that the blaze was a hot one, and before many of the would-be viewers had arrived the fire obviously was beyond control.

"They say the night crew was setting off firecrackers and that's how the fire started. Anyway, it's tough on old man Kellogg!" Such was the gist of conversation of several hundred persons as they watched the frame corn flakes factory burn. "Tough, indeed, to work a quarter-century for the San, then start a business and have it wiped out in a little more than a year."

However, as the stocky and balding Will Kellogg spoke to

various employees spotted in the milling crowd, there was nothing in his behavior to indicate that he had any thought of being "wiped out." Calmly and quietly he issued instructions:

"I want all you men to report here tomorrow morning. You will not be laid off. Some of you will be assigned to our Norka plant (an extension of the destroyed main plant) and the rest can be used in cleanup and construction work."

One of Mr. Kellogg's competitors was at the scene of the fire. Perhaps he assumed that the catastrophe would at least cripple the operations of the aggressive young food business for a long time. If he figured this, it was because he did not really know W. K. Kellogg. Holiday though it was, Mr. Kellogg had a Chicago architect at the scene within twelve hours. Before the ruins had stopped smoking, they had prepared plans for a modern, fireproof cereal factory.

"It was decided not to rebuild on the same location," recounts an unpublished *Story of the Kellogg Business,* "since it was not as conveniently located as might be. The company owned no land, and Mr. Kellogg did not know just where his new building would be put up; but he did know that the product had 'taken' with the public, that the company was three hundred carloads behind in its orders, and that the fire was not going to stop his business. Standing there in the heat from the still-glowing embers, Mr. Kellogg and the architect discussed the type of factory they would build.

"Within three weeks after the fire, a site was acquired for the new plant. In the selection of this new site, Will Kellogg revealed himself as a man with judgment and vision, for the land he chose was between the Grand Trunk and Michigan Central railroads and would place the young business in a position to ship directly over either railway."

Thus this comparatively new company president prepared to activate a cherished dream of modern factory buildings humming with activity twenty-four hours a day, with switch engines busily backing in freight cars of raw materials and strings of "empties," and hauling away loaded cars for many destinations.

First comes the dream, but though achievements beyond his wildest expectations became realities for Will Kellogg, he always retained his love for the sight of steam shovels working. As the years saw the erection of numerous domestic and foreign cereal plants, his estate at Gull Lake, Michigan, the impressive villa atop a small mountain near Pomona, California, he never was so fond of these acquisitions as when they were in the throes of construction. "The man had a positive glee in seeing a thing grow—be it an industry, a city, a forest reclamation or an orange grove," recounts a lifelong friend.

Another friend recalls that during the travel years of this energetic man, even the wild beauty of Mexico failed to hold Mr. Kellogg's enthusiasm when he discovered that it was a land of *mañana*, of people who put things off till a faraway tomorrow. There was only "today" for this man in a hurry. Always somewhat rueful that he was off to so late a start in his career, he was restlessly eager, driven by energy and ambition which he could scarcely control. There appeared to be a thermostat within him, more sensitive to change and more prompt to react than in most people.

He had supremely needed this excess of energy in the initial sixteen months of the corn flake company preceding the Independence Day fire. It was a crucial time for this middleaged entrepreneur. The era itself was a period of ferment and growth for American industry. Vociferous President Theodore Roosevelt was the current national crusader, and people in ordinary conversations spoke casually of "vested interests," "trusts" and "the Big Stick."

The new century had set a dramatic stage. Electricity heralded a future "pushbutton" era. A startled citizenry was confronted with the power of the controlled explosion of gasoline. The age held out the promise of mighty engines to propel men on land, under the sea, and in the air. In other fields, there was development of things new and revolutionary. And men with unusual gambling instincts and the necessary capital to implement such daring, were meeting the challenge of the new era.

As Putney Haight saw it: "There were other large industrial fortunes, contemporary or nearly so, such as that of Henry Ford's enterprise. In a general way the achievement of Will Kellogg was to be illustrative of the individualistic 'American way' of that epoch. His procedure was along the classic lines of industry building, practiced largely prior to World War I. It may never be invoked successfully again. The impact of two Rooseveltian crusades, plus two world wars, with income, excess profits and other taxes, price controls and labor adjustments, conceivably could terminate industrial fortune-making in the so-called 'American way'. It is conceivable that W. K. Kellogg might never have attained real wealth except under a social order and system of government placing a premium on personal initiative and free enterprise."

Bold ideas, ingenious and persevering experimentation, enthusiastic promotion, dramatic accomplishment and spectacular display were phenomena of the time and W. K. Kellogg, from a small scarcely noticed beginning was to play an increasingly important part in what has been called "the heroic age of American enterprise." Under the fire of the literary guns of Ida M. Tarbell, Lincoln Steffens, and Upton Sinclair, and the political verbiage of President Theodore Roosevelt, William Jennings Bryan, and Eugene V. Debs, the larger industries nevertheless expanded.

More and more people came into the stock market, to become in a small way partners in nationwide and even worldwide ventures. The first efforts were made toward automation, an accelerated trend in the industry of today. The "trust" and then the "holding company" became common to the corporate scene, leading to a pattern dialogue by vaudevillians Weber and Fields:

"Well, I'm broke," Weber would say. "So am I," Fields would respond. "Let's start a trust" (or a bank), they would shout.

Then they proceeded to a burlesque which was considered convulsingly funny.

But as the ordinary citizen relaxed by whistling "Sweet Adeline," "In the Shade of the Old Apple Tree," or "Everybody Works But Father," or giggled at Carrie Nation's antics or at the currently stylish "peekaboo" waist, there were more and more signs that some sort of economic lapse was in the offing. Some New York bankers even prophesied an out-and-out financial panic, and that not very far away.

The prophecy became an actuality in 1907 but, with characteristic single-track concentration, Will Kellogg ignored the sound and fury of the economic-political scene. He had a man-sized job on his hands.

For one thing, Mr. Kellogg had little practical knowledge of the grocery trade. "I was green when I started the business," he recalled. "I had handled the business affairs of the sanitarium for years, but I did not know the difference between a food broker and a jobber." To top it off, it must be remembered that W. K. Kellogg was by this time past forty-six years of age—a milestone at which many men are slowing in their business careers instead of launching new ones.

Although he had written Arch Shaw that "I sort of feel it in my bones that we are now preparing for a campaign on a food which will eventually prove to be the leading cereal of the United States, if not of the world," W. K. had to prove it to a skeptical public. It will be remembered that in the face of the collapse of the Battle Creek food boom, bankers had turned thumbs down on food companies as investments. It was only because of their belief in the integrity and judgment of Mr. Kellogg that St. Louisans, mostly former patients of the sanitarium, had furnished the initial $35,000 working capital for the new company.

Later the same belief in the quiet efficiency and honesty of the man prompted the citizens of Battle Creek to purchase stock, but Will's stock-selling activities did not meet with universal success. While the ultimate growth of the business was to make several of the city's families wealthy, some acquaintances resisted the sales talk of the company's president.

Then there were some people who bought Kellogg stock and later sold it. Among these was a prominent official of the sanitarium whose sale of corn flake holdings displeased W. K. Kellogg. Following the very successful rise of the stock with steady and good-sized dividends, a large appreciation in the market value and spectacular profits to the stockholders through splits in the stock, Mr. Kellogg was always delighted to run across this official. Out would come the little black book in which W. K. was forever taking copious notes. After clearing his throat, always an ominous storm signal, he would remind the luckless man: "Let's see, now. If you had held on to your several hundred shares, they now would be worth 'umpteen' thousand dollars." In the little black book he would have the amount all figured as to the current value of the stock that had been "disloyally" sold. There was the need in Mr. Kellogg periodically to prove to this gentleman, and to all doubters, that they had been wrong in questioning his judgment.

But if stock-selling was vital, getting into quantity production was the *sine qua non* of the new company. While the first cereal manufacture had been in quarters leased from the Sanitas Company, a purchase in the spring of 1906 made available a shanty-like factory on Bartlett Street. Though Will Kellogg knew this building to be in an indifferent state of repair and that it potentially was "an old fire trap," the Battle Creek of that day offered nothing better and the price fitted the company's slim pocketbook. Thus necessity and economy lit a slow-burning fuse to the conflagration which was almost to wipe out the fledgling corporation on Independence Day of 1907.

However, that event was months ahead and this seventh son of a seventh child was optimistic for the future. He even hoped there could be attained a production of thirty-six cases of corn flakes a day. At a profit of $1 a case, this would amount to $900 a month, or $10,000 a year, heavy money in the Battle Creek of that day!

A file of correspondence between Manager Kellogg and Arch Shaw (who handled from Chicago the advertising and selling for the company during the first seven months) reveals that in a highly competitive field this newcomer got off to a phenomenal start. It was apparent the public liked the appetizing flavor of toasted flakes made from corn. When the books were closed at the end of 1906, the company had shipped out 178,943 cases of corn flakes. Since the production rate had been only one hundred cases a day during April and May, at least one hundred and seventy thousand cases must have been manufactured during the last seven months of the year. The overwhelming rush was to cause Will to make an unbusinesslike comment to Mr. Shaw:

"I note that the St. Louis jobbers will not give more orders for corn flakes until their back orders are filled. *This is good news to me. I don't want to see any more orders for some time to come.*" (Italics the editor's.)

Because "the word 'Sanitas' partakes too much of a disinfectant," the company began to tinker with the idea of a change to the trade name of "Korn Krisps." However, when Arch Shaw suggested that the term "toasted" be incorporated into the name of the product, W. K. Kellogg quickly saw that the word would add a mouth-watering touch to an otherwise ordinary product name. So "Toasted Corn Flakes" became the favored term and the trade name was changed from "Sanitas" to "Kellogg's." The "Kellogg Company" was not to be the corporation's official name until 1925.

Concomitant with the new production line and the change of trade names was "a big, bold splash" in company advertising, to be discussed in a later sequence of this chapter. In addition, Will Kellogg was not overlooking the personal touch in building up his business. However, before he could inaugurate the first of many selling trips which must have, at first, been anathema to this shy man, the Bartlett Street fire was to precipitate a crisis to command all his energies for some time.

2.

You would never have known from Mr. Kellogg's impassive face or from his seemingly unhurried demeanor that he was a man tormented by worry. The fire meant a big opportunity for competitors to get into the market with their "imitation" products. Hence the next move after planning the new building with the Chicago architect was to obtain money to supplement the $64,000 of fire insurance proceeds. A call on a Battle Creek banker obtained the assurance: "All right, you can have a loan of $50,000."

Construction of the new plant began only a few weeks after the fire, with the contractors working night and day. When the building neared completion, Will Kellogg stopped in at the bank to borrow the $50,000 that had been promised to him. In spite of the previously given word (perhaps the growing economic panic of 1907 was the deterrent) the banker stated:

"We're sorry. We're not making any more loans to food companies."

Mr. Kellogg knew he was in serious trouble. His trips to other banks in Battle Creek were fruitless. For three discouraging weeks, he called upon the banks of Chicago, trying vainly to raise the money so badly needed for working capital. Finally, the desperate petitioner visited one of Chicago's smaller banks, the National Bank of the Republic:

"I showed them our statement and the banker said, 'We have to take chances same as other people. Your statement is good.'"

The loan of $30,000 on three ninety-day notes was a salvation for the corn flakes company. Later when a Detroit bank advanced some rather persuasive arguments to lure the company's account away from this particular Chicago bank, Will Kellogg was to say "No" because he remembered with gratitude the act of the small Chicago bank in his time of need.

An obstacle almost as great confronted him when he set about to equip the new factory building. At that time only one manufacturer in the United States could produce water-cooled rolls for making corn flakes. When Mr. Kellogg went to this manufacturer in Detroit, he was told that a competitor had placed an order for all the equipment that could be produced over a period of months. Thus quietly corralling the means of corn flake production, the competitor was simply putting the rolls in storage and no doubt laughing heartily at the predicament of the young upstart company. But he hadn't reckoned with the determination and persuasiveness of Will Kellogg.

Years later a coast-to-coast broadcast over the Mutual Broadcasting System told of Will Kellogg in this crisis, only one of many he faced and surmounted. He had never had a lot of money —never wanted it—but the one dream of his life was to make good. He was resolved to turn doubt and disbelief of others into conviction and success.

For the first time since he had started the factory, W. K. felt his age. He was forty-eight now. He had started too late. The things he wanted to do would never be done. As tired as he was and as much as he tried to put it all out of his mind when he returned to Battle Creek from Detroit, he couldn't keep from going to the old factory site. He walked through the charred rubble, recognizing here and there the remains of what had been a thriving business. Then, suddenly, his foot struck something hard, something long and round. He brushed the ashes away, examined the object, and then he hurried as fast as he could to the nearest telephone to call the equipment manufacturer:

"Does that contract of yours say anything against repairing *broken* machines. . . . You could get around the contract that way, couldn't you?"

Then Mr. Kellogg reminded the Detroit supplier:

"We helped you get started in the cereal roll business. Now you've got to help us."

On the pretext that he was repairing the rolls damaged in the fire, the supplier was able to get around his contract with the would-be monopolist. Mr. Kellogg personally bought some acid and marked the five rolls he was returning to be repaired so they could not be appropriated by the competitor. When the rolls were ready for reshipment to Battle Creek, Mr. Kellogg had a man accompany them in the freight car. He was taking no chances!

Kellogg was mad now, fighting mad. He had a new determination, a new right, from which was born a new industry that began to flourish and spread and was to become a vast network of Kellogg plants, from Canada to South America, from London to the heart of Europe, from Asia to Africa, to Australia, around the world.

Five months from the date of the fire, the pulsating rhythm of factory machines vibrated the new plant. In six months production was in full swing in a modern, fireproof factory. When the new factory was running smoothly, W. K. Kellogg contentedly looked at the rolling machinery and remarked to his son John L. Kellogg: "Now we can turn out 4,200 cases a day and that's all the business I ever want." By 1920, with improved rotary ovens, those same rolls were turning out twenty-four thousand cases a day. Of course, today's production of corn flakes and other cereals by the Kellogg Company is many times the latter amount.

Shortly after this, Mr. Kellogg set about to improve the flavoring of the corn flakes. His superintendent, H. G. Butler, had learned of an enhanced flavor process in England based upon the use of malt, and W. K. Kellogg, determined to know more about the malting process similar to that in brewing, borrowed the full-time services of John L. Kellogg who was then working part time for Dr. Kellogg and part time for the corn flake company. John was sent to the Wahl-Henius Institute and the Stein-

The accelerated sales of the Corn Flake Company didn't just happen. Planning, advertising and salesmanship were involved. Determined W. K. Kellogg could be a master salesman as can be seen from the above shipment of an entire trainload of cereals sold by him in a visit to one food broker.

hoffer Brewery in Chicago during May of 1908, gaining practical experience in malting which paid dividends in the form of a new nutlike flavor for the corn flakes. Shortly after this, John became a full-time employee of the corn flake company, working up to the presidency before a disagreement with his father caused him to resign in 1925.

With the new production lines operating at an accelerated pace, W. K. Kellogg made an extended selling trip to line up brokers who, under the then prevailing pattern, resold the corn flakes to jobbers. These in turn supplied the retail grocers. By this time the company was doing quite extensive magazine advertising and it was essential that corn flakes should be on sale in all large centers in order to care for the demand.

Kellogg's whirlwind trip took him to Pittsburgh, New York, Boston, down the East Coast to Florida, then through Mississippi, Alabama, Louisiana, and Texas. He then went to California, Oregon and Washington and returned through Minnesota. Traveling night and day for five weeks and literally living on trains, he recalls sleeping in hotels only three or four nights on the entire trip.

It was on one such journey to visit the trade that the manager-salesman put pressure upon a reluctant broker in an eastern city and "as a result I recall that we received one order from him in excess of twenty cars. These cars were loaded, decorated with banners stating they were from the Kellogg Company of Battle Creek and were being shipped to the city under discussion." This volume contrasted strongly with the wee trickle of production at the start of the new corn flake company, according to an employee who recalls:

"Before I went to work for W. K. Kellogg, I was checking in freight for the Grand Trunk Railroad. The new Toasted Corn Flake Company would bring to the railroad station two cases of corn flakes. I would say to the Kellogg man, 'Do I get both of them?' He would reply, 'No, the other goes to the Michigan Central.' Then there grew to be three cases that were brought over. Finally a whole load . . . all that could be piled on a van."

Of course, the accelerated sales didn't just happen. Planning, advertising and salesmanship were involved. But how could a "shy, cold" person be a master salesman as W. K. Kellogg proved to be on his visits to the nation's jobbers? Perhaps a chief answer to the question is that he was not a "shy, cold" man in a business transaction with his peers. Out of his natural element once he left hardheaded, practical matters, his determination and enthusiasm in the arena of business made him quite different from the reserved, diffident figure that he was in almost any other environment. With the mantle of business around his shoulders, he was able to transcend his inhibitions and to become what he dreamed of being, a leader of industry.

When it came to direct action toward a goal that he felt was right, Mr. Kellogg never bothered about anybody else's opinion. He went straight ahead like a bull moose to battle!

A long-time associate further analyzed W. K.'s salesmanship:

"Any salesman with strong convictions about the value of his product is a long way toward becoming a supersalesman. Mr. Kellogg believed that in furnishing corn flakes and other products to the people he was performing a health service."

As W. K. Kellogg became more successful, his black, shiny and baggy suit was replaced by a custom-tailored wardrobe and thereafter he was the epitome of neatness. Otherwise, he wore prosperity lightly. Even the stubby, blue bow tie shown in his early photographs lingered through many years, as characteristic as his laconic speech. Only in reminiscent moods during his late years did he ever use two words where one would do. When he spoke in his medium register voice, that quiet voice which would become weak and scarcely audible when he was not feeling up to par, his paragraphs were brief and his sentences shorter. Often he would take refuge in clichés such as "Once seen, never forgotten" or "What cannot be cured, must be endured."

A veteran employee recalls a story current at the Kellogg Company some years back. This pertained to a piano salesman who was called to Kellogg's Gull Lake estate to relate some facts concerning a grand piano possibly desired. The salesman took from his brief case considerable literature and talked and talked about the virtues of his particular piano. The food manufacturer just sat and said nothing. After the salesman had been talking for about a half-hour, W. K. interrupted him, simply saying "Send one out," thus dismissing the vendor. The man went away shaking his head over the way in which the order had been placed.

Will Kellogg was a man of action rather than of words. Yet while he was thrifty with words, he could say a tremendous lot with just a few of them. His business utterances were nearly always succinct and pithy in nature. For instance, one could have talked all afternoon about volume business and not have said it as well as on an occasion when the company was starting to make a shredded wheat biscuit. Kellogg, watching the hand operation, turned to a visitor and said:

"I don't like this hand packaging. I want products that run off conveyor belts into packages."

This was no idle remark. It was completely characteristic of the simplicity and boldness of his thinking. It explained his success. At the time, some of his company associates were talking about cases and that irritated Mr. Kellogg who thought in terms of carloads. Before long he began to think in terms of trainloads.

Mr. Arch Shaw once likened W. K. to another friend, former president Calvin Coolidge "who had two languages, the language of statesmanship and the language of the country store on Saturday afternoon. . . . Now and then W. K. would coin a phrase, a sentence which was succinct and complete, expressing in a few words what others might spend pages in delineating."

Another long-time friend of the food manufacturer, Attorney Burritt Hamilton of Battle Creek, remembers:

"His customary telephonic salutation was 'This is W. K. May I see you a minute?' His minutes were sixty seconds. In a few words he was able to express clearly the essentials of a five-million-dollar contract. When he signed a contract he performed it as written. I do not recall anyone's ever asking him for a guarantee of performance."

3.

If "advertising is the lifeblood of American business," then Will Kellogg and his counselor Arch Shaw were the "doctors" who prescribed many transfusions of ads for the health of the corn flakes company.

It is the opinion of Battle Creek's daily newspaper, the *Enquirer and News,* that "Much of the initial success of the company was the result of a decision at the outset to advertise extensively and intensively." Mr. Kellogg appreciated the power of the new force that was beginning to be used by progressive businessmen—the force of consumer advertising. Visualizing his foods on breakfast tables in millions of homes, he knew that the entrée to these homes was chiefly through advertising.

House-to-house sampling, the package itself, the principle of repetition and continuity in advertising copy—these were ear-marks of the progressive attitude not only of Will Kellogg but of most of the breakfast food pioneers. As industry historian, Gerald H. Carson, reviews the early years:

"Modern advertising and selling matured early in this field. The men were colorful. Competition was keen. The methods were rough and ready. Problems were solved with fresh and original thinking under field conditions. Many of these new ideas

This early advertisement shows that Mr. Kellogg was quick to sense the importance of sampling his product. It urges the reader to "listen for 3 rings and get the dandiest breakfast ever."

are standard techniques today. . . . Vigorous men with novel suggestions appeared in many fields, but there is abundant evidence that an extraordinary virtuosity and propaganda skill appeared among the breakfast food pioneers. . . . To the public the prepared cereals became product personalities—a composite of the way the food tastes, the radio and TV programs, the dietary preachments we get from advertisements, those jolly package faces and the famous, often whimsical names, as familiar as one's face in a mirror."

Canny Will Kellogg knew that most of us like to get something for nothing. Right from the beginning, therefore, he had his corn flakes cases made oversize so that he could pack a few full-size samples in each case for the grocer to distribute free to customers. (In addition the salesmen employed by the jobber received a bonus on any order of five cases or more.) More than four million samples were distributed by the company in its first year, and while this figure was to be dwarfed later, it represented no mean accomplishment for a comparatively wee organization.

House-to-house sampling, first utilized by Will Kellogg in 1903, was used extensively from 1908 to World War I. Taking the food to the people was not without hazard for, occasionally, sampling crews were arrested because of municipal anti-peddling ordinances. Placid Moberly, Missouri, through an exciting story written by a newspaper reporter, deduced from small cross marks found on gateposts, sidewalks, and house stoops that the town and, in particular, the marked houses, were to be invaded by a band of outlaws. The excitement abated when it was discovered that the chalk crosses had been placed there by Kellogg samplers so that other members of the crew would not cover the same territory again!

Mr. Kellogg early made a decision to stake everything upon the biggest advertising campaign his limited capital could buy. The decision was influenced by the very satisfactory results from a trial run in the newspapers of Dayton, Ohio. This was, perhaps, one of the earliest applications of today's standard practice of test-marketing products in one or two cities. The sum of $150 thus used (the newspaper insertions were supplemented by a "walking ad," an eight-foot papier-mâché ear of corn made ambulatory by a man inside) was not the last $150 in the company treasury, as has sometimes been stated, but it was an appreciable sum for the little business. Subsequently, W. K. almost depleted the slim financial resources by contracting for a full-page advertisement in the July, 1906, issue of the *Ladies' Home Journal.* No periodical today dominates the field so completely as then did the *Journal* and, as John L. Kellogg related the story:

"The company was sold on a big bold smash in advertising as against a timid, piecemeal policy. W. K. Kellogg could have gone along advertising in a small, conservative way, letting the campaign naturally build itself up from the profits. But he wanted

Violates All Rules.

In Mr. Kellogg's first magazine advertisement for the new company, he calmly admitted that "This announcement violates all rules of good advertising." The ad appeared in *The Ladies' Home Journal.*

to get his product across in a hurry and he believed in it to the extent of literally risking his business on that one-page ad."

The ad itself was a letter, probably one of the most extraordinary advertisements that has ever been published. It could not ask readers to buy corn flakes at their grocers because 90 per cent of the grocers did not carry the product. There was not even a sales force to introduce the product to the grocers. Written with the assistance of Arch Shaw (who became one of the first directors of the new company and was a stockholder from the beginning) the announcement calmly admitted that it "violates all the rules of good advertising." Advising that the company had orders which it could not fill for nearly half a million packages, it expressed the hope that the production lag could be remedied by July 1. Then by a coupon offer of a season's supply of free corn flakes, the ad sought to recruit the housewife-readers of the magazine as saleswomen to pressure their grocers to stock Kellogg's corn flakes.

This ad reflected important policy decisions: that corn flakes were to be advertised as a delicious breakfast food rather than as a health food; that the slogan WINS ITS FAVOR THROUGH ITS FLAVOR was to be widely used, and that readers were constantly to be warned to "look for the signature, W. K. Kellogg" to be sure to get the "original and genuine" corn flakes instead of imitations. (By 1912, there had been placed on the market 107 different brands of corn flakes, although by this time many of these had fallen by the wayside.)

In October of 1906 an ad playing on the theme of the original, rather than imitations, was carried in seventeen national publications, with nearly six million readers. The ad underlined a sentence "The original has this signature—W. K. Kellogg" which subsequently became a dominant theme in company advertising. The cost of the space was $8,000. By the end of 1906, total advertising expenditures reached $90,000, almost three times greater than the company's initial working capital! By June 1, 1907, the company had spent approximately $300,000 for adver-

Although W. K. Kellogg feared that to illustrate a woman winking was quite daring for 1907, neither St. Louisans, Chicagoans nor New Yorkers resented the novel advertisement and in New York City corn flakes sales rose from 2 carloads monthly to a carload a day!

tising, nearly $200,000 of this in the first twelve months of the year of the fire. The results can be abstractly measured by a statement in a letter which Mr. Shaw wrote to Mr. Kellogg upon learning of the July 4 factory catastrophe:

"The fire is of no consequence. You can't burn down what we have registered in the minds of the American women."

Keen-witted Will Kellogg was ever conscious of the fact that even an excellent product must be consistently and well advertised if the world is to "beat a path to your door." Despite the revenues from increasing sales, there were to be occasions when, with hat in hand, he had to abdicate his pride and beseech financial aid to cover the costs of one of the greatest of corporation advertising outlays. Mr. Shaw recalls the time that he and Mr. Kellogg went to one of the larger banks in Chicago and were given an audience with the president. At that time, the bank head said "No" to their request for funds. In a later year, the banker explained to Mr. Shaw:

"The trouble with W. K. and you was that you were too honest.

[135]

When you said you wanted to borrow $300,000 and I asked you what you wanted to do with the money, you told me you wanted it for advertising. Conservative as we had to be in those days, I had to say "No," but if you had said you had wanted it for a plant, I would have lent it to you."

But Will Kellogg would never misrepresent a situation to gain an advantage and he obtained loans elsewhere to finance his up-to-then almost unparalleled splurge of advertising.

Among notable advertising campaigns of the early years was the "Winking Campaign" telling newspaper readers to "Wink at your grocer and see what you get." Of course, the winker received a free sample of Kellogg's corn flakes. At first, Mr. Kellogg feared that the ads might prove objectionable, for the illustration of a woman winking was considered quite daring for the times. Fortunately, however, the relatively unsophisticated public of those days was intrigued by the novelty of the campaign, particularly when mysterious initials "K.T.C." were made a postscript to the ads.

Much as "LS/MFT" stimulated curiosity in a widely different field years later, so did "K.T.C." whet the imagination of the public. Eventually it was revealed that the initials referred to Kellogg's Toasted Corn Flakes, and the effect of the Winking Campaign may be gauged by the increase of corn flake sales in New York City from less than two carloads a month to more than a carload a day!

Later the growing company actually had the temerity to tell its Chicago customers, via another ad, to "Please Stop Eating Toasted Corn Flakes for Thirty Days" so that the company production could catch up with its sales and people would not have to eat the products of a "host of imitators."

The year 1907 saw an even more important development in Kellogg advertising. One spring day a salesman for the Ketterlinus Lithographing Company of Philadelphia walked into Mr. Kellogg's office with a drawing that had been made up for a farm implement company but not used by it. It originally

The sweetheart of the corn

Almost as familiar as the W. K. Kellogg signature has been the Kellogg "Sweetheart of the Corn." Since the first "Sweetheart" appeared in 1907, the healthy, pretty country girl has been slenderized and modernized.

showed a buxom lass in a gingham dress clutching a sheaf of wheat in her arms, but when the implement company turned it down the artist substituted a shock of corn for the armful of wheat. Will Kellogg saw the possibilities, bought the drawing and later the smiling lass was christened "Sweetheart of the Corn." Through the years this illustration in appealing colors has been used intermittently by the company in advertisements and on its corn flake packages, although the appearance of the healthy, pretty country girl has been slenderized and modernized several times by later artists. A company executive once stated:

"At the present time the Sweetheart figure is probably printed over one hundred million times a year. How much is the Sweetheart worth to us? That is entirely problematical. Our Sweetheart is not for sale."

Only a full-length treatise on advertising could do justice to the promotion of Kellogg products through the years. Pioneer in the use of color for its magazine ads, the company has often featured children in its advertisements and the "Kellogg children," painted in the earlier days by J. C. Leyendecker and more currently by Norman Rockwell, have set standards for advertising art.

In 1912, Kellogg's invaded the Great White Way of Times Square in New York City with the then-largest advertising sign in the world, 106 feet in width and 50 feet in height. About the same time, a moving electric sign was installed atop a building at State and Adams Street in Chicago. It showed first a closeup of a sobbing youngster saying, "I Want Kellogg's." By a change in lighting, the youngster's expression altered to a smile and the caption became, "I Got Kellogg's."

For many years, the Kellogg Company offered $1,000 in prizes for the best ears of corn submitted at various expositions and county and state fairs. An excellent home economics department, which was an innovation among cereal manufacturers, maintained contact with educational institutions of the nation, suggested recipes to housewives, and arranged food demonstrations. A "Funny Jungleland Moving Picture" book was a 1910 folder of animal cartoons. Eight carloads of these books were distributed within a few months. (A modernized version was given to children in 1948.)

Although Mr. Kellogg and many of his associates were not completely happy over the use of premiums for sales promotion, such has been the promotional trend in the cereal field. The Kellogg Company, in acceding to the demand for premiums, has always followed an early admonition of Will Kellogg that "the 'self-liquidating' premiums must be profitless —that is, distributed to children at actual cost or even below such cost." Of course, many of the premiums are distributed gratis to the consumer. America's children through the years have oh'd and ah'd over the premiums in cereals packages which have ranged from lapel pins and celebrity pictures to a baseball game. The most popular recently has been the atomic submarine, a miniature of the *Nautilus*. The "kids" also shrill with glee over the many cut-outs which regularly appear on the Kellogg packages.

With the advent of radio and its later cousin television, the company has used the air waves to tell the story of its product. Of great appeal to children in early radio days was the "Kellogg Singing Lady" who interspersed fairy tales with songs. Many famous concert artists were also brought into the nation's homes by Kellogg's via radio. Such programs added to the sales of the growing number of Kellogg breakfast foods (by this time Shredded Wheat [1912], Krumbles [1912] and Kellogg's All-Bran [1919] were supplementing corn flakes, which always has been the *pièce de résistance* of the line). However, Will Kellogg obtained almost equal gratification from eavesdropping on resultant conversations such as one which he heard in a crowded Los Angeles streetcar. A man obviously from a rural area was discussing a Kellogg-sponsored broadcast of a Fritz Kreisler concert the previous evening:

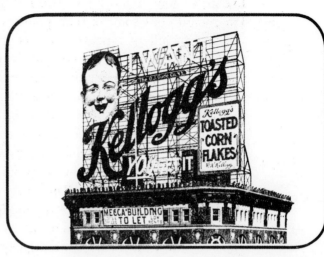

This Kellogg sign, formerly on a roof in Times Square, New York City, for a time held the distinction of being the largest electric sign in the world.

"That violin playing brought tears to my eyes and even though I've never gone in much for these newfangled breakfast foods, I'm going to buy some of that sponsor's products."

The principle of repetition and continuity in advertising is particularly evident in the company's use of the newest communications media, television. In recent years, Kellogg-sponsored TV programs have been many and varied, bringing into the nation's darkened living rooms the faces of entertainment stars whose names have become household words. In addition to the "name" programs—which largely appeal to adults—circus, Western and other fast-moving programs have attracted a great audience of children. Thus, each week the brand name "Kellogg's" becomes increasingly familiar to millions.

As important as the themes of the early magazine and newspaper ads was Mr. Kellogg's willingness to stake every last dollar upon the "big, bold splash in advertising." Early in the company history he budgeted a certain amount, per case produced, for advertising. The advertising budget grew as rapidly as production expanded. Actually, sales increased so fast that the advertising expenditures never quite caught up with them.

By 1940 company figures showed that the company had spent approximately $100,000,000 for advertising—a huge amount for a thirty-four-year period. Although no figures for advertising since that date have been released by the company, the numerous references to Kellogg products through the media of radio, television, magazines and newspapers indicate that the company continues to believe that "Advertising Pays."

Certainly Will Kellogg always held this belief. An advertising executive recalls that, after one of Mr. Kellogg's sleepless nights, several memoranda would be received relative to advertising. Listing ideas which had occurred to him through the long night, Mr. Kellogg would conclude his notes on advertising with a characteristic "These items may not be worth anything. If not, throw them in the waste basket."

Only once did Mr. Kellogg advocate retrenchment in advertising expenditures. As a part of the aftermath of World War I —when raw materials were securable only at exorbitant prices; an acute shortage of freight cars hampered transportation; the company's bank accounts were exhausted and there was more than $1,000,000 in unpaid bills—the Kellogg business was admittedly in danger. Kellogg, returning from a trip around the world, sensed the situation at once and resorted to drastic measures to save the company. He canceled all color pages in magazines and other contracts for ads, and stopped sampling operations, to put every ounce of his and the organization's energy toward getting food products out and money in to meet the financial emergency. As Horton and Henry recorded this dark page in the company's history:

"Will Kellogg made a quick trip to Chicago to try to persuade the banks to extend the company notes. The bankers were reluctant to do this because the Kellogg Company had not been able to maintain a two-for-one ratio in quick assets.

"Once again as in other critical times in the company history Mr. Kellogg's persuasiveness won out. The bankers agreed to extend the notes for a month or two—by which time the manufacturer assured them the company would be operating at a profit."

For six months neither W. K. Kellogg nor John L. Kellogg drew a salary. "Every day," Will Kellogg once related, "George McKay (then treasurer of the Kellogg Company, now chairman of the Board of the Security National Bank in Battle Creek) and I would go through a horrible stack of unpaid bills, deciding which ones to pay immediately and which ones to postpone. We'd write the creditors and say 'Here is a check for so much; another check will be sent on such and such a date.' Instead of losing our credit rating, we actually improved it. We were in debt, but we bought a reputation for keeping our promises."

While things were at their blackest the company's New York

attorney telephoned Kellogg to report that the company's leading competitor was interested in buying him out and wanted
him to name a price for his company. W. K.'s reply was typical:
"Tell our competitor we're interested in buying their company," he told Mr. Clark. "Tell them to name the price." Sixty
days after Kellogg had launched his economy campaign, the
company was back in the black. Bankers told him it was the
most remarkable comeback they had ever seen.

The suspension of advertising was only a temporary expediency, for Will Kellogg always realized it was good business
to advertise even in depression periods. It will be remembered
that after the market crash of 1929 pessimism was rampant.
Wall Street brokers jumped from tall buildings; apple sellers
multiplied on street corners. The theme of the times was "Run
for cover. The dam has broken." Will Kellogg, always the
rugged individualist, was not restrained by the prevailing fear.
Instead he told his executives:

"Double our advertising budget! This is the time to go out
and spend more money in advertising."

Again his intuition was correct. Kellogg Company sales continued to accelerate, affected scarcely, if at all, by the Depression.

CHAPTER 7

"Hope the Plaintiff Doesn't Get It"

Τ HE PREDOMINANT INFLUENCE of business upon the American scene is perhaps not duplicated in any other part of the world. As a very strong thread in the warp and woof of our social structure, business has engaged in bitter conflicts, encountering the elation of triumph, the tragedy of defeat or the irony of a fortuitous windfall.

Typical in the development of any major American company—for instance, the legal battles to separate the several Standard Oil companies or the Ferguson-Ford tractor controversies—have been disagreements with associates or competitors, conflicts as to rights, or jousts with federal administrations over interpretation of anti-trust statutes.

Several volumes could be filled with the details and crosscurrents of law suits, the legal triumphs and reversals, of Will Kellogg's company as it grew from a small contender into the world's largest ready-to-eat cereal corporation. Only students of business history, however, would be particularly interested in the minutiae of injunctions, restraining orders, crossbills, and decrees that have been a part of the life of not only the Kellogg Company but most corporations. The readers of this biography, interested largely in the story of W. K. Kellogg, likely will wish only enough of corporate detail to serve as a background for the man who is its chief character.

At the risk of oversimplification, the legal maneuverings from 1910 through 1920 in which John Harvey Kellogg and Will Kellogg alternated as plaintiff and defendant resulted largely from the fact that two able, ambitious, and uncompromising men had equally sincere claims to the use of the Kellogg name in the field of food merchandising.

Even the most compatible of relatives can become incompatible in a hurry where the pocketbook nerve is affected— and the two brothers never were congenial. They were men with divergent missions. The Doctor was wary lest his professional standing be jeopardized by commercialism. He sought to advance the cause of Biologic Living and, incidentally, the sanitarium, and he needed funds for this purpose as well as to maintain his loosely organized charities. (Forty-two children were "adopted" in one degree or another by Dr. and Mrs. John Harvey Kellogg and he for years subsidized in Chicago a "Skid Row" mission, a free medical dispensary and a day nursery.) On the other hand, in his middle years Will Kellogg at last had an opportunity to establish a long-dreamed-of business of his own, to prove that he was a peer of his elder brother, and eventually to organize a philanthropic enterprise that dwarfed the considerable charities of that brother.

Another root of the difficulty lay in the unusual and complicated business structure from which the corn flake company evolved; the conglomerate group of one-man firms the Doctor had set up to merchandise foods, medicines, medical appliances, electric baths and books. Doctor Kellogg apparently felt that many of the acts of the new company were intrusions into his own domain and that he had sold to the corn flake company only the right to make a single product (Sanitas Corn Flakes) and to sell it in a circumscribed territory. Perhaps he believed he had a proprietary right to control or curb the development of the company, only natural in a man accustomed to exercising an autocratic control over the sanitarium and his various companies. Maybe he expected his younger brother, even though now chief executive of a fast-growing corporation, to take orders as he had in the past.

The Sanitas business, owned by the Doctor, was in a marked decline, due to the nationwide business depression of 1907, the competition of the new corn flakes, and perhaps to the absence of W. K. Kellogg's business management. John Harvey Kellogg was always bewildered in the sphere of business. He never was sure he was on solid ground in a business deal, so he was inclined to take varying business advice; invariably misgivings would come and he would try to alter his course with the caprice of a March wind. Three times, for instance, he altered a decision to sell all rights to his many foods to the new corn flakes company for a lump sum and/or royalty, and this wavering greatly disgusted his more practical and sturdily anchored brother.

A series of harassing actions by the Doctor against the corn flakes company brought matters to a crisis. These concerned the use by the new company of a picture of the sanitarium on the corn flakes package and a declaration by the Doctor that he was "the Kellogg" and that any use of the name in connection with food products would be construed to refer to him. Despite the fact that W. K. Kellogg's signature had for a number of years been on various of the sanitarium companies' food packages, John Harvey maintained that his brother had surreptitiously appropriated the Doctor's name during his absence in Europe and in so doing had injured that name in medical circles.

By 1908, Dr. Kellogg decided to change the name of his Sanitas Company to the Kellogg Food Company and to adopt the trade name "Kellogg's" for his food products. Naturally, the action was a red flag to Will Kellogg.

Two other incidents fanned the flames of controversy. Dr. Kellogg announced a plan to sell the rights to some rice flakes to other manufacturers and in essence told the corn flake company that if it didn't like the idea of having another Sanitas-born flake food on the market, it could increase its capitalization to $1,500,000 (a recent increase of capitalization to $1,000,000 and a 3-for-1 stock split had increased the Doctor's holdings to 11,420 shares with a par value of $114,200) and pay the Doctor $500,000 in stock for the rice flake rights. Then, too, Dr. Kellogg had retained the right to sell corn flakes through export and by mail orders and these shipments in packages identical to those of the new company were proving embarrassing. This, W. K. Kellogg alleged, was "simply pirating on the $2,000,000 of advertising by the Toasted Corn Flake Company."

The Doctor, needing money for his various business and charitable ventures, eventually sold practically all of his corn flake company holdings to W. K. Kellogg, who from that time on held considerably more than the 50 per cent of stock needed for control. John Harvey's gradual disposal of this stock naturally made him less interested in the new company's future and his opposition, based on both business reasons and the brothers' personality conflict, could become more overt.

Voluminous letters and memoranda were fired back and forth between the brothers. W. K. alleged that the doctor's salesmen were misrepresenting themselves as agents of the new company. Even Arthur Brisbane, the famous columnist, was drawn into the controversy when he, at first interested in the Doctor's Rice Flake Company, refused to have anything to do with it after W. K. Kellogg spent two hours to explain the factors involved.

The younger brother filed a suit on August 11, 1910, in the Calhoun County Circuit Court, to enjoin Dr. Kellogg from using the name "Kellogg" either in a corporate name or as a descriptive name of a food. John Harvey Kellogg filed an answer on August 30. An uneasy armistice was arranged in 1911 but this truce lasted only a few months, and it was a "Battle of Bran"—a conflict over selling a then relatively unimportant cereal, bran food, that precipitated the renewal of legal activities.

An injunction suit filed in New York City by the Kellogg Toasted Corn Flake Company against Dr. Kellogg's company —followed by answers on the part of the doctor; an application for a trademark by W. K. Kellogg on the facsimile of his signature; the filing of opposition to the trademark by John Harvey Kellogg and an injunction suit in the Calhoun County, Michigan, Court by the Doctor against the corn flake company— signaled the start of a series of law maneuvers not finally adjudicated until December of 1920.

During the years there were innumerable postponements, long, drawn-out court proceedings, and many instances of drama. On November 20, 1919, the final decree was handed down by Judge North of the Circuit Court and his rulings were unanimously upheld by the eight justices of the Michigan Supreme Court on December 21, 1920.

The corn flake company, headed by Will Kellogg, won every major point in the suit, perhaps partly because of the excellence of this new company president as a witness. An idea of Mr. Kellogg's stature on the witness stand may be gained by this memory of an observer who witnessed a court session of one trial:

"Mr. Kellogg was put on the stand and was so good a witness that the other side asked for a recess in order to have a conference. During this recess, a person sympathetic to him was not recognized and was sitting so near the conference that she heard one of the attorneys for the other side say, 'Don't ask him anything else. He is too smart.' Thereafter, at the conclusion of the conference, the opposing attorneys said, 'We have no further questions, Your Honor.'"

The 1920 decision held that the corn flake company had the

exclusive right to use the word "Kellogg's" except that Dr. Kellogg could use it in the corporate name, as permitted under the 1911 "armistice." (A later court order prohibited the Doctor from using the name "Kellogg" in the corporate name of its food company.) Other than that, Dr. Kellogg was forbidden to use the word "Kellogg" as any part of the name or title of any food product, and the corn flake company was entitled to collect all profits Dr. Kellogg had made from the infringement of the Kellogg trade name.

According to John L. Kellogg, "Dr. Kellogg proposed that he pay the attorney fees for both sides and that any further accounting of damages be waived. W. K. Kellogg agreed. The legal costs, duly paid by the Doctor, totaled $225,000."

From the human aspect, the greatest damage came from the estrangement of the two brothers, an estrangement which was never healed. During the ensuing years, they saw each other only two or three times annually and these encounters were usually very brief.

Similar complicated issues were fought out in the courts of Canada, but this time the Doctor was not a party to the suit, although he was called as a witness by Canadian plaintiffs. The legal proceeding grew out of the early sale by the Doctor of the Canadian rights to sell corn flakes and, although this suit was lost by Will Kellogg, he turned defeat into victory through his purchase of the Canadian rights from businessmen of the Dominion. He paid exactly ten times the amount the Canadians had paid for the business a decade earlier but, after moving the business from Toronto to London, Ontario, the operation became so profitable that the purchase price was repaid in a little less than three years.

In the years that followed there occurred various legal proceedings incidental to the life of a corporation, issues related to patents, copyrights and trade practices, but none which had comparative significance to the aforementioned battles over the use of the Kellogg name.

As with other unpleasant aspects of living, W. K. Kellogg was philosophic about the Kellogg Company's quota of lawsuits, even those which obviously were of a nuisance nature. And relatively large litigation did not cause Mr. Kellogg to become excited or impel him to many words. There was the time when an attorney told the company head that the corporation was being sued for $2,000,000. Mr. Kellogg's only comment was: "Hope the plaintiff doesn't get it."

2.

Unless the parental instinct is completely atrophied, most fathers look back to regret that more of their time was not spent with their children. The many-faceted breakfast foods business was a monkey on the back of W. K. Kellogg in varying degree for three decades. Included were those years when his offspring left adolescence for adulthood. By the time his grandchildren became numerous, Kellogg had more time to indulge a real love for children but he never could shake a sense of guilt with regard to his own sons and daughter. This can be seen from a letter he wrote to his elder son, Karl:

"I have always regretted that I did not spend more time with you and Lenn and Beth when you were little, but the pressure of work was such that it seemed almost a physical impossibility to do any differently than what I did. I think, however, I have in some ways tried to indicate to you my interest in your welfare.

"When you get to be a father, if you ever become one, you will be better prepared to appreciate some things which you can not appreciate fully at this time. Above all things I want that my sons should develop into conscientious and truthful men, and even should you never be able to acquire a large amount of money, I shall appreciate the attributes of sincerity, honesty and trustworthiness above all other things."

From the time that health foods began to evolve to breakfast foods, the weary Will Kellogg was not in a physical state to be an emphatic parent and husband. The dinner conversation, if there was conversation at all, revolved around his all-engrossing ambition eventually to build a nationwide company. The aura of the food business surrounded the family in the dining room and followed them to the living room to the exclusion of the trivia so important to children. There was only the mother to whom the two sons and the daughter could take their joys and their troubles and Ella Kellogg, devoted and understanding, was fighting a losing battle against ill health.

On an occasional Sabbath (Saturday) the father found the time to walk and chat with the youngsters but, as a close relative recalls, "The rest of us went walking with Uncle Will, but his wife never did."

Even the business, however, could not inhibit Mr. Kellogg's love for family celebrations on Christmas. He never would play Santa Claus but on a few occasions hired someone to do so, and the suppers on Christmas Eve were an oasis in an otherwise somewhat barren family life. Sometimes just the immediate family and the grandchildren were present. At other times, Will's beloved sister Clara was at the festivity along with some nieces and nephews. In the billiard room of the 256 West Van Buren Street home all lights were turned out except those adorning a Christmas tree which dominated the basement room. Everyone was commanded to march downstairs, keeping eyes closed until reaching the chairs which circled the tree. Then Karl or Lenn officiated in the presentation of the gifts and afterward a big supper topped off a perfect evening.

But Christmases are few and far between, and children need a father on the ordinary days of a year. There was a loneliness, too, in that Mr. Kellogg never permitted his children to go to the public schools. (Possibly this was because half of Mr. Kellogg's own limited education was in a church-sponsored school. Also involved may have been "a sense of class" sometimes evidenced by individualistic Will Kellogg in spite of his growing and sincere concern for underprivileged children.)

In any event, Karl, John Leonard and Beth went only to private schools or had tutors. This, of course, limited the association they had with children of the town and some of the companionship craved by them had to be satisfied by housemaids and nurses.

So grew the sons and daughter to manhood and womanhood. Karl was a studious, frail lad who had the familiar Kellogg liking for the practice of medicine. After gaining his M.D. at the Detroit School of Medicine, he was a physician in Montana, and for a time was associated with the small medical staff at the Kellogg Company. Married in 1905, he contracted tuberculosis between 1912 and 1913, and though the lesion was healed sufficiently to permit service in the U. S. Army during World War I, his health thereafter was never robust. This caused him to make his home in the balmier climate of the West Coast. Dr. Karl died at his home in California on December 22, 1955, and is survived by his wife, Etta, and two sons, Karl Landram and Will Lewis.

John Leonard (Lenn) had as much energy as his father, and the similar drives of the father and this son found them sometimes in association, sometimes in conflict. Mr. Kellogg's wrath over a boyish Hallowe'en prank (Lenn had assisted in the hoisting of a small cow to the belfry of the Battle Creek College Building) had scarcely subsided when the lad's venture into an independent drayage business rekindled his father's temper. Somehow, despite Will Kellogg's admiration for business acumen, the sight of Lenn's dray pulled by two huge Percheron horses was a red flag to the father. Perhaps it was because the lad had not consulted him before entering into the short-lived business.

Considerable insight into the relationship between this strict father and a son who had a will of his own can be had from a letter which John L., then fourteen years old, wrote on October 3, 1897:

W. K. Kellogg

"When I made you thos (*sic*) promises I did not make them way down in my heart. I did not like to make them and so did not keep them. But now I will make some promises that will be kept.

1. I will not go away from home without asking you or telling where I am going.
2. Will not smoke.
3. Will not stay out late at night.
4. Will do what you think is all O.K.
5. Will work and go to the College school.

"When I make a promis (*sic*) that I make way down in my heart I will keep it.

"I ask your forgivenes (*sic*) for the things that I have donn (*sic*) in the past. Good night."

But when eighteen-year-old Lenn eloped with a pretty Swedish girl who was in Mr. Kellogg's personal employ, W. K.'s wrath knew no bounds. It was father against son and adamant will against adamant will, and W. K. Kellogg met defeat for one of the few times in his life. Later he was to employ his son in the factory and to grow quite fond of his new daughter-in-law, Hanna, with real regret over the divorce which occurred in 1924. Two sons were born of this union, Will Keith II and John Leonard, Jr. The latter was destined to be the food manufacturer's favorite grandson and to be groomed for the key position in the Kellogg dynasty.

The youngest child of Will Kellogg, his daughter Beth, grew up to look more like her father than his other children. Even-tempered, she always was patient with her father even when he tried to dominate her thinking. She was married to Norman Williamson, a pharmacist at the sanitarium, in 1911, the year before the death of her mother. From the marriage came five children: Kenneth, Eleanor, Norman, Jr., John Harold and Elizabeth Ann.

Another member of W. K. Kellogg's household was Pauline, a little red-headed girl taken into the home at the age of three.

While she never was legally adopted, Mr. Kellogg felt a measure of obligation toward her for many years, helping her to secure an education, training as a nurse, and also paying for her medical care subsequent to the failure of her health in 1931. Since the latter date, Pauline has been hospitalized at an Ontario institution.

The death in 1912 of Ella Kellogg, the beloved "Puss" of Mr. Kellogg's adolescent diary, was a great blow to the food manufacturer, even though he was forced to neglect her in the formative years of his business. This neglect did not extend to his efforts of several years to find a cure for her illness. He spared no expense in the engagement of physicians, in a trip for her to the milder climate of the South, and in the hiring of special nurses during the last months of her illness at the sanitarium.

Will Kellogg's grief was quiet but it went deep. Several years later, a relative, pitying the loneliness that was not erased despite a hard regimen of work, said to him:

"Uncle Will, you should get married again."

His only reply was, "I made one woman unhappy. Why should I inflict myself upon another?"

Later, loneliness was to modify his reaction against the thought of marrying again, but triumph in business and sadness in his personal life were the fate of W. K. Kellogg for nearly a decade after his fiftieth birthday. Another tragedy contributed to the sadness in those years, an event occurring ten months after his wife's death.

Beth's first child, Kenneth, just toddling and learning to walk, lost his balance and fell through a second-story window onto a concrete driveway. The news reached Mr. Kellogg as he returned to Battle Creek from a trip and he dropped every thought of his business as he summoned medical specialists from Chicago in an effort to save the boy. With a fractured skull, Kenneth was suspended between life and death for three weeks and was totally blind for three months. Eventually the child regained 60 per cent of his sight and a measure of health but the grandfather, with all his money, was not able to secure for the boy treatment which would bring him back to total health.

Will Kellogg's deepening love for his unfortunate grandson, and the inability of medical science completely to erase the results of the accident, were to have an important effect upon his thinking as to the proper stewardship of the increasing Kellogg wealth. He wondered what difficulties were in the path of needy parents who needed help for their children in catastrophes of similar nature. A resultant idea took almost two decades to come to fruition, for Kenneth was about twenty years old when the Kellogg Foundation, "for the welfare of children and youth," was founded. That, however, is a story for another chapter of this biography.

Meanwhile, W. K. Kellogg found solace in a return to his work, a never-abating effort to make his business a leader and himself "King of Corn Flakes."

CHAPTER 8

"Kellogg's of Battle Creek"

Dᴜʀɪɴɢ ʜɪs active years with the company, W. K. Kellogg was an indefatigable worker who expected those associated with him to work long and hard hours. He asked his executives only to match his own efforts and, as a kind of personal penance, would take his work home with him, not often in the tangible sense but in the equally harrowing fact that his keyed-up mind would continue to mull over the problems and worries of the business far into the night. He definitely was not an office pacer, and the worries and tensions that he had were usually kept hidden by his face which seldom betrayed any emotion.

A prominent Battle Creek businessman, formerly an official of the company, recalls that:

"He had the greatest memory of any man I ever knew. He would remember the birthdays of all my grandchildren, a surprising trait in a man so busy as he. He never forgot figures and could reel off data and statistics by the page, sales, carloadings, the price of grain."

His photographic memory, remembered by employees as both a scourge and a blessing, was particularly effective in periodic trips through the Battle Creek plant. He refused to be exclusively a desk man and made it a point to tour the factory at least once and often several times weekly, usually in company with the superintendent and other officials. Such inspections, always unannounced, created undulations through the

Mr. Kellogg refused to be a desk man exclusively and toured the factory several times each week. His mechanical curiosity often impelled him personally to test new factory equipment, as he is doing here in a new power plant of the factory.

factory almost as pronounced as the waves from a disturbance of the ocean floor. He could not have been the "clubby" type of executive even if he had so desired. While he knew a number of the veteran employees and occasionally would stop to talk to one about some technical aspect of the particular job, he exuded strength, not warmth, and few of these employees felt comfortable in his presence.

Kellogg's eyes were wide open on these trips and, often to the surprise of his companions on the tour, he would garner sufficient information for the writing of copious memoranda about what was wrong, suggestions for rectifying the errors, and ideas for improvements. A disabled employee who was retired on a pension remembers some of these tours:.

"The first time I got to know Mr. Kellogg was after the new plant was built. He was in the plant only now and then, but some way or other he knew where everything was and what was going on. I recall that one time we discussed a new food conveyor just installed, and he told the head millwright 'I don't think this conveyor is going to be practical.' When asked why, he continued, 'Because I think it is going to break up our flakes. I am sorry to tell you but we will try the conveyor out no longer than necessary to see whether it is practical or not.' It turned out that Mr. Kellogg was right. They had to junk the machine."

Not always were employees so sanguine about W. K. Kellogg's plant observations. Perhaps as an aftermath a luckless department head might receive a memorandum pointing out that "The steam radiators in your department were all turned on full force on a day when the weather was so warm that it was necessary to have a window or two open."

Another incident epitomizes Mr. Kellogg's propensity for detail and economy. A price change by competition had occurred on a Saturday morning, and the company immediately made ready to meet this change by arranging with the printers to work Saturday night to get out a new price list for quick mailing. The mailing necessitated that an executive and some of his office colleagues come to the plant on Sunday. This particular day Kellogg happened in at the factory and he stepped in to the department. He said not a word to the executive, but with emphasis walked over to a corner where a light had been left burning. Still saying nothing, he gave a mighty pull of the cord to extinguish the light. His habits of frugality were so strong that, to him, the fact that the men were working hard on Sunday did not excuse an unnecessarily burning light.

"Despite his ruthless streak, which primarily was evidenced during his fierce concentration upon company success, Mr. Kellogg had underneath a rather grim mask a softer heart than one might imagine. Many employees besieged by a family illness or by financial catastrophe were to know the comfort of a doctor's bill marked 'Paid,' the reassurance of a well-stocked food larder, or the warmth of a load of coal, gifts anonymously made and often from Will Kellogg's own pocket. While he would not keep a man a long time at a loss to the company, he did have attributes of mercy and hidden kindness. He was glad to pay earned wages, but they had to be earned. The wages he did pay were better than average. While he could be arbitrary under special circumstances, he was not habitually so, but upon occasion would listen to conflicting testimonies before registering a decision. He was a rather well-balanced individual if one would accept his lack of gregariousness. . . . His preference was to be generous, but not in any flamboyant way."

The above is an observation of a man who knew W. K. Kellogg for many years. It confirms that, after his own fashion, Kellogg was a man of rectitude, of justice, and of good will but, like a true son of the Puritans, he believed there was only one straight, unwavering path of virtue. Only infrequently did the plaintive, human side of the man break the fetters of his iron self-control. One such occasion was after the Battle Creek plant had added building after building to sprawl over many acres of the original factory site. Very earnestly he turned to his son John L. Kellogg, who was then president of the company, to say:

"John L., you're making this plant too big for me. I'm not comfortable in it any more."

Nevertheless, the business was Mr. Kellogg's life for many years, to the continued neglect of his health and his over all personality. Although he somehow found time to visit sick friends and relatives at Battle Creek hospitals, and a listing of his financial aid to persons during the period covers several pages of records, his main crusade of those years was a fiercely held pattern of competitive action. Fight and drive your people to a peak of efficiency. Sometimes you make a talent achieve a height never dreamed of although, conversely, hearts may be broken in the process.

Intuitively W. K. Kellogg could select a man with his heart in his work and to such he gave responsibility and opportunity for growth. Thus the man could grow with the job or go under. On the higher echelon level, you don't get fired, you resign. The bigger the job, the more desperately you try to hang on to it. And the larger grows the responsibility, the greater becomes your pride, meaning even more than the large salary you draw.

In spite of, or perhaps because of, W. K.'s Spartan tactics, this business leader gathered unto himself a great group of executives who had much to do with the success of the company, although the casualties were many along the road of the corporation's progress. The Kellogg staff of today reflects the influence of the founder of the business, for it is well-balanced, with a nucleus of veterans seasoned by experience and years and a corps of young executives who lend new and zestful ideas for pragmatic testing.

A one-time department head at the company recalls with rueful admiration " . . . Mr. Kellogg's way of terminating an interview very quickly. With a quick, dismissing handshake, W. K. could usher a person out of his presence before he realized he was exiting."

This was expressive of the tempo and the prevailing mood for, while W. K. Kellogg was at the helm, the company staff meetings were never relaxed, companionable affairs. Yet—

"You sat in a meeting and if Mr. Kellogg was there, whether he took part in the discussion or whether he did not, you seemed to feel the strength of the man. It manifested itself some way in your feelings. Perhaps it was due to his natural dignity, but, more likely, you sensed an interior reserve of strength, and this caused you to think that anything decided in that meeting when he was present was going to be achieved

100 per cent and was going to be backed up 100 per cent. Contributory to the emanation of his strength of character, I think, was the fact that in the realm of business he had perfect self-confidence. You also gained a renewal of courage because he obviously secured a great deal of enjoyment in the game of competition, that determination to outplay the other fellow in a deal. When he was able to achieve a *coup d'état,* he would afterward sit in his office and chuckle for minutes at a time."

At one time in the company's history Robert R. Updegraff, a prominent business consultant, was retained in an advisory capacity. In the course of time the executive who had retained him resigned from the company and Mr. Updegraff brought up by letter the question as to whether the management desired to continue the consulting relationship.

"We will discuss the matter on your next trip to Battle Creek," wrote Mr. Kellogg with his usual economy of words.

Mr. Updegraff relates that he arrived in Battle Creek one morning two weeks later expecting to sit down for a talk with Mr. Kellogg. "Instead, to my surprise Mr. Kellogg ushered me into the Board Room, where the entire top executive group was seated around the table, with vacant chairs at either end. Mr. Kellogg took one of the chairs and indicated that I was to take the other.

" 'Gentlemen,' said Mr. Kellogg, with his characteristic directness, 'I recently received a letter from Mr. Updegraff asking whether he could still be of service to our company.' Then, turning to me, he said, 'Mr. Updegraff, the meeting is yours.'

"I was completely unprepared for such an introduction. Gathering my wits, I ad-libbed briefly on the value of outside perspective, and the fact that one with a broad background of service to companies in a variety of industries could sometimes suggest simple and obvious solutions to problems that were beyond the experience of an organization schooled in operating in a single industry. I went on to add that 'dissatisfaction' was another contribution I tried to make.

" 'What do you mean—dissatisfaction?' demanded Mr. Kellogg.

" 'Perhaps I should have called it *un*satisfaction,' I replied. 'I am never satisfied that anything is being done as well as it might be done.'

"Mr. Kellogg arose abruptly. 'Gentlemen,' he said, 'that is what we need in this business—more dissatisfaction.' Then, turning to me, 'Mr. Updegraff, we will continue our relationship.' The meeting was over. No one else said a word."

By this time, Kellogg sales offices had blanketed the nation and the Kellogg salesman with his breakfast food samples was also seen in several other lands. W. K. Kellogg placed great premium on an efficient sales force and kept his sales managers and sales offices on their toes by reviewing copies of all incoming and outgoing telegrams. Eventually such copies would be returned to the proper company official with inscriptions such as "Why wasn't this done? What was this done for?" Even in his active days with the company, he was a great traveler and his journeys were pinpointed by notes that would be received by the sales manager, "Could not find Krumbles in Plattsburg or Oneida." This, of course, stimulated the sales department, but a complicating factor was that Mr. Kellogg's wanderings would surprisingly take him sometimes to "greasy spoon" restaurants where one never expected him to breakfast (and to ask for a favorite cereal) or to localities where it had not seemed to be advantageous to have sizeable distribution at the time.

"Expediency is the mother of invention" and many were the strategies developed by harassed sales executives to keep Mr. Kellogg happy with the widespread distribution of his products. Through friends in the traffic departments of railroads coming through Battle Creek, the executives would learn of the travel reservations of their boss. Then, fearful lest the dining car menus carry only two or three of the Kellogg cereals, they would persuade the steward to stock the entire line of products for the run on which the big boss was to be a passenger and patron of the railroad's cuisine.

The ax, which Mr. Kellogg could and did wield, was to fall more often on sales managers than on executives of other departments. One such unlucky individual, in a telephone call to Mr. Kellogg who was vacationing in California, made the mistake of saying, "Times are bad here right now. Business is going to the dogs." Immediately he was discharged because Mr. Kellogg believed that "The company can't afford to have in charge of its sales a man with that pessimistic attitude. Such pessimism would be communicated to our salesmen."

One day Mr. Kellogg had augmented reason for the optimism he always recommended. A leading banker of Battle Creek, George C. McKay, who for many years was Treasurer of the Kellogg Company, recalls that he was requested to go over Mr. Kellogg's personal books, to bring them into better shape. In returning the books, he said to his boss:

"Well, these books indicate that you are worth a million dollars!"

W. K. gasped and said, "I am no such thing." Then, convinced by the figures, he continued, "Well, I never expected to be worth that much." He went on to tell his Treasurer about the time he had mortgaged his own home to obtain money for financing the company.

With the success of the company and corollary personal prosperity, Mr. Kellogg began to have time for more leisure, although even after California became his winter home starting in 1925, he maintained relatively tight reins on the management of the company. (This *in absentia* control was possible through an ingenious cross-continent telephone hookup, one of the first of its kind.) Even before wealth, Will Kellogg had a taste of the joys of travel for he was able, through a due bill owed to the sanitarium, to journey to Europe in 1896. From the standpoint of personal indulgence, the wealth that subsequently came meant additional opportunities for travel and he made many trips abroad, as will be detailed in a subsequent chapter. Increasing stock dividends also allowed him to engage permanently a combination nurse-masseuse and he built a large home near Battle Creek, with other homes in California and Florida.

For many years he managed the great Kellogg Company from his winter home in California. His impression upon his staff was powerful; his word was law in his institutions. His policy was one of honest and careful dealing in all departments. If a department head became overzealous, Mr. Kellogg discovered the fact and applied correction timely and justly. Nothing was permitted to drift.

From his villa in California when he desired to interview an important department head, he sent for the man. He liked eye-to-eye interviews. He was not wordy. When he expected an interview, he prepared for it. Nothing relevant was overlooked. Whether in California or in Battle Creek, the hand of W. K. Kellogg always was on the pulse of the business.

Yet in many ways Mr. Kellogg set no great store on the acquisition of money, although his evolving sense of stewardship was evident in a speech which he made to company long-time employees in 1930:

"In the early days we passed through many strenuous times and had many anxious hours, not always knowing where funds were coming from to take care of the next week's payroll. I never, at any period of my life, aspired to become wealthy, but the fierce competition perhaps developed a fighting spirit, and in the effort to secure our share, the business has succeeded. It is my hope that the property that kind Providence has brought me may be helpful to many others, and that I may be found a faithful steward."

2.

The name "BATTLE CREEK" has been printed on many billions of breakfast food cartons and enunciated by dulcet-voiced announcers over most of the radio and television channels of

Ever a Home-Town Booster—

—was W. K. Kellogg. Note the inscription "This is Battle Creek" on the first building erected by the Company at its present location. The locale-designation "Kellogg's of Battle Creek" has appeared literally billions of times on packages of the various cereal products.

the nation. As fond of his native scene as any hometown boy, the grownup Will Kellogg had a vehicle through his advertising to put Battle Creek on the map. Along with the familiar "W. K. Kellogg" signature, the legend "Kellogg's of Battle Creek" is familiar reading in magazine and newspaper ads as well as on packages which can be found on most of the pantry shelves in the nation.

In part, the hometown mention à la breakfast food packages was only reciprocity, for if Kellogg's and the local plants of competitors did publicize Battle Creek to the world, the health center reputation of the city made it a natural place for the launching of cereal businesses.

As grew these businesses, so grew Battle Creek, which today has a metropolitan area population of nearly one hundred thousand people. Doubtless, this southwestern Michigan town would have become a city, breakfast foods or not, since it is a part of the large industrial belt between Chicago and Detroit, currently a stratum of smoking factories and destined by the St. Lawrence Seaway project to become much greater industrially. However, the Battle Creek of today owes much of its growth and relatively stable prosperity to Kellogg's (which has,

by far, the largest factory payroll) and the five other packaged breakfast food plants along the tracks of the New York
Central and Grand Trunk railways.

In growing into a city, the town changed greatly from the
scene of Will Kellogg's boyhood, but he never was to lose the
nostalgic thrill experienced when he alighted from a train to
see the name of B-A-T-T-L-E C-R-E-E-K proudly displayed
in a floral piece on the lawn of one of the railroad stations.
Though California's balmy weather lured him away from the
Michigan winters, W. K. ever remained a loyal son of Battle
Creek, hastening to his home town each spring. He once said:
"I do not know of any place in the world where the spring,
summer and fall are more attractive than in Michigan."

Oddly enough, Mr. Kellogg was never to be as well-known
by Battle Creek citizens as was his doctor brother or C. W.
Post. Although the citizens appreciated and used extensively
the municipal auditorium, the farmers' market, the Youth
Building, Kellogg Forest, the school buildings and improvements made possible by Mr. Kellogg's gifts, the donor was a
reticent man and almost a legendary figure to the average
resident. Even many of the town leaders knew him only in a
business way, for in his strong influence upon civic, school and
even political affairs, he worked behind the scenes, using emissaries to put over his points.

As with any strong personality, Mr. Kellogg suffered some
unpopularity, this in spite of the aforementioned gifts to the
city and the usual ethical motives back of his maneuverings.
A long-time associate thought this was possibly because "he
made the mistake of making a success in his home town. Here
was a man in very modest circumstances, not too active in
community affairs. All of a sudden, he hits the jackpot and becomes extremely successful in a field in which twenty-five or
thirty of the town's leaders had gone broke. There was a natural resentment toward an 'upstart'."

W. K. Kellogg definitely was not the mixer type and always

shunned the limelight. Indeed, he once remarked, "I don't care greatly to be seen of men." Speaking in public on one of the few occasions he could not avoid would cost him several nights of preappearance anxiety. He seldom appeared at public gatherings, avoiding even the dedications of the numerous public buildings that he gave. Any awards given him usually had to be done *in absentia,* and if he did attend a public gathering, he always asked to have a seat reserved for him in the last row. He would not sit on a stage.

Before Mr. Kellogg became blind in his later years, he was very nearsighted and it was quite possible for him not to see the faces of people he passed on the street. He had a compensation in that he could immediately place a voice, but his failure to recognize faces and thus to speak to passersby worried him lest he be thought "snobbish." He was once characterized by a friend as ". . . actually the most humble man who ever lived but a factor implying 'snobbishness' was that he was often lost in thought as he walked along the street."

While Mr. Kellogg was an executive of direct and fast action in his business, he preferred to work by indirection in affairs involving his home town (although he was a member of the city's original Charter Commission and once gave $12,500 to defray the cost of an independent analytical survey of the city government). Illustrative of this approach was the difficulty he had in persuading the city to pave a rough road near the Kellogg Company offices. An idea caused him to invite his friend and then mayor of Battle Creek to take a ride in his car. On the way to pick up Mr. John Bailey, the food manufacturer conspired with his chauffeur, Speck:

"Now when we pick up the Mayor, I want you to drive to the plant. However, when you get to Porter Street, don't slacken your speed. In fact, when I tell you to slow up, then I really want you to go all the faster."

With the city official next to Mr. Kellogg in the back seat, Speck did as he was told and bounced and jolted the two heavy-set men as the tires and springs only partly offset the impact of the rough street. Several times Speck was instructed to slow the car, but he apparently did not hear the admonitions. When the ride was over and the Mayor was catching his breath while seated in Mr. Kellogg's office, he remarked: "Well, that street is a little rough, isn't it?" and W. K. quickly pursued the point by asking, "What about getting it paved?" Both Mr. Kellogg and Speck as parties to the conspiracy got great zest out of the way they succeeded in getting Mayor Bailey to macadamize Porter Street!

Mayor Bailey, a serious man himself, was one of a few men of the city with whom W. K. Kellogg had a kidding relationship. A chauffeur recalls the chuckling of these ordinarily grave men, and that "once Mr. Kellogg was so overcome by mirth that the tears ran down his cheeks." Mr. Kellogg, who as a requisite of employment preferred "a man who can smile," seldom smiled. However, on occasion his sense of the ridiculous would "cause him to chuckle, his tummy would shake, and the tears would course down his face." For a brief moment, there had been breached the dam by which he held back long-pent emotions.

A leading minister of Battle Creek, who has an effervescent sense of humor, tells of a time Mr. Kellogg was a victim, not a conspirator, in a stratagem. Just prior to the Great Depression, "W. K. had purchased the ground for what became Kellogg Field airport. The Depression hit, and there was nobody flying out of that airport. The airmail contract was lost and local pilots had no gasoline money for flying. About once a month, W. K. would telephone to the airport, informing them that 'I am coming out to make an inspection and am considering giving this thing up so that there will be an airport no longer.'

"Hastily the man at the airport would telephone me, knowing that I had a private pilot's license and a ship on the field. I would rush out to the airport twenty minutes ahead of Mr.

Kellogg, jump into my ship and circle the field. Two other pilots would usually hurry to join me and to make up what we hoped was an impressive 'wing'. When we saw W. K.'s Lincoln drive up to the main hangar, we would land and rush over to the car, saying, 'We're glad you're out here today. Don't you want to come for a ride?' Mr. Kellogg wasn't much on flying, and he would say, 'No, thanks' and would leave. His inspection was completed and the airport saved for another time because Mr. Kellogg had seen it as a going institution which, of course, it later became in a big way."

Unlike Henry Ford, his contemporary, W. K. Kellogg had a mind which was complex and on occasion presented quite a study in contradictions. If he met old friends in carpenters' overalls, the garb made no difference, but he would never think of striking up an acquaintance with an unknown person so dressed. Contrariwise, he was a real friend to several of his secretaries, "with no condescension or any evidence of a master-servant relationship."

As a Kellogg Company executive once put it, "W. K. was always for something that he thought was better for the people. On the other hand, he was strictly Hamiltonian in his economics and political outlook, believing that the people needed leadership from men superior in leadership qualities, and that some men were made to be followers and others to be leaders."

Like many personally managed businesses of an earlier day, the company at times could be a "nest of intrigue." This melodramatic phrase refers to the fact that there were people in the employ who were not averse to carrying tales about this or that other employee and who tried to advance their position in the company by being a sort of "state's witness." W. K. Kellogg would listen to some of these employees and sometimes would take action impelled by half-truths or colored versions of what had occurred, or seemed to occur, in the plant or elsewhere.

Although it was a characteristic of Mr. Kellogg to be kindly, he never was demonstrative or flowery in his social attitudes. A delegation of Republicans called upon him during the administration of Governor Groesbeck of Michigan, and though Kellogg was likeminded in politics and economics, he was not inclined to waste much time with the politicos. Commandeering Treasurer George McKay to do most of the honors, he advised that "I will step out in the hall and just say 'hello' and then excuse myself."

But when W. K. came into the hall, he saw that a member of the group was an attorney who had pleaded several of Dr. Kellogg's cases against the Kellogg Company. He shook hands all around the group, with the exception of the attorney whom he ignored. Thinking to bridge the awkward silence, Mr. McKay said to Mr. Kellogg, "Don't you know Mr. ———?" Looking straight ahead, the manufacturer replied, "Yes, I know him. That is why I did not shake hands with him." W. K. was no diplomat and could be blunt if the occasion seemed to call for bluntness.

His moods were often derived from whether or not he liked a person. A former company executive recently stated: "I have always believed that Mr. Kellogg actually wanted to keep his employees in awe of him. For instance, I can remember at banquets of company managers and executives in the social hall, the gathering would suddenly hush when Mr. Kellogg would come in, and contrariwise, when he departed the chattering and mood of relaxation would expand."

On occasion, W. K. Kellogg, as did Jove of old, would heave bolts of lightning at erring mortals when they incurred his resentment. Sometimes this resentment was over major happenings, sometimes over what to most people would seem minor incidents. One could never quite predict when the bolts were going to be thrown.

Yet this was the same W. K. Kellogg who took any possible spare moments to visit his sick friends and relatives and who, in spite of his abhorrence of funerals, always went to pay his respects to a deceased friend. In terminating his visits to the sanitarium hospital or the home of an ill or impecunious friend, he had a habit of extending for a handshake a hand in which he previously had minutely folded a twenty dollar or larger bill. Thus the bill was left with the recipient, apparently in tone with Mr. Kellogg's wish to spare other people any embarrassment relative to benefactions and perhaps also to give the donor a chance to get away before any effusive thanks were given.

There was in Mr. Kellogg's makeup a high degree of intolerance, as there is in the outlook of many strong men. Few of his executives were ever comfortable in his presence, and when it came to competitors, W. K. Kellogg was not of the "forgive and forget" school. For instance, a contemporary recalls that "W. K. never had any love for Mr. Post. He always had the feeling of wanting to surpass this gentleman."

Actually there was very little contact between Mr. Kellogg and Mr. Post. "They largely hissed at each other over the fence." Each company zealously kept track of the other's hard-to-hide daily carloadings and had more than casual interest in new products and the trends followed in advertising. Today the two plants are comfortably adjusted neighbors, only a long block apart, but for a decade or more the rivalry extended beyond the bounds of business.

However, Mr. Kellogg (largely confining his athletics to spectator sports though he did a mild bit of golf, swimming and, for a while, horseback riding) used to exult in the victories of the Kellogg baseball nine over "our friends down the street." The plant employees, too, were elated over victory and dejected over defeat. The baseball teams of both rivals were made up of pros and semipros, some of whom had competed in the majors or upper minor leagues. While a number of these athletes later became valued employees, the majority had a main function of playing winning baseball and only ostensibly held productive jobs in the plants. In addition to a league schedule, the company sponsored the visits of barnstorming teams from the big leagues. A former Kellogg employee still remembers dining across from Rogers Hornsby after one of these barnstorming games and his request for sugar via a "Squirt the sand to me, sister."

The Battle Creek plant of the Kellogg Company is a huge cluster of buildings extending over approximately 113 acres in the southeastern section of the city. The construction of the plant and of its beautifully landscaped grounds was strongly influenced by the model National Cash Register Company plant at Dayton, Ohio. Parklets, fountains, and rose gardens ornament the west portion of the grounds while some of the interior features of the plant and its social and employee relations programs echo several visits and consultations with the aforementioned cash register corporation.

Prior to the modern change away from regarding one's company as the center of a social orbit, there was a considerable program of "extracurricular" activity at the plant. Besides the already mentioned ball games, there was a many faceted program of entertainment. A social hall permitted dancing during the noon hours. In this same hall were often scheduled traveling concert attractions such as the Fisk Jubilee Singers, and there were minstrel shows, vaudeville acts, banquets, and Christmas celebrations.

The program also included parties and picnics, the latter often at Gull Lake, a seven-mile body of water fifteen miles from the plant. Once on the eve of a picnic, W. K. Kellogg discovered that a saloon on a hill near his Gull Lake estate had been arrayed in colorful bunting to attract the picnickers. When the saloonkeeper told the food manufacturer that he did not have enough money to persuade him to stay closed all day, Mr. Kellogg retaliated by distributing a bulletin to the employees to the effect that "I hope you will not patronize the saloon."

An early-comer to the picnic was amazed to see Mr. Kellogg

enter the saloon with two companions, but he found that the three "drinkers" were imbibing soda pop and apparently maintaining a patrol so that employees would not be lured to the saloon. Later, Mr. Kellogg bought the land on which the saloon stood and thus got rid of this "den of iniquity."

As great as was Will Kellogg's aversion to liquor, he had an even stronger animus regarding tobacco. Eugene McKay, a long-time plant superintendent, can recall a number of occasions where only his intercession persuaded Mr. Kellogg not to "Fire that man who is smoking a cigarette out on the dock." Woe be it to any executive who was caught smoking on the company premises, and it did his standing no good if he were known as a smoker at all. This made indulgence in the weed a precarious business for "the boss had a very keen sense of smell" and was hard to fool with respect to the use of tobacco.

While John Harvey Kellogg and Will Kellogg were at odds on a number of things, they were in complete agreement relative to liquor and tobacco. They believed that smoking, on the whole, was more dangerous than liquor because many people smoke most of the time whereas indulgence in liquor is only now and then. W. K. Kellogg thought that smoking certainly had no place around a food factory.

This was to place in daring perspective a joke played by an executive of the company. It was understood that at company luncheons and dinners Kellogg preferred that his associates not smoke. At this particular gathering the practical joker had wooden imitations of cigars laid at each plate. Mr. Kellogg was uneasy throughout the meal and only smiled sourly when the joke was revealed by the joker's burlesque attempt to light one of the wooden cigars.

3.

When his signature first appeared on a package of corn flakes, it is doubtful if W. K. Kellogg realized that this signature would one day be known throughout the civilized world, or that

(Reproduced by permission. Copr. 1936 by The New Yorker Magazine, Inc.)

HISTORIC MOMENTS IN THE ANNALS OF AMERICAN INDUSTRY

An efficiency engineer discovers that printing will save Mr. Kellogg from
having to sign his name on each of the Corn Flakes boxes.

A far cry from the Bartlett Street shanty is to-day's array of Kellogg Company plants. Three other U.S. factories supplement the output at the Battle Creek plant (pictured later). Five additional plants are operated by the Company in Canada, Australia, England, South Africa, and Mexico. Other foreign plants operated for the Company are in Ireland, Sweden and Holland.

Kellogg cereals would be sold and consumed in the far corners of the earth.

Yet today, the Kellogg Company does business in approximately one hundred countries and the slogan "Wherever you find people, you find Kellogg's" has become a truism. The company's advertising and promotional matter appears in seventeen foreign languages. Three other large U. S. plants supplement the Battle Creek output, with these factories located at Omaha; Lockport, Illinois; and San Leandro, California. Foreign plants operated by the company are at London, Ontario, Canada; Sydney, Australia; Manchester, England; Springs, Transvaal (South Africa) and Querétaro, Mexico. In addition, foreign plants operated for the Kellogg Company by other concerns are at Dublin, Ireland; Uppsala, Sweden; and Wormerveer, Holland. Another plant at London, Ontario, represents a joint activity of the Kellogg and Pillsbury companies in the manufacture and sale of Pillsbury cake mixes in Canada.

Although there have been many mergers in the cereal field, the Kellogg Company over the years has refused a score of attractive offers for merging with a wide variety of large companies. To the offers for combination which occurred during his active business years, W. K. Kellogg turned a deaf ear. From the day that he was convinced that he had worked out the proper formulae for success, he was never diverted regardless of the allurements offered. The Kellogg Company was still young when the wave of forming trusts and gigantic combinations of units engulfed the country. The practice had the laudable economic purpose of concentrating management, but there were some points which did not appeal to a man as practical as Kellogg.

Almost unbelievable offers were made to him, but he never entertained them seriously. With all due regard for the abilities of master minds intent upon merger, Will Kellogg did not believe it would do what was claimed for it in the long run. He was an individualist and believed in the competitive system.

He thrived on competition, regimentation was abhorrent to him, and as to managerial concentration, he flattered himself that he had worked out that phase to his satisfaction and profit.

Only the most discerning of acquaintances would have labeled W. K. Kellogg as a "very human man." However, those who saw through the cold mask of this excruciatingly shy person knew the quality was there. One might even have thought the company credit policy established by him to be "sentimental" if it had not worked so well in execution. The Kellogg credit policy, as related by a company historian, "might be said to be one of these human policies. Intuitively Kellogg felt that the human factors in judging credit risks were if anything more important than the cold facts-and-figures of a credit rating. The figures might represent a temporary situation: the facts of character and vision and courage and stick-to-itiveness were more permanent and reliable. On these W. K. Kellogg built a credit policy which serves the business to this day. In spite of the breadth of this policy, the Kellogg business has operated on a loss ratio which few businesses can equal."

One reason Kellogg's succeeded where half-a-hundred companies failed in Battle Creek was the "intuition" which aided W. K. Kellogg to make quick decisions. Executives of the company agree that from him you would get an answer "Yes," or "No," quickly. Often Mr. Kellogg would pull a worn coin from his pocket and say, "Well, I will flip this lucky penny to see what we should do." Few, however, believed that the decision was left to the caprice of a coin toss but rather that their whimsical boss arranged to have the coin corroborate a quick decision he had already made.

"I will never forget a time," relates an executive, "when a sales manager was discharged before he had his year's program planned. W. K. called me in and told me to go ahead and get together a program, samples, promotions, etc. Later when I laid the projects in front of Mr. Kellogg, I was aghast at the totals reached by my calculations. Hesitatingly, I called off what seemed to me to be enormous figures, but as fast as I could get the words out of my mouth, the boss would say, 'Okay on that item; what's next?' In five minutes he had okayed several million dollars' of sales and promotional expenditures!"

An early Director on the Kellogg Board corroborated this salient feature of Will Kellogg's business administration: "He was not afraid of ciphers. If a proposition appeared to be sound, he was as ready to entertain it in terms of millions as other men would be in terms of thousands."

If Will Kellogg thought fast, he also thought long. When the company launched another new product, Kellogg's Corn Soya, in 1945, the research back of the product represented more than twenty-five years of Mr. Kellogg's faith in soy beans as a valuable source of protein. The germ of that faith had occurred in a trip he took to the Orient in 1919–1920 and, though some executives were to grow dubious of the difficult task of integrating this protein with other constituents to make a delicious and valuable breakfast food, W. K. Kellogg never did. He literally prodded his Experimental Division for a quarter-century, and his faith and persistence paid off. (The Special K high-protein breakfast food first marketed by the company in 1955, four years after the death of Mr. Kellogg, is another product which over many years evolved from an idea of and an urging by this man of ideas.)

One day in 1927 three members of the Kellogg organization drove to Mr. Kellogg's estate at Gull Lake with two packages of a mysterious new cereal. They poured some of it into a bowl for him to try. It was crisp and had a good flavor. It "ate" well, either dry or in milk or cream.

"You've got something there," said Kellogg laconically. "That will be a successful product." That was enough for the three callers. They knew that if W. K.'s judgment, based as it was on an almost infallible intuition, indicated that a food would "go," then the food would be a success. The product was Rice Krispies.

[180]

Three times Mr. Kellogg came back to the company, out of the semi-retirement which he desired because of a recurrent gall bladder condition and several resultant operations. The first time was during a financial crisis of the company. The second time he picked up the reins from a beloved son with whom he had conflict. And the last time, he wrestled with a complex situation wherein the morale of his staff had fallen to a low ebb and the earnings in a year had dwindled from millions to practically nothing. W. K. Kellogg always exhibited a capacity and a tendency to act quickly and drastically, and perhaps there was no more graphic illustration of his "immediate practicality" than at this period when he set about to put his house in order. Years later, a Kellogg employee was carrying forward a job evaluation in the Battle Creek plant when a veteran foreman said to him:.

"Did you know that the last man who made such a job evaluation got fired? In fact," he continued, "do you see that whole row of offices up ahead of you? Back in 1938 when Mr. Kellogg got through with his housecleaning, every office in that row was empty!"

Why was it that this unassuming and reticent man, "who had practically none of the extrovertic traits usually associated with the so-called captains of industry," was able to pilot the company over rocky shoals and on to success? More than twenty-five business leaders who knew W. K. Kellogg intimately were interviewed on this subject. They ascribed his success to varying reasons: "His was a one-man industry and he could move quickly, unhampered by any need for consultation with an absentee board." . . . "He had determination and will power, bulwarked by an ability to go straight down the road." . . . "He had an excellent product and, à la Shakespeare, he 'seized the tide.'" . . . "From his great courage emanated a strength that inspired his well-chosen helpers." . . . "He had learned the food business from a practical angle and knew the ins and outs." . . . "His continual activity of mind at the sanitarium had taught him to forecast needs, to plot, to plan and follow through." . . . "He had ideas and ideals, much drive and intelligence; his particular qualities would have catapulted him to success in fields other than the food industry."

And a psychologist-psychiatrist said of him:

"Dominated as he was by an older brother for many years, Will Kellogg developed what is known today as an inferiority complex. In overcompensating for this complex, Mr. Kellogg went to limitless bounds and it is likely this was the greatest driving force behind the success. He was going to show his brother, himself, and the world that he, too, had superior qualities and that only an unfortunate set of circumstances had prevented him from being as eminent as the Doctor. Those circumstances he eliminated."

To analyze W. K. Kellogg's success, perhaps one must take into account all the above allegations. If we cannot be certain of the cause, we can be certain of the effects. "What Henry Ford did for the automotive industry, Will Kellogg did for the food business. Look at any type of food production, particularly processing, and it will be seen that much of the impetus came from Battle Creek. Machinery designed currently in that city for bread-wrapping, the Kellogg Waxtite package to keep products fresh, are only two of many ingenious devices designed in Battle Creek cereal factories or allied specialty manufacturing plants. It is also true that many of the advertising ideas of the food industry, particularly dynamic packaging, slogans like 'Sweetheart of the Corn,' premiums and unique promotional campaigns, came from Battle Creek."

Because the growth of the company and the cereal industry were parallel and there was rapid acceleration of food know-how in a comparatively brief span of years, many times Will Kellogg and his company faced a dilemma of "No machinery to facilitate the planned improvement of this particular breakfast food." However, such situations hampered an improvement for only a short time, for through the driving

A cereal flaking room.

When "no existing machinery" was the obstacle to a desired improvement in breakfast foods, W. K. Kellogg, his son, John L., and veteran employees fashioned machinery to conquer the dilemma. The ingenious devices born of necessity furnished real impetus to the nation's food processing.

impetus of W. K. and the mechanical genius of J. L. Kellogg and several veteran employees, machinery was fashioned right-on-the-job to conquer the dilemma.

Thus this pioneer of the mass production of cereals used the inventive genius of his cohorts, and ingenious processing through constantly evolving machinery and a well-staffed and equipped experimental laboratory, to gain added flavor, form and texture for his foods. He found that grains could be flaked, rolled, extruded in filaments through orifices, baked and ground up, exploded and shredded. But, best of all, according to W. K. Kellogg, "the ready-to-eat cereals taste fresh and crisp, and not like the old-fashioned must-be-cooked cereals which taste like cold mush even though the housewife spends several minutes cooking them over a hot stove."

So that crisp and fresh food could be quickly produced, adequately packaged, and rapidly shipped, there came into being improved traveling ovens, stainless steel cookers, long lines of conveyor belts, and many other ingenious devices. Because of the company's experience in the design and improvement of packaging and the continued ingenuity in meeting with evolving situations, the Kellogg Company was selected by the United States Government to package much of the K rations used by the armed forces during World War II.

Cameron Hawley's book and motion picture, *Executive Suite,* were focused on a business leader who had many of the driving tactics of W. K. Kellogg as an administrator. Although Kellogg was not from the usual "captain of industry" mold

A modern packaging room.

and was quite different in personality from Edison, Bell, Eastman, the Wright Brothers and Henry Ford, he had firm control
of the stock of his company. Therefore, the business, during
his active years, had "one-man government" rather than the
multi-person management more common in corporations of
today.

A case in point particularly illustrates the fact that Mr.
Kellogg gained enjoyment from his majority holdings of company stock. In the years prior to 1937, the annual stockholders'
meetings of the Kellogg Company were very brief indeed.
W. K. seemed to take particular pride that a current year's
meeting was shorter than that of the year before and consumed
only a few minutes. This, of course, contrasts with today's annual meetings, not only of the Kellogg Company but of most
corporations, for modern corporate meetings are of considerable duration and quite comprehensive and informative in
nature.

A typical stockholders' meeting in Mr. Kellogg's heyday
would largely consist of a reading of the tally of the proxies,
indicating that so many stockholders were present, so many
proxies were being voted, and giving an accounting of the total
percentage of the stock. With the puckish sense of humor he
occasionally exhibited, W. K., as chairman of the meeting and
holder of a wide majority of the stock, then would give a
characteristic shrug of his shoulders and say, "Well, I guess
it is safe to proceed." There would follow a very brief presentation of the facts and figures of the year and a gracious statement by the chairman, "I am very well pleased at the manner
in which you gentlemen are conducting the business and want
to congratulate you all on this."

Contrariwise, it was somewhat unusual for W. K. Kellogg to
congratulate an individual on some outstanding achievement.
There was rather a tacit conclusion on the part of all concerned
that if an executive stayed on the payroll, he *was* doing outstanding work.

Executives of the company in close association with Mr. Kellogg learned to appreciate the value of time. Their boss had an addiction to promptness. If he set an appointment for 10:55 o'clock, he really meant it. He was ready at the appointed time and he expected the other party to be there on the dot. A long-time chauffeur for Kellogg once made the mistake of keeping his employer waiting on a street corner of a Florida city. He brought the car by an hour late, and this error cost him his job.

When consulting with his executives, Kellogg quite often would give them just a moment to express themselves. Then, almost before they knew it, they were being ushered out of his office. It is anyone's theory as to why he placed such a premium on his time. Perhaps he had some burning ambition over and above that known to exist for his company; possibly he lacked a sense of proportion.

According to mood, W. K. Kellogg was a singular combination of democrat (the small *d* should be emphasized since he voted the straight Republican ticket) and autocrat. A conservative in business and economics, it was natural that he regarded with unconcealed irritation the growing tendency of the federal government to "interfere" with corporate operations. It was galling to him to have government lawyers tell him how to run his business. His long-held "Square Deal" sales policy was based on his personal ideas of what was efficient and fair, and opinions falling within his sense of *lèse-majesté* would cause him to voice apprehension about the "Socialistic trend."

This rugged individualist, as were most of his business contemporaries, was completely intolerant of his competitors. However, his tendency and ability "to drive straight down the road to a goal" never represented a compromise of the ethics in the rigid code evolved from the religious atmosphere of his boyhood.

A Battle Creek attorney recalled: "W. K.'s actions and his

articulation depended upon his mood. If some salesman came in with an unfortunately expressed proposition, Mr. Kellogg would make this salesman a likely candidate for the insane asylum. He would laugh a man out of his office. He was not particularly humorous but he could turn a smart aleck type of salesman inside out, with an American admixture of sarcasm and humor. He had no trouble in getting rid of offensive salesmen. However, he did not make a business of ridicule, reserving his guns for the more boorish offenders. Basically he was a kind man."

If, in his determination to be "King of Corn Flakes," W. K. Kellogg could be stern with competitors and salesmen, he sought to be more than fair with his employees. True, he was a conservative but he eventually became an enlightened conservative and his company's employee relations may be judged from the fact that there has been a minimum of labor disturbance in the history of Kellogg's.

Perhaps one might characterize the liberality of Kellogg to his employees as benevolent paternalism, stemming from a desire to be liked, from a feeling of gratitude toward loyalty, and from a sense of *noblesse oblige*, the hallmark of all benevolent paternalists. As one intimate observer saw it:

"When the company was small, he found comparative happiness in sponsoring company picnics and parties. He built a gymnasium in Number Five building for their pleasure. He had the benevolences such as coal at cost, money given to employees in distress, and because he was away from the business at a time of great industrial change, it was hard for him to understand upon his return that employees might want security as a guaranteed contractual thing rather than as largesse from the hand of a benevolent paternalist. . . . But he was ahead of his times, for instance, on the matter of unemployment compensation.

"As a case in point, a very modest retirement scheme for employees had fallen by the wayside and, at a time when security plans had come strongly into our economy, our people had absolutely nothing for security. When the idea of a rebirth of a security plan was mentioned to Mr. Kellogg, he at first was at a loss, for he had never considered or perhaps even heard of contractual employee security plans. Perhaps the idea was even repugnant to him, for he was a rugged individualist who believed that he and all other people should work hard and save for their own old age. It took quite a while to obtain his sanction for a good employee security plan, but when the whole thing had been traced through, he saw its real merits and characteristically said: 'Go ahead. Your idea will be good for the employees and for the company.' "

It was W. K. Kellogg himself who, during the Great Depression when spread-the-work was imperative, set up a six-hour day at the Battle Creek plant. "If we put in four six-hour shifts," he said to Mayor William Penty who was also a Kellogg employee, "instead of three eight-hour shifts, this will give work and paychecks to the heads of three hundred more families in Battle Creek."

Of course, unemployment was a serious condition not only in Battle Creek but over the nation at the time. President Herbert Hoover saw in the Kellogg experiment some real potentials for a badly needed increase in the country's employment rolls. He, therefore, summoned Kellogg and Arch Shaw to the White House to give full details. Mr. Hoover, in recalling that discussion during an interview accorded the author of this biography on February 1, 1955, related:

"I was very interested in the experiment carried on by Mr. Kellogg. He inquired whether we thought it was a good plan and we told him we thought the results would be very worthwhile."

Another weapon used by W. K. Kellogg to soften the effects of the Depression upon his employees and his city was his instructions to the company personnel department to hire men or women on the basis of the size of their family so that

A ten-acre park on the Battle Creek grounds was built only partly for aesthetic reasons. Much as Mr. Kellogg loved to see steamshovels working, he decreed manual labor for the construction of the rose gardens, lily ponds, ornate fountains, tennis courts, the children's playground and wading pool. The park, fashioned during the economic depression of the early '30s, helped to make work for many of the economically distressed of Battle Creek.

breadwinners for a large family might have a paycheck. A corollary policy of the company, during the years before the demand made necessary round-the-clock shifts on practically every day of the year, was to lay off single persons instead of married people when slack times necessitated any layoffs.

The construction of a ten-acre park on the Battle Creek plant grounds was only partly for aesthetic reasons. Kellogg also saw the construction as an opportunity to mitigate the economic distress in his home city and issued a command that wherever, at all practical, the work on the park should not be machine work but hand labor. Much as W. K. Kellogg loved to see steamshovels working and much as he worshipped efficiency, he decreed manual labor for the building of the rose gardens, the lily ponds, the ornate fountains, the tennis courts, the children's playground and wading pool. The employees

An outdoor "foyer" leading to an expansive
rose garden, softball fields and tennis courts.

were "our people" and the dictates of his conscience obligated him to aid them in times of need.

Very dear to the heart of W. K. Kellogg were the veteran
employees who made up the company's "Twenty-five Year
Club." He even forgot his repugnance for making speeches
when the various occasions came to give this or that veteran
a gold watch symbolizing long years of service. A good many
of these employees have been helped by benefits ranging from
groceries and coal to the payment of large medical bills and,
to insure the continuance of such benefits, Will Kellogg in
1944 gave 21,400 shares of Kellogg Company common stock
to a Twenty-five Year Fund which now has a market value of
more than $1,000,000 in assets.

Perhaps his gratitude for the loyalty of these veterans is the

Very dear to the heart of W. K. Kellogg was the Twenty-Five-Year Club, an organization of veteran employees of the Kellogg Company. In 1944 he endowed the "Twenty-Five-Year Fund" with a large block of stock, and the Fund now has for "rainy day" benefits to its members assets totaling more than a million dollars. At top, Mr. Kellogg is shown in attendance at a club picnic when he was eighty years old. In center, a later picture shows the then-blind club sponsor shaking hands with new members. (The President and General Manager of the Kellogg Company, Mr. W. H. Vanderploeg, is in the left background.) At lower right, Mr. Kellogg, on the eve of a seasonal trip to California, says "Goodbye" to two veteran employees, Edward Huon and Charles Peterson.

reason that he considered a happening in 1950 as a high point in his life. At that time, he was presented a Forty-five Year pin by the Battle Creek factory unit. The diamond pin came to him near his ninetieth birthday and, as an observant grandson put it, "He exhibited more emotion than I had ever seen on his part." With tears in his eyes, Mr. Kellogg said, "I don't deserve it. After all, I don't work there any more." Of course, he accepted the pin and wore it proudly, not only as a symbol that he was remembered, but also as a talisman appropriately to be worn by a man who did not entirely disbelieve that there was a charm in being a seventh son of a seventh child.

CHAPTER 9

"Haunted by a Promise to a Small Boy"

ALTHOUGH THIS is a biography of W. K. Kellogg, it would be unrealistic to tell of the growth of the Kellogg Company without further mention of Mr. Kellogg's second son, John L. Until the two men came to a parting of the ways in 1925, John L. (Lenn) was a tower of strength to the company, "the driving, dynamic, indefatigable spark plug of the manufacturing end of the business."

Perhaps his forte was in experimentation with foods, but he also was a mechanical and inventive genius, responsible for many ingenious devices used in cereal production. Long after John L. had left Battle Creek for a Chicago business of his own, W. K. Kellogg recalled that "I do not know the exact number of patents and trademarks which were taken out by J. L. and assigned to the Kellogg Company, but with foreign patents, all told, I think they must have numbered in excess of two hundred." Among the processes developed by this second son were those for making a shredded wheat biscuit,

[193]

From 1908 through 1925, W. K. Kellogg's second son, John L., was "the driving, dynamic, indefatigable 'spark plug' of the manufacturing end of the business." During his seventeen years with the company, he developed more than two hundred processes and devices for which trademarks and patent rights were assigned.

(Photo by W. R. French.)

cereal coffee, beverage extracts, bran food, soybean food, and cereal confections.

The young man left a job as foreman of Dr. Kellogg's food factory in 1908 to join his father's company and by 1912 was made superintendent of the Kellogg Company factory. With as much drive and energy as his father, it was not unusual for John L. to put in a busy day as plant superintendent, then to work in the experimental rooms until 1:00 or 2:00 A.M. Or he might awake in the night with an idea, and, with no streetcars running, hike across town to the factory laboratory.

By 1913 this experimenter had developed a Waxtite package, a valuable innovation which made the food flakes moisture-proof and pollution-proof, giving Kellogg's a tremendous com-

[194]

petitive advantage. Later he was responsible for a further evolution in food protection, an inner seal package which saved the company about $250,000 annually.

Like his father, John L. had a stern face but his was the warmer personality and he was liked and admired throughout the factory. However, he was efficiency-conscious and "If you did your work, you knew it and J. L. knew it. If you did not, he also knew that too."

The son had some of the father's directness. A veteran employee recalls that John L. had suggested to a foreman that an old, non-working clock be removed from a wall and replaced by a new one. The foreman procrastinated and on the next occasion which brought the superintendent to that part of the factory, he strode over to the clock, ripped it off the wall, and let it fall to the floor with a crash.

W. K. Kellogg, always plagued by insomnia, could sleep better on an ocean voyage than at any other time, and in 1919–1920 he took a five-month trip to the Orient, leaving the business in the hands of his son. When Mr. Kellogg returned, he found the company in serious financial difficulties. The trouble largely had resulted as an aftermath of World War I and a subsequent recession, but the father, perhaps unjustly, did not completely exonerate the son from blame.

A man of temper, John L. resented criticism for what seemed to him an unavoidable situation. Perhaps a duodenal ulcer increased his irritability at another fatherly criticism, this time relative to a minor vice, smoking, anent which W. K. Kellogg wrote John L.'s son, John, Jr.:

"Your father spent most of the last week in Miami. He returned Sunday and called me up the same night. He told Barney (a long-time Kellogg chauffeur) that his stomach was troubling him again and that he was going on a diet. Barney suggested to him that in going on a diet, he should omit cigarette smoking. I think he gives up cigarettes quite regularly."

Another source of irritation between *père* and *fils* was the son's increasing tendency to disappear from the factory for weeks at a time without leaving information as to his whereabouts. Then the father, ever disposed to manage the lives of his relatives, attempted to interfere with an important personal decision of John L. This represented a culmination of a series of events stemming from the strong personalities of the two men, and the conflict resulted in a request for the resignation of the son. John L. presented his resignation at a special meeting of the Company's Board of Directors on September 1, 1925, insisting that the minutes carry the notation:

"Upon the express condition that the tendering and acceptance of my resignation shall not at any time or in any manner be construed to be a voluntary withdrawal by me from the service of the Company, I hereby tender my resignation as a member of the Board of Directors of said Kellogg Company."

Father and son respected each other's ability and there really was much love between them. However, they were both men of considerable ego and resented any restrictions on their activity or reflections upon their dignity. It was John L. who added to "Kellogg-icana" by telling of the time he and his father sat in a Chicago theatre box listening to an entertainer. This ad-lib artist was creating songs relating to people in the audience, the lyrics mentioning "the lady with the red hair" and various other distinctive attributes of the listeners. The man literally had Mr. Kellogg shaking with recurring chuckles, that is, until the ad-libber stepped over toward his box and chanted, "I see a little short, fat man in the box, with a bald head." John L. related that "W. K. got so mad at this, I had to take hold of him and pull him down in his seat."

The severing of the business relationship between him and John L. was a blow to Mr. Kellogg who naturally had dreamed of the continuance of the Kellogg name in the business after he was gone. Fortunately, the agreement to disagree was relatively amicable. The father was instrumental in an assignment made John L. by the Board of Directors whereby the latter was employed to make investigations of coffee flavor in France and Germany. Later, after John L. had set up his own businesses in Chicago, there were frequent visits between the two, and W. K. gave considerable counsel as well as loans to his son at a time of financial trouble in the businesses.

Perhaps one may best judge W. K.'s feeling toward John L. in later years through a story related by Attorney Burritt Hamilton. Mr. Kellogg had told this attorney that he had made an arrangement with John L. whereby the son would not contest the father's will giving the bulk of his money to the Foundation founded in 1930. Mr. Hamilton recalls saying to W. K. Kellogg: "That is all right, but your agreement with John L. is only oral. I would recommend that it be put in writing." But Mr. Kellogg insisted, "No, that is not necessary. John L. has given me his word and his word is good. I prefer to take it that way without any formality of writing. John L. will never go back on his word."

2.

Mr. Kellogg, with the loss of his son as a business associate, did not give up his hope for a company dynasty. He simply revised his dream, with its focus now on John L. Kellogg, Jr., a fourteen-year-old who obviously was a favorite with his grandfather. Both John, Jr., and his brother Keith were frequent visitors at the W. K. Kellogg home and there increasingly grew an affinity between the grandfather and the youngest son of John L.

The neighbors on Van Buren Street were both amused and touched by the sight of the elderly man and his slim, dark-haired grandson conversing earnestly as they walked or drove down the street. Perhaps they were talking of the Kellogg Company's winning baseball team or their like hobby of fishing. More often, however, they talked of the business which seemed to be a mutual love. Mr. Kellogg was never too busy to take young John to the plant and to explain to him the

"The neighbors on Van Buren Street were both amused and touched by the sight of the elderly man and his slim, dark-haired grandson, conversing earnestly as they walked down the street. Perhaps the talk was of baseball or fishing but, more often, they discussed the Kellogg business which seemed a mutual love."

(Photo by Doty.)

intricate processes of cereal production or to give him an insight into the mysteries of the buying of raw material, advertising, selling and shipping.

Before John was sixteen, his grandfather had promised him that "Some day you'll be at the head of this growing business," and it was increasingly obvious that he was the only one of the grandchildren who was to be tutored for this leading role. According to a grandchild, such distinction between the grandsons came to a head when a University of Pennsylvania psychologist gave these boys "a comprehensive set of forms to fill out, and then he interviewed us. The test was an outgrowth of the directional school of psychology. John, Jr.'s results in the test showed a very high aptitude for business, and Grandfather was a little obnoxious in holding him up as an example to us other grandchildren. It was a little hard to take, for Grandfather always presented John, Jr. as a shining light who was going to become a great business leader."

With renewed belief that there would be a Kellogg to succeed him in the business, the grandfather's elated and mounting hope is shown by letters written during the next few years to the lad's father in Chicago:

"With reference to John and the Ferris Institute, on account of John's heart, I have thought best not to push him too hard along various lines. He is only a boy of sixteen, and it seems too bad to get him into the business so early that he will have difficulty in remembering that he ever was a boy. He is a wonderful chap, and the more I see him the more I appreciate the foundation that he has for becoming a first-class executive. . . . It is rather amusing to think that John takes so much interest in the plant. I agree with you that his radio speech went over fine. I, too, was proud of the boy. . . . Surely John has an old head, and I am very proud of him. He has a good head as well as a good heart, and I feel that I could trust him with everything that I have."

On October 23, 1929, Mr. Kellogg wrote a letter to Paul de Kruif, famous author and long-time friend, which read in part:

"I am also feeling quite high-hatted over an offer that came to us yesterday from a very large concern, with assets of over $100,000,000, offering to take us into partnership with them. We have had a lot of such offers during the last several years, but I think this last offer is somewhat more complimentary than the others, due to the fact that the company is a very large concern and nationally known. We turned down the proposition because we have all of the money that we need, and are saving the business for John, the grandson. If my life can be spared to see John develop into a businessman during the next four or five years, it will be worth more than several million dollars to me."

The letters reveal the well of sentiment which was not far beneath the stern façade of this business statesman. He knew he was placing a heavy yoke on very young shoulders but he regarded John, Jr., as possessing "a business instinct as strong as any I have known." Eager to develop this innate talent, his methods of training the lad were perhaps more zealous than psychologically wise. So that John might become familiar with the operation of the stock market, he established a fund of $25,000 for stock transactions which became the property of the boy but was supervised by the grandfather.

A veteran employee of the company recalls an incident

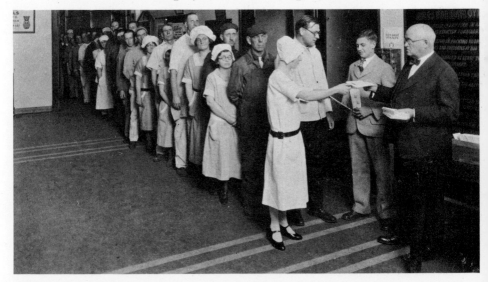

As a part of his grooming for future executive responsibilities, John, Jr. aided his grandfather in greeting company employees and passing out life insurance policies as Christmas gifts in 1925.

which illustrates the pressure placed on young John, Jr., in the effort to mold him as an executive. It was at the Christmas season when W. K. had the young man stand with him in the lobby of the company administration building to shake hands with employees in a long line as they left the building for the holidays. "The young grandson appeared ill at ease and frightened, not enjoying the occasion at all, and several times I heard Mr. Kellogg admonish him: 'You stand right here now, and do as I say.'" At the time the lad was probably seventeen or eighteen years old and to have to shake hands with literally hundreds of adults must have been a traumatic experience.

By the time John was eighteen, his grandfather enrolled him in Babson Institute for an intensive business course. A classmate remembers the lad as—

". . . a well-built young man, of swarthy complexion, with very dark hair. He was about 5′ 9″ tall, weighed 160 pounds, and always wore glasses. . . . He was always like a flea on a griddle, very intelligent but with more nervous energy than his power plant could accommodate. . . . At this training ground for sons of rich men who were to inherit industries, many of the sons had more money than brains. However, this was not true of John. He dabbled in college politics, was business manager of the Institute's annual, and he was always characteristically scurrying to carry out this or that special project."

Following graduation from the Institute, the grandfather gave the grandson a five-month trip around the world, in company with a classmate who had also become an employee of the Kellogg Company. Shortly after the trip, John, Jr., was made a vice-president of the company. He sat in at all board meetings and functioned as a member of the Budget and Merchandising Committees, and at one time listed the additional activities of "the Control Committee; development of more efficient departments, machines and methods; followup on advertising and sales; watching bond switches and foreign exchange; remapping territories and plans; development of

[201]

work standards; bringing Canadian and Australian matters to the fore!" As if these were not enough, he became involved in a number of extracurricular activities: the formation of a Junior Chamber of Commerce, pioneer work toward a railroad grade separation in Battle Creek, and the organization of a land company to build homes for working class folk.

An observer recalls:

"John, Jr., was somewhat of a grasshopper, an idea man, but usually wanted someone else to follow through on his ideas. He had tremendous nervous energy, a very active mind, and these kept him continually on the go, leading him into many highways and byways that wore him out physically."

During the period, this same observer was relatively close to W. K. Kellogg and he knew that—

"John, Jr., represented a last burning hope for his grandfather. He had hoped to establish a Kellogg dynasty in the company. So the old man put all his chips on this one boy who seemed a strong possibility for the Kellogg mantle. He gave the young lad a tremendous responsibility and tried to develop John so fast that his resources were taxed to the utmost. John not only wanted to take up where his grandfather had left off but, if possible, to exceed his grandfather's achievements. For instance, because Mr. Kellogg had built on the highest crest of land around Gull Lake, John was elated when he purchased some land supposed to be three feet higher than the holdings of his grandfather.

"There was great affection between grandfather and grandson. However, there was something about the Kellogg breed . . . apparently there was no organization, house or other thing big enough to hold two male Kelloggs. John always liked and admired his grandfather, but he was ever in a wind-shadow. He knew the fate of the company hinged on his young shoulders."

If W. K. was an unrelenting mentor, he did have for his pupil a concern which was an amalgam of affection and ambition. With all the concentration of a mother hen on a lone chick, the grandfather showered counsel orally and by memoranda and letters upon the evolving executive. An example of the latter is a letter written by Mr. Kellogg to John, Jr., on November 11, 1931, which epitomizes the former's philosophy. The gist of the counsel is in this excerpt:

SUGGESTIONS FOR ONE WHO WISHES TO HIT THE TRAIL SUCCESSFULLY, MAKE THE GRADE, PLAY THE GAME, AND WIN

1. First of all, get plenty of sleep and recreation and try to have your nerves in such a condition that you will not be working under a tension.
2. At no time appear to be rushed, even if you are in a deuce of a hurry; the impression is bad.
3. Do not scatter your ammunition; concentrate and you may get your bird.
4. Finish as far as possible one job before taking up another.
5. Do not have too many tag ends. In other words, have few irons in the fire at one time.
6. Try to lead the other fellow; do not push him.
7. Do not dominate your elders. Age gives people lots of experience.
8. In conversation with people forget the word "I."
9. Have patience with people. If things seem to go wrong occasionally, remember that time cures many things.
10. Do not dictate to your elders; better endure and let the other fellow boss. After all is said and done, we are all striving for results.
11. Consider the feelings of the other fellow and remember to do as you would like to be done by.
12. Keep your feet on the earth and your head up, but not too high in the sky.
13. Be kind to all, but choose carefully your friends.
14. Remember it took six days for Jehovah to create the earth. We should not try to reconstruct it in any less time.
15. Be humble.

P.S. The above represents fifteen suggestions, not commandments.

Not always, however, was the counsel so mild and philosophic. Various letters and memoranda, as well as the re-
membrances of company associates, reveal that the grandfather became increasingly critical of the fact that his grandson and business heir was "not taking proper care" of his
health. John was driving too hard toward the goal chosen for
him and the drive was taking its toll. The tension of the assignment, the grandson's own tendency to carry on too many
activities, caused a gradual descent toward ill health. One
close associate recalls the time that John, Jr., and two former
schoolmates were "out on the town" in Detroit. "We returned
late to our hotel that night and while two of us took the loss
of sleep without too much ill effect, John showed up at work
on Monday morning in a rather jaundiced condition. This
caused his grandfather to read him the riot act about keeping
himself physically in shape."

Emotionally, John, Jr., was a person of peaks and valleys
and possibly his moods were accentuated by a below-par
physical condition after a fall from a horse during September
of 1934. As the horse stumbled in a gopher hole, the young
man was thrown to the ground and later found only partly
conscious. In the hospital several weeks, he then went to a
ranch in Montana for recuperative reasons. Subsequently he
had some special treatment and his grandfather wrote him
on July 19, 1935:

"I had hoped that you would carry out fully the instructions that you received from your doctors, but I am afraid that
you are still carrying on in rather an active way.

"I dislike very much to be a party to these activities and I
am afraid that I am indirectly aiding and abetting you in these
various matters by allowing your salary to be continued while
you are on rest cure. I appreciate the fact that you must be
expending more or less money on account of these activities.
I have given the matter considerable thought, have lost some

sleep over it, and have come to the conclusion that the Kellogg Company had better discontinue paying your salary until such time as you are able to curb your enormous energies and concentrate on getting well. . . .

"I wish that you would talk the matter over with your doctor, after which I hope you will feel justified in wiring me that you have cut out the various business matters in which you have recently interested yourself. Don't try to do anything to surprise your grandfather or the world, but try to settle down to a quiet, lazy life for the time being. There is a whole lot of future ahead of you and plenty of time for activities later."

It is evident that W. K. Kellogg later came to some sort of a decision concerning his favorite grandson. Reasoning that he had tried to bring the lad along too fast, Spartanlike Will Kellogg took the vice-presidency away from his grandson, put the boy on the road in Wisconsin as a salesman and greatly reduced his salary. Perhaps the grandfather reasoned, "We have tried one way and it didn't work, so now we will try another route."

Mr. Kellogg's intentions were of the best, for he believed that "only drastic action would pull John out of a tailspin. He forgot or lost sight of two things: (1) that John was a Kellogg with his share of ego, temper and intractability and (2) that he no longer was a boy but an adult."

Subsequently, John evidenced a dislike for sales work so that he was brought into the plant and put to work in the company's experimental laboratory. It was here that came the dénouement.

In an early state of experiment at that time was a process for puffing corn grits, an effort to do with corn what had been done by company technicians in evolving the popular Rice Krispies. John threw himself wholeheartedly into this work. Whether the results were wholly his was a moot question but,

John L. Kellogg, Jr.

in any event, the grandson apparently tried to sell the grit-puffing process to his grandfather. When Mr. Kellogg expressed a resentment at this attempt to sell him a product developed on company time and property, John flamed in anger and resigned from the company. Apparently at the time of the resignation and even afterward, there lingered hope in Mr. Kellogg's heart that he and his grandson eventually would be reunited, for he wrote John's father:

"By the way, I received a note from your John the other day in which he asked to be relieved from his work with the Kellogg Company. The boy seems to be discouraged and thinks that in some way his grandfather has lost interest in him. . . . I wish you would look John over and see if it is time for him to have a conference with his physician. . . ."

Subsequently, however, occurred litigation over the ownership of the process ("The Kelloggs were the suing-est people") and the young man, now twenty-six, started his own company to manufacture the puffed product under the name of Nu-Korn. This was in 1937, and he was married that same year to an airline stewardess, Miss Mary Muench.

There was to be no happy ending to the story. In February of 1938, at a time when W. K. Kellogg was on a voyage taking him through the Panama Canal, the lifeless body of John, Jr., was found in the office of a small factory which he operated in

Chicago. A brief note near the body gave no indication as to the immediate reasons for taking his own life.

As soon as possible, a radiogram was sent to Mr. Kellogg, telling him of the death. The heartbroken grandfather was unable to return in time for the funeral services. However, at the hour the services were being held in the States, he went to a small Spanish chapel in Panama, there to remain on his knees in prayer while the last rites were being conducted far away.

Thus died Will Kellogg's last hope of a dynasty for his business—and forever he was to be haunted by the ghost of a promise made to a young boy.

3.

While in later years W. K. Kellogg gained great satisfaction from the continued success of his company, and from the achievements of his Foundation in helping people to help themselves, he never could completely divorce his sorrow over the fact that there was no Kellogg to run the business. Characteristically, however, he pushed personal disappointments deep into his subconscious and applied himself to the task at hand.

He saw that he was going to have to place the business in the hands of men outside of his family and he looked about for men worthy of such trust. An important ingredient in his success to that time had been his ability to pick helpers. When he employed a man, he usually had a complete dossier of his previous record. He had one or more interviews with the person and, by one means or another, practically psychoanalyzed the applicant before hiring him.

Even the best corporate head, however, can err in choosing executives who, in spite of real capabilities, do not fit into the workings of his particular organization. In this respect Mr. Kellogg slipped, not once but several times. "No one saw his mistakes clearer than did W. K. himself," recalls Mr. A. W.

Harris, founder of the Harris Trust and Savings Bank of Chicago. "He understood that only a very exceptional man could weld together the many-sided and growing operations and, as a personal assignment, he was determined to discover such a leader for his company."

So this business owner, at an age when the old rocking chair usually beckons, returned to Battle Creek and the job before him. It was not long thereafter that he came to Mr. Harris to ask him for one of the best men in the Harris Trust organization. Thus it was that W. K. Kellogg chose a management which made it possible for him to graduate from his "second life" of making money to a long-desired "third life" of investing money in people.

The reins were not dropped at once. From the new management, Kellogg required a weekly letter and, as always had been the custom, a daily statement of the cash status of the company and the car orders. Always in the Kellogg wallet was a consolidated statement of the company earnings and, by the aforementioned telephone hookup, he engaged in many

An aerial view of the present-day Battle Creek plant of the Kellogg Company. Since 1907 more than a million people from all over the world have toured this plant to see how ready-to-eat cereals are processed. The current

conversations with company executives. However, it was not long before Kellogg had a confirmed belief in the high quality of the management last chosen by him, and the easing of his mind with respect to his company helped to offset his weariness from the decline of his health and his sight.

He was to rejoice that his company maintained a wide lead in the ready-to-eat cereal field. With relish he recounted to friends that the Kellogg Company was doing (and continues to do) more than 40 per cent of the business in ready-to-eat cereals within the United States and more than 50 per cent of such cereals sold beyond the borders of our nation. And Mr. Kellogg's face came the nearest to showing animation when he had an opportunity to visit one of the company plants. The roar of modern machinery on floor after floor continually fascinated him. Though his blindness from 1941 on prevented his actually seeing the processes of cereal production, he took pride in contrasting the miles of conveyor belts, the modern packaging equipment, with the scanty machinery by which the first Kellogg cereals were processed and packaged.

facilities will store more than one and a half million bushels of grain and daily shipments of Kellogg cereal products exceed sixty-five carloads.

W. K. Kellogg

Of considerable satisfaction to him, also, was the news of
the crowds of people who annually visit the company's largest
plant at Battle Creek. Since 1907 more than a million people
from all over the world have toured this plant to see how the
cereals are processed. "Nature's gold," sun-ripened corn, wheat
and rice are the three basic ingredients in the more than a
dozen Kellogg products. Eleven of these products are produced at Battle Creek where there are storage facilities for one
and one-half million bushels of grain and where daily shipments of cereals exceed sixty-five carloads.

Approximately six million packages of cereals, including a
million boxes of corn flakes, are produced each day at this
plant. These current figures for just the one plant boldly contrast with the earlier mentioned incident when two, three
or five case shipments were parceled out as equitably as possible to the city's two railroads. Such figures also evidence that
while not all of W. K. Kellogg's dreams came true, that dream
with regard to carload and trainload business became very
much a reality.

Such has been the growth of the Kellogg Company in recent
years that it is likely that even its founder never dreamed of
the extent to which the company would expand. The business
he built was to be among the top two hundred in American industry, in volume of sales. In May of 1955, Building No. 80
(the numbering system encompasses both large and small
additions) was dedicated at Battle Creek, with the one hundred thirty-five thousand square feet of added plant space in
a five-story addition representing a portion of a $7,000,000 ex-
pansion program. As the company celebrated a fiftieth anniversary in 1956, its nine major plants and its world-wide production and distribution were tangible evidence that "Kellogg's of Battle Creek" have come a long way since W. K. Kellogg started the business in a shantylike plant on cobblestoned
Bartlett Street.

[210]

CHAPTER | 10

"He Was a Man in a Hurry!"

WITH THE CARES of his business now resting largely
on other shoulders, one might have surmised that W. K. Kellogg would slow the pace of his living. This, however, would
have been uncharacteristic of the man. Even though his general health was not good and his eyesight gradually failed in
the next few years, he drove for the goals of his diversified
interests almost as ardently as he did in the building of his
company.

He was delighted with the activities of his new philanthropic foundation (to be discussed in a subsequent chapter).
He grumbled over affairs at the sanitarium and took a leading
role in opposing brother John Harvey's plans for a reorganiza-
tion. He fumed over the "Socialist trend" in politics, and not
only aided conservative political candidates financially but
also with every ounce of influence he could muster. In between
such forays, he kept a watchful eye on his children and grandchildren and occasionally attempted to persuade them to
courses of action which, to him, seemed perfectly desirable
and logical.

By the time he had reached his seventies, Kellogg had

mellowed to a degree, but the essentials of his character and personality had not greatly changed. A prominent Battle Creek businessman, neighbor to W. K. for a quarter-century and still on the Board of the W. K. Kellogg Foundation, recalls:

"He was always a man in a hurry. When he wanted a thing done, he had the energy, intelligence and wherewithal to get it done 'pronto.' About five years after he had built his Gull Lake estate, he decided he wanted to add an orchard and explained to me, 'At my age, you can't wait for trees to grow.'

"While W. K. proved a poor prophet, in that he lived for twenty-one years after that, I remember he was a dynamo with respect to that orchard. He got in touch with farmers and professional orchard people and purchased fruit trees as large as twelve inches in diameter. Huge holes were dug to receive these trees which, wrapped in large balls of earth, were moved to the estate in the dead of winter on regular house trailers. By springtime the trees did not even know they had been moved and bore blossoms and fruit the first year. Perhaps to many the obstacle of moving mature trees might have appeared so great as to cause abandonment of the project, but the difficulty only sharpened the desire of W. K. to get the job done."

A chauffeur for Kellogg in much earlier days recalled that "in our many trips to New York, California, and to points north of Battle Creek, Mr. Kellogg never liked to eat the other fellow's dust. At that time, at least, he had no particular fear of speed and he would urge me to 'Open her up to seventy or eighty so that the other cars can't pass us.' "

The same chauffeur remembered that:

"On our morning drives to the Kellogg Company offices in Battle Creek, Mr. Kellogg and I almost daily would meet a bread delivery wagon which would hog the center of the street and pay no attention to toots of our horn requesting the right-of-way. Mr. Kellogg told me the next time we met the truck to toot the horn several times and then to drive right at him and try to scare him but not to hit him. I followed through on the instructions and that road hog turned to his right and gave us half the street. The boss said, 'I guess that cured him' and seemed to get a kick out of the incident."

However, if W. K. Kellogg was so determined and so in a hurry in most of his projects, he proved more cautious about hurrying back into matrimony. For nearly six years after the death of his first wife, he lived as a widower. Involved was a sense of loyalty to the wife whom he had loved and felt he had neglected. Too, he had a lack of confidence. Successful in business, he felt that he had been "a failure" as a husband. During these years, he sublimated his urge for a mate and for a more complete home by assiduous application to his work, by extensive travel, and by increased interest in his growing grandchildren.

His ever-present love of good music also proved a solace. A neighbor, Professor Edwin Barnes who was organist and director of the choir of Battle Creek's large Congregational Church, helped Kellogg to become a devotee of chamber music. It became a habit for W. K. to go to the Barnes home every Sunday night, when the professor would play a classical repertoire at the grand piano for hours. The musical evenings were just that, with very little conversation. Music was the bond and Kellogg formed a very deep attachment for this cultured musician who traveled abroad every other year.

These salon-type evenings were forever to make W. K. Kellogg a defender of the classical and a derider of jazz music. At Palm Springs, California, many years later, a Kellogg Foundation official invited the then blind Mr. Kellogg to join him in a chocolate soda at a drug store. Chocolate sodas were one of W. K.'s "vices," and he accepted with alacrity. The soda was excellent but a jazz juke box was making the atmosphere hideous with cacophony. This caused Kellogg to turn to his companion and ask: "What makes that thing run?" The reply, of course, was "The nickels that are put in it."

Whereupon Kellogg plaintively wondered: "Do you think we could put some nickels in it to keep it quiet?"

On one occasion, W. K. Kellogg was able coincidentally to aid the Barnes family and to indulge his dry sense of humor. A wedding ceremony at the First Congregational Church united Miss Gertrude Barnes, daughter of the professor, with Carleton Brooks Miller, pastor of the church. The couple and the wedding party then went to the Barnes home for a reception. Previously Kellogg had conspired with the young newlyweds: "If you want to get rid of any charivareers, just sneak out to the back door in the late minutes of the reception. Then jump over the hedge between our two houses. I will have Henry, the chauffeur, in the driveway with the car all ready to go."

As Dr. Miller recently recalled the incident:

"Just before the young folk were ready to inflict their fun upon us, Gertrude and I dashed to the back of the house and through the door to the back lawn. Henry helped the bride over the hedge and we were in the car and being driven swiftly down the driveway before the would-be pranksters knew what has happening. Ours was a clean getaway and the charivareers were very chagrined. For years thereafter, Mr. Kellogg would recount with glee the way our friends were foiled."

In almost every man's life, there is a period when he cherishes the male prerogative of not being rushed into a state of matrimony. Conversely, it is not unusual, when the right mood and the right woman come along, for this selfsame male to leap into connubial bliss. W. K. Kellogg proved kinship to his fellow men in the late months of 1917 when, almost impulsively, he proposed marriage to Dr. Carrie Staines, a woman physician on the staff of Dr. John Harvey Kellogg's sanitarium.

Always having great respect for the practitioners of medicine, Mr. Kellogg had real admiration for Dr. Staines' professional attainments and her quiet personality appealed to him. Perhaps his proposal was partly actuated by Dr. John Harvey Kellogg's opposition. The Doctor had informed Carrie Staines that she would be discharged as an employee of the sanitarium if she continued to go out riding with Will Kellogg.

On New Year's Day of 1918, Carrie Staines became Mrs. W. K. Kellogg in an unpretentious ceremony at Grand Rapids, Michigan. Present with them were two close friends of the couple, Dr. and Mrs. Rowland H. Harris, both former physicians at the Battle Creek Sanitarium. A somewhat small, introversive brunette, the new Mrs. Kellogg was more of a career woman than a housewife type and "two people who never say anything spontaneously must have found it difficult to communicate orally any feeling toward each other." Nevertheless, there was mutual respect in the marriage and there was a natural conclusion that the specter of loneliness was banished for these middle-aged newlyweds.

In the years ahead, the couple was to take a number of trips abroad. Oddly enough, however, Mrs. Kellogg did not accompany Mr. Kellogg on his first major travel after the marriage. For some months prior to the wedding, Kellogg evidently had planned a trip to the Orient in the company of A. K. Detwiler, a Los Angeles financier with whom other journeys to Hawaii, South America and Alaska had previously been taken. In a letter of September 20, 1918, Kellogg wrote to Mr. Detwiler:

"In regard to a trip to the Orient, I will talk this matter over with you when I see you in October. I am not sure but what I would prefer to go with you alone, if I can get away. I am not much used to traveling with ladies and am not sure that I would care to form a habit. In making a long trip there are so many things that men can do when they are by themselves in regard to accommodations, etc., that women would not care to put up with. I think Mrs. Kellogg would be quite contented

W. K. Kellogg was fifty-eight
years old at the time of his second marriage.

to have me leave her in California while making the trip.
However, please do not take this as a promise, as I may not be
able to get away at all."

Four months later, in January of 1919, another letter told
Detwiler "If I am able to get off for a trip, it is not my purpose to take Mrs. Kellogg with me." Perhaps there would have
been a change in the trip plans had not Mrs. Kellogg's father
become ill, making it impossible for her to take a long trip.
In any event, the trip to the Orient was embarked upon by
the two men on November 26, 1919, and they did not return
from this visit to Japan, China and India until May 1, 1920.

Letters and a diary written by W. K. Kellogg during the
long trip indicate that he proved not so confirmed in his "bach-
elor-widower" habits as he thought he was. Six months inces-

[216]

Dr. Carrie Staines who became
Mrs. W. K. Kellogg in a ceremony at Grand Rapids, Michigan, on January 1, 1918.

santly in each other's company evidently wore on the nerves
of both the men travelers. The more travel weariness and nostalgia bore in on W. K., the more he wrote home to Mrs. Kellogg. His letters were not mere travel notes but were six and
seven pages long and quite affectionate in tone.

In the course of the journey, Kellogg contracted a severe
cold while in the Philippine Islands and by the time he had
reached Hong Kong in China, the cold had deepened to pneumonia. Hospitalized for nearly four weeks, he had a telegram
sent into the interior of China requesting that Dr. A. C. Selmon, an Adventist medical missionary formerly at the Battle
Creek Sanitarium, hurry to the bedside. Ten years later, when
planning the establishment of his philanthropic enterprise,

Mr. Kellogg remembered the abilities and loyalty of this physician and made him the first president of the W. K. Kellogg Foundation.

In a letter written to his friend, A. W. Harris, Kellogg recalled not only this bout with pneumonia but also an illness suffered on a previous foreign trip:

"Some years ago when making a trip to Alaska I suffered a severe gall bladder attack and found myself three hundred miles from a physician. The Yukon River steamer made only three miles an hour. On arriving at the hospital, I was laid up for a few days and sent back up the river. The hospital and the nurse certainly looked good to me when I reached Fairbanks. I also had another experience with pneumonia at Hong Kong. I firmly resolved that the next sickness I had would be at home and not in a foreign country or an out-of-the-way place."

Despite this resolve and an observation of a friend that "The best part of a trip to W. K. was getting home again," Mr. Kellogg subsequently went abroad numerous times. Mrs. Kellogg was his companion on a second trip to Alaska, two West Indies cruises, two trips to Europe, a journey to Honolulu, two trips to South America, a voyage to Africa and one to Australia. Kellogg's daughter Beth was with the couple on trips to Australia and to South America. A nurse, Miss Helen Abbott, also made several of the journeys and Kellogg's secretary, Mrs. Bessie Young, was on one of the West Indies cruises.

Will Kellogg shared with most human beings the desire actually to see the historic and scenic spots described only inadequately in books. He wanted to marvel at the sovereign sights of the world: the Sphinx at dawn, the Rockies at dusk, the beautiful harbor of Acapulco at sunset. Although his eyes were never strong, he had an acute sense for color and picture composition and was a camera enthusiast for a number of years. However, it was more than his yen for the picturesque and aesthetic and "to see beyond the curve of the road" which motivated him to take an unusual number of travels.

Egypt was a port-of-call during the extensive journeys of Mr. and Mrs. Kellogg. With the desert as a frame and the enigmatic Sphinx and an age-old pyramid as a background, they brave a cool morning to pose on their skinny "ships-of-the-desert."

In the dining salon of the S.S. Georgic, bound for the West Indies. At the center table, and wearing festive hats, are Mr. Kellogg, to his left Mrs. Kellogg, to his right Miss Helen Abbott, his nurse. Across the table from Mr. Kellogg is Mrs. Bessie Young, his secretary.

W. K. Kellogg

This very modest and self-deprecating individual always felt his lack of formal schooling and, therefore, more regularly than most sought the broadening influence of journeys to various parts of the world. (Actually his business contacts, his extensive reading of both nonfiction and fiction, and his travels erased his educational deficit. A friend recalls that "Mr. Kellogg was as articulate in his speech as anyone I ever knew. He had a nice command of the English language. His grammar was excellent and he could be a very nice conversationalist when he was in the mood for conversation.")

W. K.'s insomnia also made ocean voyages particularly at-

Subsequent to the purchase of his first automobile, a Franklin with an air-cooled motor, in 1908, W. K. Kellogg had many cars but none which afforded him more pleasure than "The Ark." Purchased in 1923, when the "long, long trailers" of today were not even a dream, it possessed many of the comforts of the current homes-on-wheels.

With a body especially built on a White truck chassis, "The Ark" possessed its own sleeping berths, a galley-kitchen, an ice machine, shower bath, lavatory and toilet, intra-communications telephone, electric fans, superhetrodyne radio and even a 16-foot folding motor boat.

"The Ark" was a custom-built job, constructed according to detailed specifications furnished by Mr. Kellogg. He evolved these specifications over a period of five years in an effort to design a practical and comfortable automobile camping outfit. Mr. and Mrs. Kellogg toured several states of the Union in "The Ark" and, distinct as the vehicle was for its day, it attracted much attention in many of the highway towns of the early 1920s.

In this picture of "The Ark," near a California park, can be seen the chauffeur, Dr. and Mrs. Karl Kellogg, and W. K. Kellogg.

Almost invariably Mr. Kellogg wore a cap during his many auto trips. Here he is shown on Main Street of a western town, a tourist who liked touring because "Motoring has been of very great benefit to me, making possible many a good night's sleep and rest that I would not have had but for the hobby."

tractive to him. The first item of the daily entries in the diaries which he kept of his journeys always concerned the quality and quantity of his sleep:

"Slept seven hours last night. First time for some time." . . . "Had wonderfully good night of sleep." . . . "Slept poorly; only four hours; very light sleep, too."

Usually his slumber on a ship was more satisfying than in any other environment. It is deducible that during his business years this was partially because he could not be frequently contacted and thus business cares seemed far away. Since he took an intense interest in business and went to the excesses of a devotee, one can understand the reason for Mrs. Kellogg's note to a relative: "Mr. Kellogg is very busy and I will be glad when he gets on a boat to Honolulu so that he won't be bothered with telephone calls, wires and visits."

On another occasion she wrote a friend:

"Mr. Kellogg is not well and does not sleep much, and has been working like a man of forty. He may try to get away for a rest. He will be away from people who are always after him to buy something or are begging for something or have some marvelous scheme to unfold."

With an inner sight much stronger than his failing eyes, W. K. Kellogg was also looking bravely and philosophically into a darkening future, for he once wrote a former secretary: "Blindness may not be far ahead and that's why I am traveling so much. I want to store up memories of the scenic beauties of this wonderful country, and of the faces of my old friends who are scattered over the world."

Always on the eve of one of his many journeys, whether to California, to the Orient, to Europe or over the world, Mr. Kellogg liked to have certain of his close friends drop in for a short chat. (He also would make "farewell" telephone calls and visits to many company executives and to a few Battle Creek civic leaders.) It was a sort of leave-taking which he cherished, not so much that he had any premonition of not seeing them again but rather that he wanted them to feel he would miss them while he was gone. Doubtless, he too wanted to have the reassurance that here were friends who would miss him a little.

A letter to Mrs. Frances Starkey Cooper, who was his secretary in the early company days, expressed real gratitude because she was the only one who sent him flowers on the start of one ocean voyage. "While Mr. Kellogg would rebuff any effusive thanks for his various generosities," remembers a psychiatrist and long-time friend, "he was a man literally starving to death for appreciation, understanding and compliments."

W. K. Kellogg quite often traveled incognito, using such pseudonyms as "Will Keith," "A. Mann" or "W. Kellogg." He was a typical tourist and took in all the sights. However, he did not care to go with the crowd and, instead of sightseeing in a public conveyance, would hire his own taxi or carriage. Once in Peru, his party boarded a train for a mountain trip but "W. K. could not take the smoke and sudden stops and starts. Therefore, he contacted someone and hired a driver and a car proving that he could get things done even in a foreign situation."

During his journeys, Kellogg was able to shed a few of his repressions and to become more of a *bon vivant*. Sometimes this temporary change of personality led to minor crises as, for instance, on a voyage where he indulged his appetite for chocolate bars and chocolate sodas. After complaining that the ship's laundry had shrunk his shirts, he weighed himself to find he had gained fifteen pounds! His love of lobster (a food which was taboo for him) caused him deliberately to dine earlier than the rest of his party on a South American cruise so that his nurse could not veto his order for this sea delicacy. As a consequence, he had a recurrence of gout!

Mr. Kellogg reverted to his comparatively rigid personality, however, over an incident on this same cruise which concerned his daughter Beth and his nurse Helen Abbott. With the ship anchored in Guanabara Bay, the beautiful harbor of Rio de Janeiro, there was an opportunity for the two young women of the party to see something of shore life. They accepted an invitation of some of the ship's entertainers to go to a café in the city where these musicians were to play for a dance. The evening lengthened more than had been anticipated and Beth and Helen did not get back to the ship until 3:00 A.M. They found W. K. Kellogg pacing the deck and in a fury. He told these grown women that if there was any way to ship them home, he would do it, and he was quite cool to the young ladies for several days.

Contrariwise, this man who could be stern, also could show exceptional consideration for those in his travel party and particularly for the stay-at-homes in his family and circle of friends. His return from journeys meant the showering of gifts upon relatives and sometimes even on mere acquaintances. He was an inveterate souvenir hunter and, while occasionally proving a "fall guy" to some sharp vendor of an Eastern bazaar, he could be a canny shopper and usually his selections evidenced good taste. For instance, his daughter Beth (Mrs. Norman Williamson of Monrovia, California) still treasures some exquisite Swiss, French and Austrian dolls brought back by her father from a trip to Europe, and the homes of W. K.'s grandsons and granddaughters all contain exotic art objects which came from this or that Odyssey of their grandfather.

2.

As previously related, the much-traveled W. K. Kellogg also was a great homebody, often in the midst of trips pining for the springs and summers of Michigan or the balmy winters of California. His growing assets did not become real wealth until about 1925 and it was from this year on that his home became homes—a number of palatial dwellings. They were substantial evidence that, for a period, the characteristic frugality of Will Kellogg was tossed to the winds.

During the first decade in which he built his company, Will Kellogg lived well, but not lavishly, in a large two-story frame structure, adorned by a Michigan fieldstone enclosed porch, at 250 West Van Buren Street. This house he sold in 1915 to his son, John L. Kellogg, and then moved one door west to 256 West Van Buren Street. The French provincial house, which fronts McCamly Park in the western section of Battle Creek, still stands in marked contrast to its Midwestern gingerbread-and-Gothic neighbors. For ten years it was the only residence of the food manufacturer but, in the early 1920s he started visiting California, staying with friends and relatives for short periods and a portion of one winter at the Desert Inn in Palm Springs.

The Golden State began to have great appeal to W. K. Kellogg, and from 1926 on he was to divide most of his years between his winter residences in California and summer residences in Michigan. Apparently he reached a decision along these lines which made 1926 a "steamshovel year" for sure so far as he was concerned. That year saw the construction for him of two palatial homes, one named Eagle Heights on a high hill overlooking Gull Lake, fifteen miles from Battle Creek. The other, a nineteen-room villa atop a small California mountain, looked down upon the eight hundred acres of the W. K. Kellogg Arabian Horse Ranch which had been purchased in 1925.

The construction of the two large houses represented an uncharacteristic spending spree for Mr. Kellogg and, of course, a division of his interests. As intimated previously, he perhaps received his greatest satisfaction from the places during their construction. However, an old friend recalls that Kellogg enjoyed his Gull Lake estate more than any other home, even more than the great horse ranch in which he took real pride.

Mr. Kellogg had always wanted a home out from Battle Creek and regarded the seven-mile-long Gull Lake as the most scenic of the many lakes in the area. After choosing a promontory for the thirty-room, nine-bath house (which he often called his "cottage") and a lake shoreline of some 1,600 feet, he eventually acquired a thousand or more acres in the vicinity. These later were used for the bird sanctuary, a reforestation project and an experimental farm, which he constructed and subsequently gave away.

During the construction of the dwelling, actually a manor house rather than a cottage, Mr. and Mrs. Kellogg were frequent visitors to Eagle Heights. There was the thoroughness with which he approached every project in W. K. Kellogg's preplanning of the home and the many nights spent in going over blueprints with the architect. His busy work days and the building of the ranch home in California precluded daily inspections of the progress at Gull Lake. However, his visits were often enough so that he could detect any deviation from his careful planning and it is recalled that "he was happy over the progress and was as enthusiastic over the whole thing as he would permit himself to be over anything."

The busy activities of masons and plasterers and the ring of carpenters' hammers superseded the roar of steamshovels and in only a few months the building of the large home came to a conclusion with the installation of a $25,000 pipe organ. (A similar organ was installed in the new California home.) Many oil paintings, imported tapestries and oriental rugs supplemented the interior decoration and furnishings suggested by decorators from Marshall Field and Company in Chicago. Then

Exterior (above) and interior (at bottom of page) photographs of the manor house of the Gull Lake Estate which was constructed in 1926.

it was that, with a natural pride, Mr. Kellogg could survey the interior and exterior of the English-type home, and from its long veranda exult in the majestic beauty of the landscaped acres which swept to the blue waters of the lake.

The place lacked only a moat and a drawbridge to resemble a feudal manor and the resemblance was heightened by the five-foot, chain-link fence which encircled the spacious grounds and led to two impressive, iron gate entrances. At one time, there were twelve men working full time on the property and the lawns, with the grounds and a four-section greenhouse

under the supervision of a head gardener who hailed from England. The rolling hills of the fifteen acres in the front lawn were insured a green turf through an underground sprinkling system for which the piping alone cost more than $100,000, and to fertilize the turf Kellogg had carload after carload of stockyard manure shipped from Chicago. In addition to the

(At top of page) Aerial view of the Kellogg Estate on the shores of Gull Lake. The manor house is obscured by the trees. The picture at right is of a Dutch windmill imported from Holland and placed on a peninsula of the Estate.

(Windmill picture by Department of Information Services, Michigan State University.)

lawns, there was a sizeable fruit orchard made to bear the first year through the tree-moving incident earlier described. The greenery included many rare shrubs, vines and trees and a grove of English walnut trees was, for a time, an engrossing hobby of the owner of the estate.

Practically all the construction at Eagle Heights—including a guest house, a chauffeur's house, a caretaker's cottage, an auxiliary cottage, the greenhouse, a seven-car garage, a two-story boathouse, beach and docks, facilities for tennis, croquet, pitching horseshoes, and a patio with outdoor Dutch oven— took place at the time the manor house went up. The one exception was a large Dutch windmill which, transported from its original site in Holland, was placed on a small peninsula of the estate.

In addition to the Gull Lake home, W. K. Kellogg leased, for the quarter-century till his death, Apartment 601 in The Inn, a seven-story apartment house which he built in 1924. This large apartment, which corresponds to the penthouse suites in the hotels of some of the larger cities, was used by Kellogg partly as a convenience but also to bolster his assertion that he was a *bona fide* resident of his beloved home town, Battle Creek.

3.

W. K. Kellogg's California villa spread over the summit of a high foothill almost as quickly as did Eagle Heights over the Gull Lake bluff. This "Big House," as Mr. Kellogg usually called it, sits nearly five hundred feet above the west end of Pomona Valley, and the huge windows of its sixty-foot living room afford a magnificent view of the ranch and the remainder of the valley as well as of the San Jose Hills which are flanked by the San Antonio Mountains. The house itself is about 150 feet long and has an air of grandeur with its statue-adorned fountains, its landscaped grounds and the numerous large and exquisitely decorated rooms.

Under the direction of famous architect Charles Gibbs

Adams, the 800-acre ranch quickly became one of the beauty spots of Southern California. The many buildings on the ranch are all of Spanish design, including a large home (with swimming pool and patio) originally built for Mr. Kellogg's eldest son Karl. In addition to the various barns, garages and machine storage sheds—all with red-tiled roofs—there is a spacious Administration Building. This houses the offices which had as their main order of business the supervision of the Arabian Horse Shows held each Sunday, as well as the provision of facilities and convenience for the proper rearing and development of these distinctive horses.

Large stables of Moorish design are joined to the Administration Building to form a U and in the middle of the U is a green, landscaped plot of grass surrounding a tinkling Spanish fountain. Within the stables are élite stalls for approximately thirty Arabian horses, and the éliteness may be judged from the fact that each stall has its own patented watering device, producing water at the touch of the horse's nose.

Among other features of the ranch, which is on U.S. Highway 99 about five miles west of the City of Pomona, are numerous avocado, olive, grapefruit, orange, lemon and pomegranate trees. Decorative touches include winding drives and walks, various ornamental pools, clever landscaping of descending rivulets, and great varieties of trees and shrubs. In Sycamore Canyon, which with Palm Canyon had the special attention of landscape architects, is one of the world's largest sycamore trees which majestically overlooks bamboo, ginger and eucalyptus groves.

It was on this site which W. K. Kellogg picked as an ideal place for his California home that he decided to carry out his dream of boyhood days to develop the purebred Arabian horse. As the memory of "Old Spot" came loping out of the past, he determined to memorialize this equine friend through the perpetuation and improvement of the Arab horse, which had endured the adventures of daring sheiks in the sands of Arabia's

The W. K. Kellogg Ranch

deserts and through the years had figured so largely in the romances and wars of the Near East.

During the period of building the Pomona ranch, Kellogg frequently discussed his plans with A. W. Harris, a Chicago banker friend who sometimes spent his winters in California. Harris was the owner of a fine strain of Arab horses which he rode and loved. One day, Kellogg proposed that he purchase several of the horses from Harris for foundation stock to establish a stud at the Pomona ranch. He mentioned Old Spot, saying

[230]

near Pomona, California.

he thought he would do something of this sort in memory of his old friend and at the same time provide and preserve for American stables this noblest of all horse blood.

Mr. Harris agreed that the idea was a good one and that the Pomona ranch was an ideal location for such an enterprise. The plenteous sunshine, the valuable mineral content in the forage grown in this area, and a climate resembling that of Arabia provided a perfect setting for the venture. However, Harris was not inclined to sell any of his horses and, instead, his

[231]

The Three Graces

Mr. Kellogg's pride in the beauty of his Arabian colt twins, Calamyr and Calamyra, was accentuated by their biological rarity since the odds against the birth and survival of Arabian twin colts had been estimated at 150,000 to 1. Here Mr. Kellogg helps the twins celebrate their first birthday.

suggestion for the purchase of the Chauncey D. Clarke Arabian stud near Indio was acted upon. As soon as Kellogg had built some spotless white stables, a training ring and, eventually, added a spectator grandstand large enough for several thousand spectators, the animals were moved to Pomona.

This proved only the first step, for W. K. Kellogg then undertook to improve the strain by adding to what became the third largest stable of Arabian horses in America. Although some of the horses were from Poland, Egypt and even faraway Arabia, most of them came from the Lady Wentworth stables in England where horse fanciers of the English nobility had built up studs through thirty years of negotiation with Bedouin breeders of these distinctive horses.

The photograph at left—taken at the W. K. Kellogg Arabian Horse Ranch and titled "The Three Graces"—catches the beauty and poetry-in-motion of the distinctive Arabians.

W. K. Kellogg

The Arab is a distinctive horse "anatomically different from the ordinary horse. He has one less vertebra; much larger nostrils and greater lungs and fine bone structure like ivory. He is as fearless as a lion is supposed to be (and isn't), and ordinarily is as docile as a house dog. The Arab has great speed for short distances and almost incredible endurance."

Accustomed to subsisting on scant water and forage, subjected to the burning heat of the desert, the Arabian is capable of carrying heavy loads for long distances. Powerful and swift, he is raised almost as a member of the family of desert tribes and is invariably gentle, affectionate and tractable.

However, the Arabian never has been easy to obtain. Desert owners are true lovers of their horses and seldom are willing to part with their stock. Stubborn Will Kellogg leaped this hurdle by sending letters and personal emissaries over the world, for he was determined to propagate on the California ranch the finest Arab strains that could be bred. Size, height and conformation were to be developed with painstaking skill, with an over all goal of preserving the endurance and stamina as well as the gentleness and docility of the breed. Thus the ranch was to play a real part in perpetuating the Arabian horse in America, helping to provide better mounts for cavalry, pleasure riding and polo.

While Mr. Kellogg received some help and advice from Mr. Harris and from W. R. Brown of Berlin, New Hampshire (probably the original Arabian breeders in this country), he actually knew very little about horses, particularly Arabians. Characteristically, he did not let this stop him but sought to purchase expert advice through the hiring of horse trainers. With one of these trainers, Kellogg had a series of misunderstandings which caused the blood pressure of the ranch owner to rise to a high level on more than one occasion.

The climax of the relationship between the two came when the trainer was sent to England for the purpose of purchasing additional Arabian horses. Carrying a general letter authorizing him to make these purchases and a check for $2,000 expense money, the trainer just before embarkation wrote Kellogg telling of plans to extend the trip to Arabia. Very incidentally he added that he had purchased an expensive movie outfit and a large silk flag as gifts for Arabian sheiks and to facilitate barter for the horses and had commissioned an artist to paint some Arabian horses. Too late to stop the purchases, W. K. Kellogg was able to veto the extension of the trip to Arabia.

Arriving in England, the trainer consummated a deal for fifteen Arabian horses at a total cost of approximately $80,000. W. K. expressed great dissatisfaction with the horses and their general condition when the steeds arrived in California. As an epilogue, it was found that the trainer had committed Mr. Kellogg for a $1,200 prize for the Richmond Horse Show in England and for a $1,500 gold cup as another horse show prize. For a year or two after Kellogg parted company with this promotionally-minded representative, the ranch owner had on his hands two custom-built German watches for which he had to pay approximately $3,500 plus 40 per cent duty. The watches were purchased by the trainer to "soften" the King of Arabia so that the purchase of Arabian horses in his country might come easier. After the smoke of the conflict had subsided and Kellogg's blood pressure returned more nearly to normal, the harassed ranch owner arranged through a physician of New York City to give the ornate watches to the King of Arabia because "The doctor thinks there is a good probability that Ibn Saud will present us, in exchange for our gift, one or more Arab horses." There is no record as to whether or not this strategy worked.

Even though the Arabian horse venture brought some headaches to W. K. Kellogg, there is reason to believe it also brought him much enjoyment. He grew to love the handsome horses and looked upon them as a real contribution to the lighter and sporting side of American life. He had great pride in his stable which encompassed approximately ninety Arabians at

The Stables and Horse-Ring
of the Arabian Horse Ranch

The Sunday afternoon Arabian
Horse Show has been a weekly
feature of the Kellogg Ranch for
thirty years. Usually 2,000 to
3,000 people are on hand for the
two afternoon showings.

its peak. Several of these horses were broken both to saddle and to harness, and along with the polo and jumper horses were a few outstanding five-gaited steeds.

Kellogg took a quiet but deep pride in the noble horses. For him, the frosting on the cake was the Sunday afternoon Arabian Horse Show, a weekly feature now in its thirtieth year at the ranch. The Sunday shows were held at 2:00 and 3:30 with the stands at the show ring usually holding from two thousand to three thousand people. A loudspeaker system enabled a narrator to supplement the showing of Arabian jumpers, gaited horses, draft and stock horses, trick riders, gaily costumed riders and the climax, a Ben Hur chariot race. So great was his zeal with respect to the Arabians, that Mr. Kellogg banished his shyness to appear on an April, 1939, NBC blue network broadcast which featured the ranch and particularly a set of Arabian colt twins reputed at that time to be the only set in the world.

About three times each week when he was in California, Kellogg would bring visitors to the stables and have the horses displayed to them. A chief hostler recalls, "You never knew how much he knew about horses because he never talked much, even when showing horses to the guests. He would let the manager or the horse hostler do the talking."

Many guests of contemporary or lasting fame made visits to the ranch and Will Kellogg took a pardonable pride in consorting with the famous. Colonel Lindbergh dropped in and had a horse named after him—"Hawaragil," which in Arabian means "airman." Madam Schumann-Heink was entertained at dinner. Tom Mix, Rudolph Valentino, Lois Wilson and Bonnie Gray were film luminaries pictured riding Arabian horses on a plaque in the corridor leading from the administrative offices to the stables. Other notable visitors included Clara Bow, Gary Cooper, Laura LaPlante, Olivia de Haviland, Will Rogers, Fred Stone, Douglas Fairbanks, Mary Pickford, Wallace Beery and Marlene Dietrich.

Kellogg apparently gained considerable satisfaction from his contacts with various luminaries of the motion picture field. In a letter of March 17, 1927, to Mrs. Hanna Kellogg he related, "Tell John that I had my photograph taken yesterday with a half dozen different movie people, including some of the owners. One picture was taken with Colleen Moore. I asked Colleen if they were going to name it 'Youth and Old Age.' I also had my picture taken with Hal Roach's 'Our Gang.' I think they are going to send me some prints and I will bring them with me."

Kellogg's idea of starting a New Year in the proper manner was to see several of his Arabians mounted by Bedouin-robed riders in the annual Tournament of Roses parade in Pasadena. He also received much satisfaction from the fact that his Arabs took part in several motion pictures, including Valentino's "Son of the Sheik," "The Garden of Allah," "Lives of a Bengal Lancer," "Beau Ideal," and "Madame Du Barry."

In the spring of 1926, a telegram was sent by the movie idol, Rudolph Valentino, to Mr. Kellogg at Battle Creek, reading in part:

"I am anxious to show your marvelous stallion, Jadaan, to the world through the medium of the Arabian motion picture which I am making. Sincerely believe this will help Arab horse cause in America. It will show the people for the first time the appearance, color, style, gentility and nobility of the true Arab which you have so wonderfully set out to save for posterity. I ask for Jadaan because I consider him the embodiment of the finest Arab, knowing your heart is in the preservation of the breed and because I also love these wonderful aristocrats."

This request for the use of Jadaan in "Son of the Sheik" was granted but subsequent correspondence between the two men reveals that Kellogg did not hesitate to scold his celebrity friend when he thought the occasion merited it. Apparently the borrowing of the horse exceeded the time limit set for the loan and therefore the horse owner wired Valentino on May 4, 1926:

"Am informed by my son, Dr. Karl Kellogg, that the arrange-

In the winters, California became Mr. Kellogg's adopted state and during twenty-five seasons there he gained considerable acquaintance with the movie colony. This 1927 photograph shows Mr. Kellogg with Hal Roach's "Our Gang" whose currently reissued films are again finding much vogue. In the group are Farina, at the far left, the little blonde is Mary Kornman, "Freckles" is behind Mary, and Joe is at the far right.

ment made with you for the return of Jadaan May 1 has not been carried out and that Jadaan is still absent from the ranch. In my business dealings I am not accustomed to treatment of this sort. I made a definite and positive engagement with you for certain things; have carried out my part and you have failed to carry out yours. Shall ask that you return Jadaan to the ranch at once. An immediate answer advising me of your compliance is expected."

W. K. Kellogg even rode some of the Arabians in the early years of the ranch. He was never a Teddy Roosevelt type of rider. However, he did get a great deal of enjoyment from horse rides to the far reaches of the property until an accident and

Distinguished Visitors at the Horse Ranch

(Valentino picture courtesy of Spide Rathbun, "Calarabian"

several narrow escapes caused him to abandon this exercise in favor of hikes around the ranch.

If the accident dimmed his enthusiasm for riding, it deepened his love for the Arabian horse. His favorite mount had been Antez, a chestnut stallion with blond mane and tail. One day while Kellogg was riding in the company of one of the caretakers of the ranch, he with Antez lagged behind the caretaker who was out of sight beyond a hill. As the ranch owner later recalled the incident:

"There had been a rain a few days previous which had softened the narrow path up the quite steep hill. The mud caused Antez to slip and as he endeavored to regain his feet, I fell from the saddle and found myself on the ground with Antez over me. I expected that any minute he would step on my body and, with my foot caught in the stirrup and my body in an upside-down position, I was helpless. However, the trembling horse stood fast in his steps and remained in this position for four or five minutes until the caretaker came back to investigate our delay and then rescued me from the perilous situation."

"Love that Horse" would never have been in Mr. Kellogg's phraseology but, nevertheless, it aptly described his affection for Antez and his amplified admiration for the intelligence of the Arabian breed. After the ranch was turned over to the University of California, Antez was sold to the Polish government. Learning of this belatedly, Kellogg used all the resources of his energy and finances in the effort to trace this horse which he always fondly remembered. Years later, he was glad to be able to repurchase the horse because "Antez saved my life once, and I feel he ought to be retired in his old age and given good care." Antez was thirty years old when it died on a ranch in California.

Even after the narrow escape with Antez, W. K. Kellogg continued to ride. Particularly was he anxious to continue this

At upper left are shown comedian Will Rogers, Governor James Rolph of California, and Mr. Kellogg at the ceremony during which the ranch was given to the University of California. At upper right is screen star Rudolph Valentino as "Son of the Sheik" with a Kellogg Arabian, "Jadaan." The photograph at center left shows Mr. Kellogg and Tom Mix admiring a young Arab horse. At center right, actor Victor McLaglen is shown on a Kellogg steed. Clara Bow poses beside an Arabian at lower left, and, at lower right, actress Laura La Plante is shown with Mr. Kellogg.

exercise when he had several visits from his son John L. who was a lover of horse riding. Red-letter days of Mr. Kellogg's years at the ranch were the visits of Lenn and the opportunities for father and son to reform their intimacy after the severing of their business relations. It was on a ride into the hills with his son that W. K. had another accident, suffering a broken rib when his horse stumbled. He rode very little after that.

A new friend was to be a constant companion in the daily walks which superseded the horse rides. Ever a lover of dogs, Kellogg was delighted with his acquisition in 1927 of Rinson, a son of the famous German shepherd dog of movie fame, Rin Tin Tin. The dog was acquired from Lee Duncan, well-known trainer of dogs for motion pictures, and was the first of three German shepherd dogs which made happier the latter years of Will Kellogg's life.

W. K. and Rinson had several favorite walks at the ranch and daily could be seen on these trails. Although Kellogg used to say that "I get plenty of exercise going up the hill from the stables to the house, a five hundred foot, almost vertical ascent," often the master and his dog would stroll through Sycamore Canyon, with the former admiring the many varieties of huge cacti; a wash, beautified by rocks and other landscaping; the previously mentioned enormous sycamore tree; and the attractive ginger and bamboo groves. The whole canyon had a natural look despite the fact that the works of nature had been supplemented by some planting.

In May of 1932, the $3,000,000 ranch, with eighty-seven head of purebred Arabian horses, was given to the University of California which was to operate it for almost a decade as the W. K. Kellogg Institute of Animal Husbandry. Mr. Kellogg also presented the university with a trust fund of $600,000 to cover the expenses of ranch maintenance, reserving only the "Big House" and approximately fifty surrounding acres for his personal use. He resided there until the summer of 1942.

An event long remembered by Pomona Valley was the ceremony at which the ranch was turned over to the university. More than twenty-five thousand people overflowed the horse ring to watch the public ceremony described by W. K. Kellogg to a friend as "one of the most embarrassing days of my entire life." It was the embarrassment of a man of essential shyness at being singled out for the thanks of prominent California officials and the repartee of comedian-actor Will Rogers who acted as master of ceremonies for the occasion.

To the music of the 116th Infantry National Guard and the University of California bands, Will Rogers arrived in an ancient Concord coach driven by Captain William Banning, pioneer stage driver. Also inside the coach, a relic of Overland Trail days, were Mr. and Mrs. Kellogg, Governor James Rolph and four other California notables. After the Governor's salute of seventeen guns, there was a twenty-five minute Arabian horse show, following which Will Rogers presided over the main ceremony. Following the chief speaker of the day who said, "These Arabian horses represent one-fourth of all the Arabians in the world outside of Arabia," Will Rogers took over and, after paying his respects to the gift of the ranch, he turned his guns of repartee upon the Kelloggs:

"Mr. and Mrs. Kellogg, with all my jokes and foolishness (somebody has to act the fool) I want you to know that we all appreciate very much your generosity. . . . I have Mrs. Kellogg's coat over here that she handed me. Now the Kelloggs are very plain people. I looked at that coat. . . . These are people who have just given away $3,000,000 and Mrs. Kellogg's coat is rabbit; that is just what it is. They are plain people. Mrs. Rogers (the comedian here pantomimed a telephone call to his wife), I hope you will take notice and don't drag in anything about minks. By golly, it is wonderful, I tell you that . . ."

If the ceremony was an enjoyable, albeit embarrassing, occasion for Mr. Kellogg, there occurred during the university's administration of the ranch some happenings which aroused the ire of the donor. A long-time ranch manager was replaced

[243]

by the university, much to Kellogg's displeasure. Then, as he meticulously detailed in correspondence to the university president, he felt that the university was not living up to the terms of the agreement. Eventually, Kellogg was able to get ex-President Hoover to act as an intercessor but to no immediate avail. Later, through mutual agreement between the University of California, Mr. Kellogg and the W. K. Kellogg Foundation, the property was deeded to the federal government for use by the United States Army which established there the Pomona Quartermaster Depot Remount.

In 1948 the Army turned the ranch over to the Department of Agriculture which renamed it the Pomona Remount Station. Later that year the Department announced that the ranch would be closed the following January 1 for lack of funds and that all the horses would be sold!

W. K. Kellogg sprang into action to avert a dissolution which would have meant an anticlimactical end to his efforts to perpetuate the Arabian horse. A flood of petitions went to the federal government from Arabian horse breeders, even from Senators Knowland and Downey of California and from Representative Richard Nixon (who later became Vice President of the nation). The sale of the ranch was called off by Secretary of Agriculture Charles F. Brannan after Dr. Emory W. Morris of the Kellogg Foundation and Mr. W. H. Vanderploeg of the Kellogg Company conferred with him.

Later an Act of Congress transferred the ownership of the ranch to the Kellogg Foundation and, subsequently, late in 1949, the ranch was deeded by the Foundation to the State of California for use in the expansion of the educational program of the California State Polytechnic College.

Another area of California which greatly appealed to Mr. Kellogg was the famous resort city, Palm Springs. He liked the even climate and the wild beauty of the desert which encircles that oasis and, in May of 1929, he purchased a home in the outskirts of the city. Fifteen years later, when his eyesight was

The Kellogg home in Florida, at Dunedin Isles,
north of Clearwater on the West Coast of the state.

(Photo by Burgert Bros., Tampa.)

practically gone, he bought another Palm Springs dwelling.
This latter house, originally built for a blind woman, enabled
him to get about nicely since the construction made for ready
access from the living room to the other rooms and the patio.

Only twice did W. K. waver from his loyalty to California as
"the proper place for a winter home." In 1934, the palm-lined
shores of Florida beckoned to him and he purchased the Frisch-
korn Italian villa at Dunedin Isles, just north of Clearwater on
the west coast of the state. (For a short time, during the previous winter, Kellogg leased property in the south bay section
of St. Petersburg.) The first winter at Dunedin had ideal
weather but upon later sojourns in the state the brand of winter
weather failed to appeal to Kellogg, and he decided that he
preferred to spend his winters in the West. A subsequent
week's trial of a rambling home near Phoenix, Arizona, did not
satisfy this man of many homes. Thereafter, his California

[245]

homes were in Palm Springs and the Talmadge Apartments in Los Angeles (owned by screen star Norma Talmadge) although he spent portions of the winters of his late years at the Huntington Hotel in Pasadena.

Early in World War II, the use of three of Mr. Kellogg's homes was donated to the war effort. The Army Remount Corps used the Arabian Horse Ranch, as previously related; the Gull Lake estate was used by the United States Coast Guard as a reception center; and the Dunedin home became the Dunedin Marine Base utilized for quartering Marine personnel who tested Roebling amphibian tanks there and taught student Marines how to operate such tanks.

By the time of World War II, these large homes—even though two of them were less than twenty years of age—had actually become relics of a vanishing age. Like the upper-class estates in England, they were survivors of a time when income taxes were not confiscatory, of an age which apparently had produced thousands of individuals who thought the mode of life they knew would remain unchanged for centuries. With mounting taxes and excessive costs of personnel necessary to maintain such estates, these homes became too large to live in but were firmly built so that they should withstand destruction for many years.

Too, in the case of Mr. Kellogg and his huge homes, he began to feel that he and his wife were "rattling around in the houses." With the advent of the war, he disposed of his Gar Wood boat and several of his automobiles. More and more he was of the opinion that, in a time when the exigencies of war were causing economic retrenchments in nonwar purposes everywhere, it was "sinful" for his household to be living in luxury. The mantle of prosperity had never rested too comfortably on his shoulders. Although he grew to like luxuries, his puritanic conscience occasionally assailed him about the spending of money, particularly upon himself. It was all right to spend money on others.

This uneasiness over too many luxuries, particularly in wartime, was undoubtedly a prime reason for the disposal of both the horse ranch and the Gull Lake estate. The latter, after use by the Coast Guard as above related, was eventually given by the Kellogg Foundation to Michigan State University and is now a valued branch of that institution, being used as a biological experiment station and as quarters for an off-campus agricultural education program.

The last dwelling of W. K. Kellogg, only a short distance from the Gull Lake estate, was a house and grounds owned by

"The Inn," a seven-story apartment house built by W. K. Kellogg in 1924. He maintained Apartment 601 as his residence partly as a convenience but also to bolster his assertion that he was a bona fide resident of his beloved home-town of Battle Creek.

the W. K. Kellogg Foundation and leased to Mr. Kellogg. It is a large house on quite a large lawn but is small when compared to Eagle Heights. While at this property, in which he lived until his death, Mr. Kellogg kept the same number of house servants, four to five, but was able to get by with only one person to take care of the lawn.

The last residence of W. K. Kellogg, on the shore of Gull Lake, which is located fifteen miles from Battle Creek, Michigan.

CHAPTER | **11**

"A Man Whose Star Had Not Set"

It will be recalled that Mr. Kellogg went into his second marriage with some misgivings. These were not because of the wife he had chosen, for he respected this former schoolteacher who had become a skilled physician in her own right. Rather he realized his own impliability as the co-dweller of a home and feared "lest I make another wife unhappy."

Perhaps that is why he, in the first few years of the marriage, strove to be very attentive to Mrs. Kellogg. A friend recalls W. K. tiptoeing over to the chair in which sat his wife reading a book, there to turn higher a lamp so that she would have more light. Another friend recalls that "Mrs. Kellogg would look forward to the nice gifts which he would bring to her."

Mrs. Kellogg was an intellectual, a person whose dominant interests were largely professional in nature, and she took little interest in housekeeping and homemaking. That she loved her husband is evident in the many sympathetic letters she wrote to him. It is doubtful, however, that she understood the complex nature of W. K. Kellogg and it is obvious that she was not the ultrafeminine type with an innate capacity to cajole and "manage" a husband. As for running the home, she was a novice attempting to do a new job under the eye of a perfectionist who had always run his homes and who could be intolerant of too-evident shortcomings.

A friend, who knew both W. K. and Carrie Staines Kellogg as well as did almost any other person, respectfully discussed their home life:

"It was more than a marriage of convenience, although W. K. was fifty-eight years old and Carrie Staines presumably several years younger at the time of the wedding. I think he really loved her and I know she loved him. He actually did not mean anything by his long periods of silence. He, at one time, said to me: 'I have to have those times when I can be alone, when I must have a room to myself where I can spend some time thinking undisturbed.' When nighttime came, he quite often wanted to be alone. I don't believe those moments of solitude were unhappy but were constructive hours when he was able to organize his thinking toward better ways of doing things he had set out to do."

Burdened by failing eyesight and, after 1941, by total blindness, it is quite possible that Mr. Kellogg did not realize that his wife also was an ill person, continually harassed by high blood pressure. In any event, the latter years of the marriage did not see the relatively much closer union of the earlier days, although a close friend did not construe this "as the product of any lack of mutual respect or lack of love. Likely as they grew older, he got to be too much of a burden to her and she to him and this meant not a severing of respect and love but simply a mutual agreement to live their own lives without impinging too much on the activities of each other."

W. K. Kellogg always had a great concern for his health and, if one will except the recurring gall bladder attacks from middle life on and, of course, the blindness which gradually came upon him, his health was about the average up to age seventy.

He was almost a hypochondriac, insisting upon having his meals at a regular time of day and going to bed regularly to get his allotted hours of sleep. For the latter reason, he would sometimes leave evening functions when the hour grew late and occasionally refused to go to meetings or entertainments because he knew they would take him past his bedtime. His medicine cabinet was usually filled with various nostrums and, at the first hint of a cold, W. K. applied all the known remedies. He was a great believer in the efficacy of sunlight and a sun-bath was a "must" for many of the days. Rubdowns and massages were part of his daily regimen. For exercise, he had his daily walks and, at Palm Springs, Gull Lake, and at his office in the Foundation, stationary bicycles which he would "ride" two miles a day.

During his late sixties and seventies, Mr. Kellogg had a number of bouts with illness including some operations of serious nature, but his will to live and to be active triumphed over these adversities. For the last two decades of his life, he became quite susceptible to colds, respiratory complaints, and recurring foot ailments. In addition, of course, there was the trouble with his eyes to be discussed in another sequence of this biography.

As with any clan where there are several children and many grandchildren, the Kellogg family had its days of rosy hue and again those which only could be painted as a monochrome gray. Mr. Kellogg was particularly comforted by his recon-ciliation with John L. and his pride was great over the award of a Carnegie medal to Lenn after he had rescued one of his Chicago workmen from an accidental shower of searing acid.

Ever since childhood, W. K. Kellogg had deeply loved his sister, Clara Butler. After her children had grown, she had lived largely with brother John Harvey Kellogg whom she served as a secretary. However, she made occasional visits to brother Will and there was great affection between them. The sentiment that lay below W. K.'s passive exterior is graphically illustrated by a letter of thanks which Clara wrote, thanking him for sending to her a lock of their mother's hair, "which we both had combed so many times."

Occasionally there could be a short period of truce, and even fleeting tenderness, in the perennial wars between John Harvey Kellogg and his younger brother. W. K. once wrote John L., Jr.:

"I had heard of Dr. J. H.'s fall and accident. I presume that Doctor is better by this time. I am glad you are accepting his invitations. He has no grandchildren of his own, and I am sure he would appreciate a young fellow like you coming in to see him. Perhaps you can cheer him up a little."

Usually, however, the brothers continued on guard with each other and this was evident in the tug-of-war which they intermittently had over Clara. At one time Mr. Kellogg succeeded in getting Clara away from the household of the Doctor for a long visit. She enjoyed the visit there but also missed her old association with John Harvey. One day she wrote the Doctor to this effect and immediately he came to the Gull Lake estate to get his sister, telling W. K., "She wants to come back." Mr. Kellogg countered: "She doesn't need to come home. She is well cared for here." However the Doctor prevailed and Clara went home with him.

Although W. K. Kellogg never expected more from others than from himself, he undoubtedly was a taskmaster to himself, to his children and to his employees. He wanted to be a real family man in spite of his severity. He sympathized with the troubles of his children and grandchildren and exulted over their successes. Like many other fathers and doting grandfathers, he loved to recount the achievements of his descendants as, for instance, when he wrote to his daughter Beth: "I have never seen a child quite as bright as Elizabeth Ann at her age."

Long after his children had left to form their own homes, Mr. Kellogg held real concern for their futures and fortunes, but this only bolstered his determination to have a hand in their destinies. From afar he sought to influence his beloved daughter Beth, proffering advice on many details which were essentially her personal family matters. He was not quite so overt with his injunctions as far as his sons were concerned, but the "silver cord" was always there. He apparently had a master plan whereby he thought things would work out not only for himself but also for other people.

A long-time employee on the personal staff of W. K. Kellogg thinks he likely would have been a happier man had he not possessed this propensity to manage the lives of others—not only the lives of his children and grandchildren but also of more distant relatives and a few of his close friends. His determination to engineer the lives of others almost invariably led to complications and to many disappointments for him.

Mr. Kellogg was more than generous with his children and grandchildren, but as a granddaughter recalls:

"Anybody to whom he gave money had to account for that money to the penny. Even after we were married, I had to send an accounting monthly to him as to how much we spent for this or that, and ask him where to go to school, what to take and why."

A story tending to corroborate the above statement concerns a relative of Mr. Kellogg who had married. The happy couple was given $5,000 as a wedding gift from W. K. but there was no stipulation made as to the use of the money. Unfortunately, the young people did not invest the sum in a home or in what Kellogg thought was a productive manner but, instead, spent it a little here, a little there. A year or so later the couple came to visit Kellogg and a servant ushered them to a hallway anteroom of the Pomona Big House.

This hallway had a terrazzo floor and its only furniture was a hard bench with a stiff, upright back. The couple was seated there to wait for Mr. Kellogg. Intentionally, he let them sit for an hour before he even called them into his presence. This was because he knew they had come to ask for more money

The Children of Beth

This picture, taken in 1923, shows Mr. Kellogg with his daughter Beth (Mrs. Norman Williamson), and her children—John, Norman, Jr., Elizabeth Ann, Kenneth and Eleanor Jane.

and the sequel to the story is that they did not get the money. The decision was not whimsical. If they had used the original money in a manner approved by Mr. Kellogg, he would have been glad to have given them another sum to complete any worth-while venture. However, they had spent the money "foolishly" and he, therefore, was washing his hands of them. Apparently, Kellogg had read and remembered the New Testament parable of those talents which were buried and those which were used productively.

A disciple of thrift through most of his life, Kellogg taught the value of money to his grandchildren when they were but little folk. He would save all his pennies in a small pitcher and periodically would divide the money by a "Hold out your

Children of Karl and of John L.

Mr. Kellogg, in this photography of 1923 vintage, is shown with his two sons and their children. In the back row are Will Keith II (son of John L.), Karl Kellogg and John L. Kellogg. In the front row are Will Lewis and Karl Landram (both sons of Karl) and John, Jr. (son of John L.).

(Photo by Bachrach.)

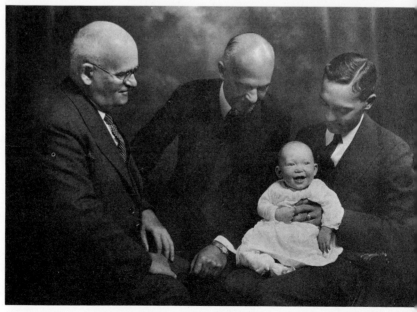

Four Generations of Kelloggs   *(Photo by Bachrach.)*

Will Keith Kellogg is shown here with his son, John L., his grandson, Will Keith II, and his great-grandson, Will Keith III.

hands" and then "Eeny, meeny, miney, moe." The children learned the money was not to be spent but was to be put in a bank. This was under an agreement that he would double whatever amount they were able to save.

When Beth's sons, Norman, Jr., and John Williamson, were living on the California ranch, the grandfather wanted them to feel that they were earning the money they received. Therefore, he left instructions for them to be paid ten cents for each gopher's tail and twenty-five cents apiece for each ground squirrel's tail. Besides this work in ridding the ranch of rodents, the lads were given tasks around the stables and W. K. paid them from his personal money. He wanted them, as well as his other grandchildren, to have a college education but he believed it was bad training for them to get something for nothing and that young people should grow up realizing the value of money and that it must be earned by the sweat of their brows.

Mr. Kellogg once wrote his son John L.:

"I do not think your boys should dress better than the majority of the boys at the school they are attending, and their allowance for dress should be moderate. If they could work part of their way through school, it would be of very material help in developing character. Dollars have never been known to produce character, and character will never be produced by money."

On June 6, 1928, Kellogg wrote in a letter to his grandson, W. K. Kellogg II:

"Now that you have arrived at the age of twenty-one years, I am sending you a final check. Very shortly you will be able to make your own way in the world without financial assistance from others. If I did not think you would be able to do this, I should scarcely want to own you as a grandson. A Kellogg should always be successful."

The grandchildren recall their grandfather as nearly always having two currents of thought in his mind: the thought under discussion and something far-off. It was difficult to carry on a conversation with him when he was in such a mood. They believed this characteristic to be the result of a hyperactive mind but also ascribed some of it to the fact that Mr. Kellogg had found that a successful technique with people was to play "hard to get."

However, Will Kellogg did have his lighter moments. A friend recalls an informal family lunch at the Gull Lake estate, "probably the only time that I saw him as a family man, a grandfather and even a great grand-father. I normally had seen him as a rather quiet, somewhat aloof man of business who felt things but didn't express them. But on this rare occasion, in his family environment I found him to be humorous, almost jovial, twitting Norman, Jr. about some escapades of the Betas, remarking for Leonora's benefit (she was living with

The First of Three Beloved Dog Companions.

W. K. Kellogg had great affection for the three German shepherd dogs which successively were his companions from 1927 on. The first dog, Rinson, was a son of Rin-Tin-Tin of movie fame, and the others were also descendants of the renowned canine. Lee Duncan of Hollywood, who has trained many dogs for film roles, is here shown with Mr. Kellogg and Rinson.

Dr. John at the time) that this was one Kellogg home where they served chicken. He had a wonderful time later that day kidding me about 'helping to lose the sailboat race.' "

Daughter Beth recalls that her self-conscious father would kiss the children goodbye only if there were a door to screen this moment of affection from other eyes. She also remembers the day that Mr. Kellogg, after carefully locking the door of the social hall at the Kellogg Company, mounted to the stage and there recited "Barbara Frietchie" with his daughter as the only audience.

Yet another recollection of Mrs. Williamson is revealing of the essentially clean character of the man:

"Father always read nearly every book that was published and occasionally would read aloud to the family portions of his favorites. One evening he told the assembled group that a friend had recently given him 'a book by Chic Sale which evidently concerns a man who made many dollars in the building business.' Norman, Jr. and other of the grandchildren, who previously had read the humorous story which largely concerns a mode of outdoor plumbing, stifled a snort at this statement. Father opened the book, read a couple of lines, and realizing their nature, stopped abruptly. He folded the book and put it away without comment. He never would have truck with reading material which was risqué or obscene or even 'shady.' "

2.

Home life for W. K. Kellogg was simple whether he happened to be in Michigan or California. After 1937 and his retirement from full participation in the company business, the routine of his days varied but little. He could have been a hearty eater because he loved good food and was a connoisseur of taste. ("W. K. was a better cook than his wife and always was the chef on his few fishing and camping trips.") Because of his weight, however, he tried to control his appetite and was able to forgo most gustatory temptation with the exception of his beloved chocolate sodas and chocolate bars.

In the later years, he ate only two meals a day, breakfast at ten and dinner at six. The breakfast usually was the typical American one of fruit juice, eggs and cereal (Kellogg's, of course). However, the dinners often reflected the influence of his earlier Seventh-day Adventist days. W. K. would drink buttermilk at meals rather than his taboos of coffee or tea. He spurned sugar for honey as a sweetener. For many years he was a vegetarian but later told a friend that "Mrs. Kellogg and I have decided we should have a higher protein diet so we are now eating meat." Another friend recalls the day he was at the Pomona ranch for lunch and that Mr. and Mrs. Kellogg, then on a reducing diet, carefully scraped away the potato in the baked potatoes and then ate the skins.

During the day, Kellogg invariably had a massage and rub-down and often a sunbath. Even then, his scratch pad was at hand to make notes concerning the Foundation, Company or other activities in which he was interested. There likely would be a car ride in the afternoon or evening, but perhaps the high spot of the day for him was his walk over the estate, at the ranch or in Palm Springs. Nearly always he was accompanied on these walks by his German shepherd dog. Kellogg agreed with Senator George Graham Vest that "The one absolutely unselfish friend that man can have in this selfish world . . . is his dog," and from 1927 on—as Rinson II succeeded Rinson I and then was succeeded by Rinette—these dogs meant as much as almost anything else in life to him. (Not trained as "Seeing Eye" dogs, because Kellogg did not have the stamina or the patience to undergo the training also required of the dogs' master, the latter two of the dogs did serve as partial guides and bodyguards to Kellogg as his sight progressively failed.)

His evenings at Gull Lake or at the horse ranch were spent much in the same fashion. He would sit on the porch if the

weather permitted, listen to some favorite radio programs, or
would have his nurse read to him. When it was not warm
enough to stay outside he would go into the living room to lie
on a davenport and the nurse would read to him until he
started "puffing," a prelude to sleep. As he lay stretched out on
the davenport, he would quite often reach over and pet his
dog who would be close by. (Rinette, the most affectionate
of the three dogs, was his last canine friend and on not a few
stormy nights her master repaid her devotion with comforting
pats and crooning words as she whimpered in fear of the fury
of the storm.)

Sometimes, but not often, there would be guests, and if
these happened to be old friends, the evening would be spent
in reminiscence. At Gull Lake the talk might center around
the business with some reference to Battle Creek personalities
and affairs. Mr. Kellogg always had a good idea of what was
going on in town through persons who kept him informed but
he did not personally mix in civic affairs. Introversive Mrs.
Kellogg, away from her talk of medicine, had but little to
contribute to such gatherings and Kellogg complained: "I
have to do all the entertaining." Perhaps she could have functioned better as hostess and "first lady" if she had not been so
in awe of her husband.

A distant relative once analyzed W. K. Kellogg's attitude
toward home life:

"I think that after he made his money Mr. Kellogg would
have liked to live differently than he did. The modern kids have
a slang phrase for it—'Live it up!' I believe he would have enjoyed more of the amenities and luxuries of life than the habits
and personalities of the womenfolk of his family made practical. If conditions had been different, if in some way he could
have broken through his wall of reserve, he would have liked
to have been more of a socialite, the life of the party, an entertaining host in the manner of the literary salon."

Kellogg once dryly commented that after living near Pomona for more than fifteen years "I have only three friends in the whole valley." This was due only in part to the awe in which people instinctively held him. There was the barrier which must be flung up by the wealthy in self-protection lest they be overwhelmed by myriad requests for gifts, loans and the extension of influence toward consummation of some pet project. Mr. Kellogg's secretary, his nurses, Foundation and Company officials, the corps of servants, protected his privacy from invasion by a strict cordon which screened all telephone calls and the missions of would-be visitors and solicitors.

However, if W. K. Kellogg felt "poor" with regard to a scarcity of new friends, he, contrawise, was rich with regard to old friends. His long held travel habit of searching out former sanitarium and business acquaintances, both in the United States and abroad, tended to maintain old ties. In a letter written from California to a friend in Battle Creek, Mr. Kellogg recounted that "I saw eighteen old-timers today, many of them Battle Creek Sanitarium people, on my way up from Palm Springs. Some of the people are very old, a few of them were bedfast and I will probably never get to see them again. I hope I was able to cheer up the old-timers a little."

A great comfort to Mr. Kellogg from 1916 until his death in 1951 was his secretary, Mrs. Bessie Young. Quiet, efficient and personable, this small brunette (who until recently was an official of the W. K. Kellogg Foundation) was a "right arm" to her employer not only in company affairs but in the expedition of the many and varied interests held by Mr. Kellogg. Of her, a member of the Kellogg family recently said:

"I think Mrs. Young was responsible for tempering Grandfather's decisive actions in connection with the family. She understood him better than anyone and we were indeed fortunate to have had her as an intercessor. She is a wonderful woman who deserves a place in any biography of W. K. Kellogg. She was kind and most considerate of us all, while always giving loyal and unstinting service to her employer."

For thirty-five years Mrs. Bessie Rogers Young was Mr. W. K. Kellogg's chief secretary. She also was an official of the Foundation for many years. When she retired in late 1955, a feature of a dinner in her honor was a gift of silver candlesticks to her by employees of the Foundation. At left, Dr. Emory W. Morris, President of the Foundation, is shown presenting the candlesticks to Mrs. Young.

Mrs. Young was also extremely helpful to the officials of the Foundation and company in interpreting and helping to implement Mr. Kellogg's desires with respect to policies and operations.

Through the years, Kellogg had other loyal servitors in his nurses who, in addition to aiding him when he was ill or blind, were also friends and confidantes. Besides several who were on Kellogg's personal staff for comparatively short periods, there were Miss Helen Abbott (now Mrs. Harold Braford) who served from 1933 to 1939 and Miss Elsie Hoatson (later Mrs. John Elbon) who was a household member from 1939 through 1951. These well-educated and empathic women, in addition to their capacities as nurses, were also secretaries, companion readers, and part-time chauffeurs to Mr. Kellogg. As Kellogg became of great age, he looked more and more to his nurse for comfort, consolation and inspiration. He talked to her of memories of his boyhood, of the joys and tragedies of his more active adult years. Perhaps the stern W. K. Kellogg was more human and less on guard with his nurse than with any other person.

This, then, was the home life of Will Kellogg. He had come a long way from the thin, brown-haired boy who lamented his fate as he weeded seemingly unending rows of his father's garden in early day Battle Creek. Never whimpering—for he always had courage—he as an adult was lonely for he knew not what. Even more than most people, he had a sense of inadequacy. Most of the time he never liked the person that he thought he was. Yet, as age began to quiet the longings of his youth, he nourished a belief that the star had not set on his horizon. Perhaps that is why great accomplishments were still possible for him.

The business district of present-day Battle Creek, W. K. Kellogg's beloved home-city. In the center background may be seen the tower and rectangle of the former location of the Battle Creek Sanitarium. Currently this large structure is the headquarters of the Federal Civil Defense Administration.

CHAPTER 12

"First Comes the Dream"

A NURSE OF Mr. Kellogg recalls that each night her employer, upon retiring, would recite the "Lord's Prayer." As a sequel, he would close his day with a simple quiet petition that he continue humble and that his family, particularly his afflicted grandson, Kenneth, might have blessing and security. "Except for this prayer," she remembered, "and an occasional Biblical quotation, he rarely made reference to religion. However, it was obvious that Mr. Kellogg had no truck with atheists and tended to regard them as fools."

He had his own brand of personal religion, although during most of the years of his life he went to church only to attend funerals or weddings. Occasionally to the closest of his old friends and to Dr. H. M. S. Richards of California's "Voice of Prophecy," he would talk of God and the hereafter. Sometimes he would recount to them a conference he once had with his friend Dr. Robert A. Millikan, the famous physicist. When Kellogg asked this scholar, "In your study of science, do you not feel there is a pattern or a guiding force?" Millikan replied, "There is no other answer."

Dr. Richards annually would come to Michigan for a state-wide Adventist camp meeting and would make it a point to bring his "King's Heralds" quartet to visit Mr. Kellogg at the Gull Lake estate. He recalls that this lover of music never grew tired of the hymns sung by the quartet and that "Little by little, I discovered that W. K. Kellogg was a deeply spiritual man. He believed in prayer, in God, and in Christ. He had a very complete knowledge of the Bible and of those intricate prophecies uncomprehended by many persons. Both of us had seen the Holy Land and we discussed its sacred objects."

After Kellogg became totally blind, he purchased "Talking Book" records which encompassed the whole Bible. Nevertheless, he did not pretend to extreme piety. Predisposed by a sensitive nature to religion, he was estranged by the organized aspects and, like occasional preachers' sons, was in revolt against an overdose of piety during the earlier years. Yet he believed in a higher intelligence and doubtless his God had the same attributes that he had: neatness, efficiency, justice and intermittent compassion.

Apparently, Mr. Kellogg did not attend the Adventist Church (or the temples of any other denomination) after the early years of his marriage. In a letter dated July 14, 1907, to Harry G. Dodd of St. Louis, he acknowledged "a clipping from the *St. Louis Times* announcing my expulsion from the Adventist Church. . . . The fact that I have not attended church for the past twenty-seven years would certainly indicate that the people did the proper thing to let me out."

An Adventist effort to move the sanitarium from Battle Creek to the District of Columbia after the fire of 1902 may have further widened the hiatus between W. K. and the church. Yet while he was divorced from the SDA Church, in his ethics, his altruism, and his business precepts he always, consciously or unconsciously, used the church for what engineers would call a base of reference. This church was to him a fixed mark from which one might measure the validity of principles and actions. The Adventists themselves were always "our people," and in Kellogg's home the maids were asked to observe the Adventist Sabbath by doing most of their work before Friday sunset and only the absolutely necessary tasks on Saturday.

As intimated previously, the Battle Creek Sanitarium ran into financial trouble after the construction of a fifteen-story, several-million dollar addition in 1928. As the national Depression deepened in the '30s, so did Dr. John Harvey Kellogg's dilemma as to how to keep the institution solvent. In 1938, it became necessary to reorganize the sanitarium under Section 77B of the National Bankruptcy Act and on May 15, 1942, the main building and other real estate and a large amount of furniture were sold for approximately $2,250,000 to the United States Government which desired the building for the establishment of a military hospital.

This sale placed the sanitarium on a more solvent basis, erased many of its debts, and permitted its continued operation on a less grandiose scale in a stone building at 185 North Washington Street. However, the remaining $725,000 of liquid assets caused a fierce and long battle within the Constituency, the governing body of the institution.

Dr. Kellogg had conceived the idea that he could combine the sanitarium with his Race Betterment Foundation, thus swallowing up the "old San." Almost gleefully went younger brother W. K. into the ensuing war, fighting both his brother and the non-Adventists in the Constituency. W. K. believed that since the Adventists had started the sanitarium, their faction should have considerable to say regarding the proceeds of the partial liquidation. Thereupon, he fought a mighty campaign through letters and personal contacts. He even offered to match up to $5,000 of the money of the General Conference of the SDA to bring to Battle Creek for the crucial vote many of the scattered eighty-one living members of the Constituency.

As a result, he helped to secure over $500,000 for the Adventists and further kindled the animosity of his brother, the loser in the internecine war.

2.

The Great Depression which seriously affected the sanitarium proved no great hurdle for the Kellogg Company. People ate low-cost cereals rather than the more expensive ham 'n eggs for breakfast and company sales stayed relatively high. Neither was Will Kellogg's aggressive business policy seriously hampered, but there is evidence that he proved not entirely immune to the virus of fear which affected most of the world's population. This was discernible only in a little private hedging, such as his consideration of a farm and vegetable garden site near Goguac Lake, two miles south of Battle Creek, "to insure that my family will have something to eat."

In one conversation with a friend, W. K. exhibited a one hundred thousand German mark note, commenting that it had been worth $25,000 before World War I and that one billion marks could be purchased for twenty-four cents after the German inflation. Clearly, Kellogg had a remote fear that his money might also fly away but, again, he proved a poor prophet, for he maneuvered his stock holdings so sagaciously that they actually appreciated during the long market depreciation.

Kellogg was able to see a silver lining in the cloud of adversity. As he wrote his friend Arch Shaw (through the years the correspondence between the two filled many Shaw-Walker files):

"I told George that I thought the whole nation had been getting soft and that in my opinion it took some knocks and hardships to develop the character of young people and to keep firm the character of us old birds."

Fear of the future never lingered long in the mind of Kellogg. As evidence there is the fact that he made large philanthropic grants in and around Battle Creek when the Great Depression was imminent or even when the nation's economy was in a deep trough. The fleeting phobia concerning the security of himself and his family was displaced by the resurgence of a long-held, almost mystic belief that he properly could be only a steward of his mounting fortune. From out of the past, the Puritan precepts against self-indulgence, the admonitions of his parents who did not believe in laying up worldly treasures, bound him to an altruistic course of action which was to affect the lives of many individuals and communities in two hemispheres.

As Kellogg prospered and was able to increase the number of his contributions to worthy causes, he decided that he should provide some systematic and businesslike method of administering these benefactions. Therefore, in 1925, he established the Fellowship Corporation, which served for the next five years as the agency through which almost $1,000,000 in donations were directed.

His major contributions through this period included a grant for the building of an agricultural school near Gull Lake, the W. K. Kellogg Bird Sanctuary, the Kellogg Experimental Farms, and a reforestation project, all located fifteen miles from Battle Creek. Mr. Kellogg celebrated his sixty-fifth birthday by making gifts to the Battle Creek community which made it a leader among cities of its size. These gifts included a civic auditorium and junior high school, a Youth Building (with many types of recreation including a large swimming pool), assistance to an Altrusa Day Nursery, a city market for farmers of the vicinity, land for a Boy Scout camp and a grant for more than half the cost of the Ann J. Kellogg School. (His Foundation later paid the balance of the cost of the construction which was completed on the one hundredth anniversary of the founding of Battle Creek.)

A principal activity of the large school, named in honor of W. K.'s mother, was and is a program of special training for handicapped children by their integration with normal children as a part of the public school system. It was hailed by educators as "a contribution which is thoroughly democratic since it strives to create an equal opportunity for all children

Through the Fellowship Corporation which preceded his Foundation, Mr. Kellogg made numerous gifts to the Battle Creek area including the pictured Kellogg Agricultural School near Gull Lake (left) . . .

the Ann J. Kellogg School in Battle Creek . . .

the Youth Building . . .

. . . and the Kellogg Auditorium in Battle Creek.

*(Photo of Youth Building by Krum's.
Photo of Auditorium by W. R. French.)*

A painting of the W. K. Kellogg Bird Sanctuary near Augusta, Michigan by Charles C. Schafer. More than a million persons have visited this sanctuary to view the many varieties of waterfowl and other birds. In the autumn more than 5,000 wild Canada Geese and several thousand wild ducks may be seen on the lake. A museum is an added feature of the sanctuary.

(From an original given the Foundation by the Franklin DeKleine Company, Lansing, Michigan.)

who may come under a single school roof—whether they be physically handicapped, unusually gifted, or average."

In this period numerous contributions by Mr. Kellogg were made through the Fellowship Corporation for student scholarships and research in various fields, and the Kellogg Radiation Laboratory at the California Institute of Technology was established through a grant.

As far back as the year 1900, a lecture at the sanitarium on birds had intrigued W. K. Kellogg and in subsequent years he picked up considerable bird lore and information about bird sanctuaries in the United States and Canada. He had become particularly interested in a refuge for birds, set up by Jack Miner in Canada and, after acquiring a thousand acres near his Gull Lake estate, he conferred with Mr. Miner as to what could be done to attract wildlife to the region. In 1928 the Michigan Legislature agreed to declare Gull Lake and the surrounding territory a bird refuge and on a tract of about 180 acres, including Wintergreen Lake, Kellogg established a sanctuary for waterfowl, a center for wildlife research, and a site for the public to view native waterfowl and other birds.

During the first two decades of the life of this sanctuary, more than a million visitors came to view the many varieties of birds which had a much greater chance of survival on long trips North and South because of this and other sanctuaries. In the autumn more than five thousand wild Canada Geese and several thousand wild ducks may be seen on the lake. Captive flocks of several species of swans, geese and ducks are maintained. Aviary pens retain numerous ornamental pheasants, native grouse, quail, wild turkeys, hawks and owls, and a number of bird houses; feeders and plantings of various trees and shrubs demonstrate methods of attracting birds and furthering wildlife conservation. Visitors to the sanctuary also find interesting the exhibits which are maintained in the museum and aquarium located on the shore of the lake.

Mr. Kellogg, with a true love for wildlife, took great pleasure in the sanctuary and was exceedingly irritated by the practice of a few unsporting nimrods who would linger just outside the boundaries in an effort to shoot at birds descending to the lake. This likely was back of his refusal to joke with a Battle Creek businessman who kiddingly said to Kellogg: "Well, I'm going to take my gun and go over to your bird preserve and do some hunting." Never a man to be joked with too much, W. K. immediately replied, "Listen, Mister, if I ever catch you in my preserve shooting any of the birds, I will prosecute you to the full extent of the law." To him the preservation of bird life was a precious thing and not a subject for levity.

In the course of purchasing Wintergreen Lake for the bird sanctuary, Kellogg acquired more land than was needed for that particular project. Casting about for something to do with this land, the idea came to him that he should set up a model or demonstration farm. He was averse to waste and this area of farming land had been under unskilled cultivation for many years and was rapidly being depleted of any value. He wondered if it were possible to take that land and bring it back to productiveness by the latest agricultural aids offered by science.

His interest can be explained by the fact that always Mr. Kellogg held a great deal of interest in the agriculture of the nation. Of course, the products of agriculture are an important factor in the Kellogg Company business and through the years W. K. Kellogg read extensively on this subject and talked on many occasions with experts in the field. He firmly believed that much of the welfare of the nation hinged upon the well-being of the farmer. Hence his worry about waste land was the product of a quasi-scientific research of the subject.

From his idea came the 832-acre Kellogg Experimental Farm, a graphic demonstration of approved practices in livestock management, soil building and conservation, with many head of livestock and poultry, and more than six hundred acres in a crop program. (A Feed Research unit was added in 1949 and is financed by the Kellogg Company.) Mr. Kellogg spent about a half-million dollars on this farm before giving it to an educational institution. The only strings attached to his gift were that he and his family should get milk and eggs for their own use. In all the subsequent years, he strictly adhered to the deal. If he requisitioned a chicken or some blueberries, he insisted upon paying for them. If he had one of his Arabian horses pastured by the farm, he insisted upon being billed for the pasturage.

His revulsion to waste prompted W. K. Kellogg to another experiment which has paid educational dividends to the farmers of Michigan and nearby states. Acquiring a rectangle a

W. K. Kellogg

mile long and three-quarters of a mile wide, he turned these
worn-out farmlands over to Michigan State University with the
request that the university see what it could do to make them
useful again. From the ensuing reforestation project, substan-

Aerial views of the Kellogg Experimental Farm. The main unit is pictured
above and the Field Research unit is shown below.

tially financed by Mr. Kellogg, came the beautiful Kellogg Forest, a monument to the fact that badly eroded land can be made productive. Through plantings of white pine, Norway red pine, Norway spruce, Scotch pine, and seventy-five other varieties of evergreen and deciduous trees, there is demonstrated to the farmer what he can do for his own exhausted fields at minimum time and cost. Such reforestation can bring a sustained yield of saw logs, poles, firewood, pulpwood and Christmas trees and an income on investment equal to that of the average farm land used for short-term crops. The project also has the major purposes of wildlife conservation and recreation, with the latter including picnicking, hiking, nutting, controlled trout fishing and hunting and trapping.

Between 1928 and 1932, W. K. Kellogg gave the three associated projects to Michigan State University and established trusts of $100,000 each for assistance in the maintenance of the sanctuary and the experimental farm. Since 1932, when the State of Michigan last appropriated money for this branch of the state institution, the experimental farm has been self-supporting and W. K., who admired efficiency, was always quite proud of the farm and the efficient way in which it was managed. Too, he retained some surprising memories of farm operation statistics. He was intrigued by the fact that a field opposite the farm superintendent's home had been made to produce

Explanatory sign at entrance to Kellogg Forest.

forty-five bushels of wheat to the acre as contrasted to its former fifteen-bushel yield. A decade after he learned of the increased yield, he was riding in a car with the superintendent and, pointing at the field, said: "Mac, that field went 45 bushels to the acre some ten years ago."

3.

One of Battle Creek's tallest buildings, now called the Security National Bank Building, was constructed by the Old Merchants' National Bank, the same bank which in earlier days had refused to make good on an original promise to give W. K. Kellogg a $50,000 line of credit. When this bank closed its doors in 1933, many townspeople said, "The cost of the new building has broken the bank." Others blamed it on the Depression of the 1930s which had a disastrous effect upon many of the nation's depositories.

In any event, Battle Creek and thousands of its people were greatly involved and excited. Ironically, a major part in salvaging the remaining assets fell upon the shoulders of Mr. Kellogg, a man who rightfully had little reason to feel obligated to the bank. A businessman and current Kellogg Foundation trustee remembers that there was considerable pressure placed upon W. K. Kellogg to put in a million or more dollars to organize a new bank. He recalls that the seventy-three-year-old man said to him:

"Dr. Pritchard and the bank president and the RFC men are coming out today, relative to my putting in a lot of money to organize a new bank. I wonder just what you think about it?"

The associate's reply was, "Mr. Kellogg, you know you have a lot of employees in your company. To an extent you were associated in their minds with the Old Merchants' National Bank. Most of your employees probably felt that it must be a pretty good institution because you were using it as your depository and, therefore, felt safe in putting their money in that bank. Perhaps you have at least an implied obligation to them to establish a new bank."

Kellogg quickly replied, "I think you are right." Subsequently, he instigated negotiations whereby four of the leading businesses of the city voluntarily accepted total liquidation payments of 40 per cent instead of the originally scheduled 65 per cent on their accounts. This considerable sacrifice left a sufficient amount in the bank coffers to pay in full more than twenty-one thousand accounts of less than $100 each. The reasons for the acceptance by the four large interests of the lower settlement are contained in Kellogg Foundation minutes which indicated that 5,491 school children accounts were in the $100 or less brackets and that some of the hardship on adults holding small accounts in the bank would be lessened by the voluntary action.

The settlement paved the way for the establishment of a new bank which has become one of the two largest in the area. Seventy-five per cent of the "big money" sacrificed was the property of Mr. Kellogg and the Kellogg Company but there could be no other course for W. K. Kellogg, conditioned as he was by association with pious, ethical people in the formative years of his life.

Perhaps the ethics stressed in the Masonic ritual explain the appeal of this lodge to Kellogg. While he was never a regular attendant at lodge meetings, he was sufficiently a student of the lore to pass every degree (including Knights Templar, Scottish Rite and the Shrine) except the rarely bestowed 33rd degree. When the Battle Creek Masonic Temple was going through financial troubles during the Depression, he made several anonymous donations to the Masonic Temple Association. He was influenced by the ethics of Masonry and would use Masonic verbiage when he wanted to make sure that what he was saying would be kept confidential, often emphasizing, "I am going to talk to you *on the level.*" (The italicized words are from the Masonic ritual.)

[277]

Long after Kellogg had taken his degrees, his interest in Masonic lore was rekindled because his grandson, Kenneth Williamson, was taking these same degrees. In conversations with Dr. Emory W. Morris (Kellogg Foundation President) who was coaching Kenneth, Kellogg kept track of the progress. Thus he had occasion to recite verbatim many of the Masonic passages several decades after he had originally committed them to memory.

For awhile, Kellogg was quite zealous with respect to another Battle Creek organization. Both he and his son, John L., were active in a new Rotary Club, according to a former president of the civic group. "Presently, however," it is recalled, "we noticed that Mr. Kellogg no longer came to our meetings. Several of the members reminded me as president that we should play no favorites but that Mr. Kellogg should be reminded of the Rotary Club's rule about regular attendance. Reluctantly, I relayed the question: 'Why don't you come to Rotary Club?' W. K. merely said, 'I pay my dues.'

" 'But that's not enough, Mr. Kellogg.' " The president sought a compromise. "Can't I tell the fellows that you'll be in attendance pretty often?" To this Mr. Kellogg replied: "I am not going to lie to you. There is too much tobacco smoke in the atmosphere down there." He never subsequently attended the club meetings.

With the advance of years, W. K. Kellogg may have grown increasingly indifferent to the society of businessmen, but he never lost interest in the business of his own company. In the collection of personal papers left by Mr. Kellogg are carbon copies of long memoranda addressed to various officials of the Kellogg Company. One of these was written when he was eighty years old and addressed to General Manager W. H. Vanderploeg. Apparently it was dictated after W. K. had heard his nurse read a monthly report of the company executive committee, and the resultant two-page memo contained thirty questions of major import.

It was at about this time when Mr. Kellogg and his son John L. exchanged letters to reminisce about the course of the company through the years. In a letter to his son dated April 29, 1939, Mr. Kellogg said, in part:

"I do not take any exception to what you write. I am conscious of having made many mistakes. I shall enumerate some, but not in chronological order."

Then his letter sketched twenty-four mistakes pertaining to business strategy and details. Perhaps most of us would not construe two dozen mistakes as "many" in the course of a dramatic business career then totaling thirty-three company years. The only emotion exhibited in W. K.'s highly objective and analytical letter was in the postscript:

"P.S. Shall be eighty my next birthday and I think it is high time that I get out of business and quit making mistakes."

For the record, it was not until May of 1946, six years later, that the elder Kellogg declined reelection to the company's Board of Directors. Even then his real interest in the company activities continued, and it is reported that he had a

Mr. Kellogg, in his early eighties, is shown with his dog-companion, Rinette.

(Photo by John H. Williamson, Arcadia, California.)

conversation about his beloved enterprise just the day before his death.

Paradoxically for a man who at his home base was never gregarious, Mr. Kellogg held a long and fervent interest in his old friends. As intimated previously, he seized opportunities during his many travels to locate friends of his boyhood or of his sanitarium years. Many of these San friends were scattered as missionaries over the world and on his several foreign journeys, W. K. would make inquiries about these people, often going considerably out of his way to look them up and to see if they needed anything. A California resident who left Battle Creek in 1900 recalls an invitation some forty-nine years later to visit Kellogg at Palm Springs and that "He never forgot old friends or acquaintances, even those whom he had not known well."

An observer believes that, while the real friendship of W. K. Kellogg was restricted to a few persons, "back of it all was the milk of human kindness, although it was hard for him to express his feelings in that regard to you in person. Instead, he went out and took care of those in need or the suffering. When a brother Mason was brought to the San to be operated upon, Kellogg stood by. When Dr. Harris underwent an operation, Kellogg was there, saying 'You were with me during my operations and now is my opportunity to reciprocate.' Characteristically, he was embarrassed if you ever spoke of this or that kindness or if a recipient ever appeared to thank him personally."

A poignant letter from the eminent physician Percy T. Magan reveals that as changes of residence (and sometimes death) took old friends away, Mr. Kellogg was unable completely to disguise his sorrow:

"I have wanted to write you a letter ever since I was at your Gull Lake home last Saturday afternoon. You will, I am sure, remember how you, Ben Colver, Rowland Harris and I were walking in the flower garden and chatting about their coming out to California. Well, in the midst of that conversation, you dropped a little remark which touched me very deeply—'What all of this means to me! What will I do when Ben and Rowland go? They mean so much to me and I need what friends I have.' There was a note of sadness in your voice which went home to my heart, and it has been echoing and reechoing there ever since."

Arch Shaw and A. W. Harris, business leaders in Chicago, were long-time, intimate friends whom W. K. made an effort to see on every convenient occasion. They were among the perhaps a dozen people in the circle of his acquaintances who were on a first-name basis with him. Most of the company executives never called him anything but "Mr. Kellogg." It was a rarely bestowed accolade when he would say to someone, "I am W. K. to you."

Helen Keller, the blind authoress, once presented a copy of her book *Midstream* to Mr. Kellogg, autographing it with the statement:

Thank you, dear friend, for lighting a candle of hope in the night of blindness. Helen Keller

Will Kellogg had great respect for people like Miss Keller who tried to be helpful to others. The respect in this case was mutual since Miss Keller thought highly of his aid to the blind.

Former President Herbert Hoover was another person for whom W. K. held undying admiration. (It was at Mr. Kellogg's suggestion that Mr. Hoover's public addresses were accumulated and Kellogg paid the cost of printing three of the seven volumes.)

A friend among the literati was Paul de Kruif. So much did Will Kellogg esteem de Kruif's book *Men Against Death* that he purchased three hundred copies to give to friends and acquaintances. Dr. de Kruif was a frequent visitor to Mr. Kellogg's Gull Lake estate and, in their many walks over the grounds, the fact that the author smoked a pipe seemed to give no offense to the usually sensitive nostrils of the host.

Although Henry Ford, as has been related, came to the Battle Creek Sanitarium upon several occasions, it is not believed that W. K. Kellogg was acquainted with him. Neither did the food manufacturer know Harvey Firestone, Thomas Edison, Henry Burroughs or Senator James Couzens, although they were contemporaries and did much of their famous work not far from his own base. Perhaps even if Kellogg had had the opportunity to consort with these personages, he would have been too modest to become friendly with them.

Yet it is evident that he did receive an understandable gratification in "walking with kings." In letters to his children and grandchildren, he occasionally made mention of rubbing elbows with celebrities such as:

"I am enclosing with this an invitation that I received a few days ago to come to Philadelphia and to meet President Coolidge. I also have an invitation for dinner by the Mayor of Philadelphia, all of which I declined with thanks."

Other celebrities whose friendships were greatly valued by Mr. Kellogg included Senator Arthur Vandenberg and Governor Woodbridge N. Ferris of Michigan, Ransom E. Olds, founder of the Olds Motor Company, Arthur Brisbane, the noted columnist, Senator Arthur Capper of Kansas, and the previously mentioned Robert A. Millikan of the California Institute of Technology.

4.

A former employee of Mr. Kellogg remembers that one time he said to her, "I never want to hear of you saying anything derogatory about Dr. Kellogg. I don't want anyone around me to talk against my brother." The startled woman, who had no intention of discussing Dr. Kellogg, was naturally quite surprised at this injunction because she had heard Mr. Kellogg say a number of things not altogether complimentary concerning brother John.

Although relations between the two brothers were never friendly after the lawsuits culminating in 1920, John and Will did have intermittent contact in succeeding years through correspondence and infrequent personal meetings. Letters from the Doctor thanking W. K. for a gift of cucumbers from the estate garden, for orchids from the greenhouse, are in the latter's personal letter collection. Another letter explains that the Doctor was "sending you some iris from plants which I transplanted from the old Kellogg home in North Hadley" and still another to Mr. Kellogg expresses the physician's appreciation of "your kind offer of a place to work in your home at Palm Springs." Apparently Dr. Kellogg did use his brother's home in California, for he later wrote that "I am starting home tonight, and am writing this note to tell you how much I appreciate your courtesy in giving me such a lovely time at Palm Springs. . . ."

Blood is thicker than water and while Will Kellogg never fully forgave his elder brother for the "indignities" of the sanitarium years, he occasionally softened in his attitude toward the Doctor. There was the time in 1942 when George McKay advised Mr. Kellogg that John Harvey had asked him to become a member of the San Board:

"George, I think it would be fine if you did go on the Doctor's Board," suggested W. K. "I think you could help him."

The frank-speaking banker, no longer an employee of Will Kellogg, replied:

"If I do go on that board, W. K., I won't be your man nor will I be the Doctor's man."

Apparently Mr. Kellogg did not resent the inference for he chuckled and said:

"Go ahead, then, George, and be your own man."

At the most, the brothers saw each other two or three times a year up to October 3, 1942. On this date, approximately six months after the sanitarium Constituency battle, the brothers Kellogg conversed for the last time and the conversation became a marathon talkfest lasting five hours. In essence, Mr. Kellogg was trying to convince Dr. Kellogg that he should not attempt to build up the sanitarium any further but should try to sell out. Further, W. K. believed that John Harvey should make appropriate provision for the older employees in the event of a dissolution. The pros and cons of the Constituency battle were thoroughly discussed and then, during the long session, the talk apparently turned to the past. Mr. Kellogg, after the conversation, dictated a memorandum from which are taken the following excerpts:

"Dr. J. H. 'fessed up at this interview. He said that he had talked too much and that during his lifetime he had wasted a great deal of time by talking unnecessarily. I mentioned to the Doctor that his visits with Magan and Sutherland of the old Battle Creek College, as well as long talks and visits with other people, were responsible for depriving me of many nights of sleep. He said he was sorry that this had happened. . . . The Doctor said he was being rejuvenated by a mixture that he had put up of malt honey, vitamins, and minerals. He said that this medicine had grown him some new fingernails, from which I took it for granted that he had reformed and quit biting his fingernails. . . . The Doctor also mentioned that the use of tobacco by the Army was likely to cause the U. S. A. to lose the war."

It is evident that, if the hatchet was buried at all, it was not buried deep in this last conversation between the two brothers, one of whom was then ninety years old and the other eighty-two. From the past of many years, their minds held memories in the corners like cobwebs, but likely the atmosphere was scarcely cleared at all by the discussion. It also is apparent that the counsel freely proffered by each found little later implementation. A Battle Creek businessman remembers a talk he had with the Doctor in December of 1942 in which the "little genius" said:

"With the San directly across from the Race Betterment Foundation buildings, we will run there until world affairs have settled down. Then later, I am going out east of town where there is a square mile of lakes and woods and will rebuild the San along the original design."

The businessman recalled that at the time of this forward look, the Doctor was more than ninety years old and the new sanitarium he was predicting would cost several million dollars! "The uncanny thing," continued the businessman, "was that you did not doubt for a moment that he fully intended to do this thing and that, if his health permitted and he lived a while, it would be done."

However, "man proposes and God disposes," and death came to Dr. John Harvey Kellogg on December 14, 1943. This short man had attained great stature through the brilliance of his talents and the iron of his will power, and it was as if a dynamo had abruptly stopped, leaving a disconcerting silence.

More than he perhaps would have admitted, the passing of his elder brother came as a real blow to W. K. Kellogg. Having a photograph made of the grave, he sent this picture to many people who had known the Doctor during his lifetime, particularly to many whom John Harvey had befriended. Several times during the years that followed, W. K. expressed deep regret that there had been no reconciliation between the two and this lasting hurt was accentuated by an occurrence on June 22, 1948, more than six years after the elder's death.

Arriving on this June day at the W. K. Kellogg residence was a seven-page letter dictated by the Doctor a considerable time before his death. This was a belated reply to a letter written by Mr. Kellogg after he had received several suggestions from prominent people relative to aiding Dr. Kellogg in refinancing the sanitarium. Mr. Kellogg noted on his brother's letter that "I heard this read for the first time on June 22, 1948" and investigation disclosed that a person in the household of Dr. Kellogg had withheld its mailing because she believed the Doctor should not have revealed that ". . . I find my memory failing . . . I thought I had about reached the end of walking and was distinctly doddering. . . ."

In the letter that arrived too late, Dr. Kellogg asserted that "I certainly am not responsible for any of the letters that have been written you (concerning aid in refinancing the sanitarium)." The entire tone of the letter was conciliatory and it traced the years in which the brothers had been associated, stating that "It was the greatest possible misfortune to the work that circumstances arose which led you and me in different channels and separated our interests.

"I am sure that you were right," continued the Doctor, "as regards the food business. . . . Your better balanced judgment has doubtless saved you from a vast number of mistakes of the sort I have made and allowed you to achieve magnificent successes for which generations to come will owe you gratitude."

In the final portion of this letter, Dr. Kellogg said:

"I am making desperate efforts to get all my affairs into such shape as to preserve as much as possible what good they may represent and to mend as many as possible of the errors I have made. I earnestly desire to make amends for any wrong or injustice of any sort I have done to you and will be glad if you will give me a very definite and frank expression of anything I

[286]

have said or done which you feel should be justly designated unbrotherly or otherwise open to criticism. . . . I hope that this note may find you more comfortable and that you may have many years left to promote the splendid enterprises that have given the name you bear a place among the notable ones of our time."

One might safely conjecture that had this magnanimous letter been delivered to W. K. Kellogg before the Doctor's death, at least a part-reconciliation of the two brothers would have resulted—but the letter arrived too late.

5.

A biography of W. K. Kellogg could only be written posthumously because the extreme modesty of the man caused him to veto several suggestions to record publicly his history during the years that he lived. A letter written on August 10, 1940, told a would-be biographer:

"From what you write I have no doubt whatever of your ability to write a biography. However, it so happens that I am not especially interested in having my biography written."

At one time, Kellogg did allow a California writer to interview him for a short biographical article but after the manuscript was developed and sent to the subject, it was held and never published. Later, apropos a three-hundred-word sketch to appear in a New York City publication, Mr. Kellogg wrote a memorandum to a Kellogg Company official:

"In the article he used the word philanthropy * several times. I asked him to cut it out and also to take out some of the 'applesauce.' He offered to send me fifty copies as I would probably want to send some copies to my friends and I told him 'No,' that I would not."

---

* Kellogg had a strange distaste for the words "philanthropy" and "philanthropist," once writing Paul de Kruif that "a philanthropist is one who would do good for the love of his fellowmen. I love to do things for children because I get a kick out of it. Therefore, I am a selfish person and no philanthropist."

W. K. Kellogg

It was this same reticence which prompted Kellogg to decline, with thanks, an offer of a prominent Midwestern university to award him an honorary degree of Doctor of Laws. He explained to company associates that "I thanked the president and told him that I did not think I was entitled to anything of this sort . . . that I was not an educated man and did not think I would feel very comfortable with a degree attached to my name. I told him that I had three or four times been offered by the publishers of *Who's Who in America* an opportunity to appear in their book but had always declined and preferred to pay for any advertising."

There was to show up some "advertising" for which W. K., with his aversion to liquor and taverns, was willing to pay so that it might *not* appear any longer than it had. A Michigan artist once persuaded Mr. Kellogg to sit for a portrait (if there was any chink in the armor of W. K.'s reticence, it was with respect to likenesses, for he had many photographs and several paintings executed in his lifetime) but when the painting was completed, the subject did not appreciate it and refused to pay for it. Several years later, as a sort of compromise, Kellogg again submitted to sittings before this artist, but again did not like the results and again refused to buy the painting. As a sequel to the dispute, the unpurchased painting was hung in the bar of a hotel in a town not far from Battle Creek!

Greatly embarrassed by this "advertising," Kellogg through an intermediary was finally able to obtain the portrait's removal from the tavern wall by a belated purchase of it.

In 1938, Mr. Kellogg sat for a formal portrait in oil by Frank O. Salisbury, world-famous London artist who painted the portraits of two kings of England and their queens and of three presidents of the United States. The original of the Kellogg painting hangs in the W. K. Kellogg Foundation offices and a copy is in the lobby of the general offices of the Kellogg Company. A smaller reproduction appears on the title page of this biography.

6.

Henry James once said: "Every life is a special problem . . . an algebra of its own."

Undoubtedly it is difficult to appraise the years which have brought wrinkles, joys and sorrows to a man of long life, and then to sum up by saying, "He was a happy (or unhappy) man." Yet if the hedonists be right and happiness is the ultimate goal of living, no summation of a man can be complete without an attempt to divine whether he struck a balance and said, "Life, as a whole, has been good" or whether, contrariwise, he told himself, "The struggle has not been worth the trouble."

More than a score of those who knew W. K. Kellogg best were interviewed on the key question: "Was Mr. Kellogg a happy or unhappy man?" As could be expected from analyses of a complex personality, there was no unanimity of opinion.

A psychiatrist, who was also a relative in considerable contact with Will Kellogg through the years, took the negative view in recalling that the subject of this biography was: ". . . deeply unhappy and frustrated. In all my long practice of psychiatry, I don't know of a more lonely, isolated individual. . . . Possibly by the time he gained success at middle age, the capacity for enjoyment of a rich life had atrophied. He had few vices and only short-lived hobbies so that he had practically no escape valves for his nervous tensions. Just a modicum of added extrovertism would have given him the capacity for an outlet which would have meant much to his total happiness. . . . Here was a man of great brain power, of practically photographic memory, who lacked the self-confidence needed to complete his being."

Yet another close observer, a man of sensitivity and intellect, would dispute any view that Mr. Kellogg did not enjoy life:

"He was happy in his own way, with a deep enjoyment and appreciation of living. Concededly, this was a quiet happiness, not exuberant, and only occasionally reflected on Mr. Kellogg's rather impassive countenance. Coming from a religious family, with high, ethical standards, he found real satisfaction in a life-long hobby of helping others. . . .

"W. K. had a method of control which he tried to pass on to me. Even when he had suffered greatly from some vicissitude such as the death of John, Jr., he would—after a period of ordeal—decide, 'Now, I can't do anything about what has happened. I can't let this happening interfere with my main project in life, so I must start again and not think about this tragedy any more.' By this control, Mr. Kellogg would annihilate from his thoughts anything that interfered with his Number One Project which in his later years was that of building a Foundation to help others. He told me, 'I never could reach that goal if I let anything interfere with my health, my energies, my strengths, my attitudes.' There was something almost Oriental in his ability to submerge the tragic or the irrelevant."

In a succeeding chapter of this book, which tells of Mr. Kellogg's formation and support of the W. K. Kellogg Foundation, will be found evidences to substantiate parts of the foregoing and contradictory theses. Mrs. Norman Williamson (the "Beth" of this biography and a philosophic and clear-thinking person) believes that both these views were partially correct. On a couple of occasions, she recalls that her father told her of his regret that he was not more extroversive, that "he could not break down, smile and laugh, and enjoy things in the manner of many people. But in his formative years he seldom had the time to be gay. He never learned to play because much of his boyhood was spent in hard work. Then came the twenty-five-year regimen at the San when he toiled eighteen to twenty hours a day. . . . However, Father did receive deep and lasting satisfaction from the accomplishment of so many things of benefit to humanity. This quiet joy was almost in conflict with the self that had never had a youth, had never been able to loosen up."

Will Kellogg's old friend, Arch Shaw, believed that "W. K. had many moments of happiness and real satisfaction from the success of his company and his Foundation. He did have two great regrets, one that he did not get started until late in life when an earlier start might have made possible still greater accomplishments. The other regret pertained to his lack of the knack of meeting and mingling with people. He once told me, 'I would give the world to be able to get along with people as well as you do.' "

A one-time nurse, Mrs. Lucille Gardner, recalls that she never heard Mr. Kellogg laugh out loud when funny things happened —pranks of his grandchildren or his dog. "He would chuckle and his stomach would bob up and down but apparently he could not laugh heartily. I would say to him, 'Really you are not a cold kind of man at all. Anyone as affectionate as you are with that dog (he would get down on the floor to romp with his dog) must simply be putting on a mask so that people will stay away from you.' Mr. Kellogg just chuckled and made no comment."

A former secretary believes that Kellogg did occasionally don a mask of harshness as a protective barrier, particularly to ward off effusive thanks for some kind act performed by him. He remembers a plea received for some money during the Depression and that the letter of declination to the person was harsh. However, in the same mail a letter went to Mrs. Young, his secretary at Battle Creek, asking her to go to the bank to buy a $200 draft which was to be sent anonymously and in a plain envelope to the person who had requested aid. '

Association with W. K. in both company and Foundation transactions prompted a Battle Creek businessman to believe that "Any happiness he may have had lay largely in the attainment of his objectives through the business and the giving away of his money. Knowing his mind, I think he must have been a lonesome man. His planning was the controlling factor. If that did not go right, then he was desolate and unhappy. I think his whole life was largely keyed to the idea of growth, a sort of law of nature which rejected any tree which did not grow fruit. He

was not seeking mere bigness but perhaps proof of a reason-
to-be. He demanded that his food must have merit. He required
the best of materials, workmanship, the best of mechanical aids
for their manufacturing. His later years were made happier
because he realized he had found two lieutenants who would
make his company and his Foundation function to an optimum
degree."

Perhaps as close to the actual as a summing up may approach
is the opinion that, like all of us, Mr. Kellogg had his happy
and unhappy moments, his great virtues and his weaknesses.
His happiness sprang from a sincere love of people, *en masse*
rather than individually, from a sense of achievement and from
the resultant prestige which he secretly treasured. Militating
against this happiness and perhaps leading at least to some "loneliness and frustration" were his personality defects, the inability
to bridge the gap between his personality and the next person's.
His austerity and control of emotions were perhaps so ironlike
because he feared that were he to open the gate even a little,
he would be unable to dam the emotions which underlay a
very sensitive nervous system. Any unhappiness, too, was partially because of the harassment of any rich man, the fear that
he is not valued for his own personal worth but for what might
possibly be obtained from him.

There was the rigid atmosphere of his childhood which led
to anxieties and deep-seated complexes. These effects continued
into adulthood. In his loneliness, there often welled within him
a yearning. He told himself philosophically that this unrest is
the toll man must pay for his evolution. As with everyone he
sought understanding, but for him there were few islands of
companionship.

He was a powerful individualist who kept his associates in
awe. He exhaled energy, vigilance and severity; expected and
gained obedience on the jump. Yet take him out of the fierce
arena of business and he thought of people in terms of the human
factor. And a strength (and perhaps a great joy) was the fact

that even in his later years, life for W. K. Kellogg was no tale of old, far-off things and battles long ago, but a forward look toward more and greater accomplishments.

7.

When W. K. Kellogg set up the Fellowship Corporation in 1925 —as a forerunner to the establishment of a Foundation of much greater scope five years later—he was not acting upon a sudden whim. Before most worth-while endeavors are launched, first comes the dream, and Mr. Kellogg for many years had nurtured a dream of "helping others to help themselves."

In a letter written on October 5, 1909, to Mr. Charles N. Crittenton of the Moody Bible Institute of Chicago, Mr. Kellogg stated:

"If I am successful in getting out of debt and become prosperous in my business affairs, I expect to make a good use of any wealth that may come to me."

Soon after he established his own company when he was forty-six, he wrote a friend that "It appears my business will be a financial success and it is my hope that anything I accumulate can be used for the benefit of mankind."

This was a modest and conservative person's way of indicating that he held a dream, not primarily for himself but for others. Perhaps because this dream was so great in its implications, W. K. Kellogg restrained his usual urge for immediate action. Instead he allowed a master plan slowly to evolve in his mind, a thread in his thinking for many years to "aid humanity in general and America in particular." A long-time friend remarked, "Mr. Kellogg was the only businessman that I knew who planned in advance what he would do with the money he might make from his business." However, deliberate as was the crystallization of his ideas, W. K. Kellogg truly was generous long before he was wealthy.

In 1906, the initial year for his company, W. K. was carrying a heavy personal indebtedness, but when one of his carton

machine girls lost her pocketbook containing a week's pay, he
insisted upon reimbursing her for the loss. Many years later the
employee, by then a middleaged woman, wrote, "I will never
forget how you came to me and insisted on replacing my lost
pay money."

Even during the sanitarium days, when Will Kellogg's salary
never exceeded $87 per month plus a quarter share of the Sanitas
Company profits, he found ways to aid hard-pressed relatives,
friends, and occasional strangers. At the very least, an indigent
relative could depend upon free board and lodging at the Kellogg home, and the impoverished ill frequently found a ray of
sunshine in discovering that a sanitarium bill had been mysteri-
ously paid or canceled.

A niece of Mr. Kellogg recalls that during a seven-week illness
at the San, "Uncle Will" made almost daily visits to her bedside.
After she returned home and wrote the institution requesting
a statement, she received the following letter from the business
office: "We are in receipt of your very courteous letter of December 20 and in response thereto beg to state that the reason
you have not received a bill is that it has already been adjusted
and you have no account on our books."

During a period of depressed economics in Battle Creek, it
is recalled that at least a dozen people in Battle Creek were
receiving monthly allowances of $50 each from this benefactor
who only asked that they not embarrass him by effusive thanks.
Not a few people over the country, friends as well as relatives,
were to have experiences similar to that of one Battle Creek
family. Borrowings on the family home had caused the total
indebtedness to reach approximately $2,700 and the woman of
the house went to a local bank to attempt to find some way to
amortize the interest burden. Passing Mr. Kellogg in the bank
on her way to the mortgage loan department, she thought little
about the contact until she received a letter from the bank a
few days later—"You will find enclosed herewith the abstract
and title to your home. . . . These papers are sent to you under

the instructions of a certain individual who further instructed us that the gift be made to you anonymously."

Someone has said, "The first thing to be done by a biographer in estimating character is to examine the stubs of the subject's checkbooks." From records kept by various bookkeepers of W. K. Kellogg, it was possible to compile a listing covering three single-spaced typewritten pages of moneys given to relatives and friends for educational purposes, house rent, hospital and funeral expenses, annuities, and even "to rebuild your burned sawmill." Spontaneously Kellogg gave away money and as impulsively he resisted what he deemed attempts to "gouge" him because he was prospering. When he went to a farmhouse to purchase fresh sweet corn and found the farmwoman had suffered a broken wrist, he thereupon placed in her mail box a $50 check. Yet he was furious to learn that his barber had raised the cost of a haircut to one dollar and told a company official that "Hereafter I'm going over to Hickory Corners for my barber work. Sixty-five cents is enough to pay for a haircut."

"That is wasteful," was one of the most severe indictments that W. K. Kellogg could utter. Setting a "good table" for his household employees, looking after their comfort even to the extent of buying an expensive television set for their personal use, he nevertheless was a strict taskmaster with regard to the wastage of food or the discard of an appliance before its period of utility had ended. In a kind but firm way, he would suggest that the cook not put more food on his plate than he could eat. This same aversion to waste was what caused him, after buying berries at a roadside stand, to return to the stand the empty berry boxes.

He was willing to pay a fair price for merchandise but would not be "held up" by a supplier even if it cost an inordinate amount of money to avoid this gouge. There was the time when a repeat order was necessary on pictorial postcards which were given away to the public at the bird sanctuary. Before placing this repeat order with the original printer, Mr. Kellogg secured some competitive bids and found the price was about half of what the sanctuary had been paying for the cards. Advising the printer of this, he asked for the plates so the imprints could be made elsewhere. The printer refused to surrender the plates. Unswerved, Kellogg paid an extra thousand dollars for new plates, being willing to assume this large expense to observe a principle of refusing to pay more than the competitive price of an article.

When Mr. Kellogg's philanthropies were more spontaneous than organized (in addition to the millions he gave to and through the W. K. Kellogg Foundation, Kellogg's personal benefactions approached $3,000,000) his giving was scattered and for various unrelated purposes. These included the financing of a "teacherage" the better to house rural teachers, thousands of dollars to clothe British children orphaned by the war, many gifts to aid the blind. Because "I like to pick winners," he helped countless talented young people to secure educations. When he thought Battle Creek needed another hospital, he gave $50,000 to his friend, Dr. Rowland Harris, to aid in starting the Maple Street Hospital. Told that his home town needed a municipal auditorium for a meeting place, he made such a structure an actuality. He remembered his Adventist friends by various assistance to the Loma Linda Sanitarium, the Azusa Sanitarium, and the White Memorial Hospital.

Many of Mr. Kellogg's donations, and particularly those through the Fellowship Corporation, had more than immediate benefit to the recipients and to the public in general. An anonymous grant to Northwestern University was for research toward restoring crushed hands that ordinarily would be amputated and subsequently the method of restoring use of the hands was introduced into a large number of clinics. A sufferer from glaucoma, Kellogg underwrote a long-time research of the causes and palliatives for the eye disease.

Perhaps most of Mr. Kellogg's personal philanthropies proved worth-while investments in people or for the public. Nevertheless, Kellogg wondered if a more formal organization, devoted to full-time planning for systematic giving, might not provide an even more beneficial stewardship for his fortune. He recalled the Bernard Baruch story of how this "advisor of Presidents" went home to his father to announce, "I have made a million dollars." When his father asked, "Well, Barney, what next?" the son replied: "I am still trying to find out what best to do with it." W. K. Kellogg himself once stated: "It has been much easier to make money than to know how to spend it wisely."

Likely his thoughts upon better stewardship of his wealth were accentuated by an ill-fated investment made in 1929 to facilitate the treatment of cancer. Two California physicians were experimenting with an extract of suprarenal cortex substance in the belief that the treatment lessened the need for narcotics, caused tumors to degenerate and made it possible for patients to gain in weight. Mr. Kellogg, naturally knowing little of the subject area, agreed to allot $500,000 of his funds because, as he said, "I am not sure there is anything in this cancer cure, but suppose there was and I did not support it!"

Seventy-five thousand dollars was spent to set up a special hospital unit and on the special treatment for patients. A subsequent investigation by an emissary of Mr. Kellogg, Dr. Rowland Harris, resulted in his belief that the extract was of little or no value in the cure or mitigation of cancer. The report issued by Dr. Harris, and subsequently printed in the *Journal of the American Medical Association,* saved Mr. Kellogg approximately $425,000, for this remainder was not used when the unfavorable report was issued.

W. K. and the three close friends who comprised the Fellowship Corporation began to believe that the best stewardship for a fortune devoted to altruism might well be a full-time trusteeship bulwarked by an expert and professional staff. The Fellowship Corporation had served its purposes; the members had been glad to relieve Kellogg of the time-consuming pressure from seekers of gifts and loans, and checks carrying only the corporation name served to conceal the identity of the modest donor. These members, sacrificing time from their own businesses and professions, had followed through on Kellogg's desire to turn many of the benefits toward children, particularly underprivileged children.

As early as 1926, Kellogg had discussed with the Fellowship Corporation members his desire "to get a child welfare foundation established and set in operation during my lifetime." In August of that year, Dr. Harris had turned over to Mr. Kellogg the results of his research concerning child welfare and this might be regarded as the actual start of the W. K. Kellogg Foundation even though the Fellowship Corporation was the vehicle for his philanthropies until 1930.

Although he was from a long-lived family, W. K. in the period of his late sixties and early seventies had no intimation, of course, that he would live to be nearly ninety-one. Perhaps he did have some premonition of the illnesses, ranging from the chronic to the severe, which beset him in his seventies. In any event, he set about to "put my own house in order."

An old friend, Attorney Burritt Hamilton of Battle Creek, recalls that, without preliminaries, Mr. Kellogg came to his office one morning and said:

"I want you to draft a will for me. It will contain about thirty trusts. It must be carefully drawn. It will dispose of property of the estimated value of $50,000,000."

Mr. Hamilton concluded this recollection with the observation: "That order was a memorable shock to a country lawyer!"

The trusts evidenced the great interest of Kellogg in the financial affairs of his children, grandchildren and great-grandchildren and some of his needy friends. During his lifetime, he created about fifty-five trusts, including twenty-seven which were for the benefit of relatives or friends, twenty-four in which the beneficiaries were institutions (colleges, universities, the bird sanctuary) and three trusts for needy friends and distant relatives.

One of the largest of the trusts was that of $3,900,000 for the benefit of relatives and employees with the residue to go to the W. K. Kellogg Foundation. Two trusts for the grandchildren totaled $600,000 and $950,000 respectively. Kellogg even provided for great-grandchildren, including those yet unborn at the time, through a $275,000 trust. A trust for the benefit of specified needy persons was financed by five hundred shares of common stock of the Kellogg Company, now worth $38,500.

The educational trust created for the grandchildren and great-grandchildren exemplified a strong premise of the philosophy of Mr. Kellogg. Many years previously (in 1902) W. K. Kellogg had written his son John L.: "In assisting you in the past I have always had in view that you would sometime take up studying again. I am myself lamentably ignorant, and am exceedingly anxious that you should know at least as much as your father, and I am afraid that you do not. My work is of such a nature that it has assisted me in some respects, and I have gotten a practical education which has been a great help to me. . . . I want to put myself on record as having offered to furnish you with such help as will enable you to secure a good practical education. I would not care to recommend you to take Greek or Latin, or anything that would come hard to you and that would not come practical. There are many other things one needs to learn. The competition in the business world is such that the people with good educations are usually those who succeed."

Forever regretting his lack of an extensive formal education, W. K. Kellogg hoped that his descendants would not suffer a similar deprivation. Regardless of how successful his grandchildren should prove to be, he wanted to insure that his great-grandchildren—those already born and those yet to be born—would have opportunity for a well-rounded education.

By the trust he deemed that he was fulfilling an obligation

yet, at the same time, he did not propose to leave large amounts of money to the youthful members of the Kellogg clan. He believed that "these young people should stand on their own legs." This trust—which was prepared under the guidance of Matthias Concannon, a Chicago attorney who long was both a legal and business advisor to Mr. Kellogg—did provide that if any of the beneficiaries should suffer physical impairment, a portion of the funds could be used to help to surmount the resultant problems. Another trust was created by him for the lifetime benefit of his grandson, Kenneth Williamson, who was injured in a previously mentioned infantile accident.

It is recalled that "Mr. Kellogg handled the matters of estate in his usual meticulous and capable manner." Some of the trusts were revocable and others irrevocable, with a number of the former to be affected by changes made in 1935, the time when W. K. Kellogg became convinced that the Foundation bearing his name was on the right track insofar as stewardship of the great bulk of his fortune was concerned.

This man-in-a-hurry—who never was sure he had enough time to follow through on the myriad ideas in his teeming mind—had almost a morbid fear that he had too few years remaining for the disposition of his fortune so that it would be of optimum benefit for the welfare of people. He was determined that this fortune should not disintegrate to dust as other great fortunes had done, and perhaps no wealthy person planned more diligently than he for the proper disposal of his money. He did not realize that the sands of time were to run for twenty years more of his own life, representing two decades of "a third life" and personal observation of the widening scope of his Foundation. He thought he was working against time which was running out when on June 7, 1930, he addressed a letter to Mr. L. J. Brown, Mr. Eugene McKay and Dr. A. C. Selmon. Even though years of careful thought and a life aim were involved, he was characteristically laconic in using but two sentences to express his wishes:

[300]

W. K. Kellogg
Battle Creek, Michigan

June 7, 1930

Mr. L. J. Brown,
Mr. Eugene McKay,
Dr. A. C. Selmon:

In an effort to carry out some of the
projects which I have in mind, while still
on earth, Mr. Hamilton and I have decided
that it is desirable to establish a child
welfare foundation.

Would appreciate it very much if each
of you would act as a director of this foundation.

W. K. Kellogg

tg

An important factor in Mr. Kellogg's decision to "invest my money in people" was his love of children, and the originally-stated purpose for the creation of his Foundation was "the welfare of children and youth."

CHAPTER 13

"I'll Invest My Money in People"

——THE FOUNDATION IS ESTABLISHED

O CCASIONALLY ARCH SHAW, with the presumption of an old friend, would offer a bit of advice to his business confrère, W. K. Kellogg. An instance of this kind occurred in 1929 when Mr. Shaw ventured:

"Apparently, W. K., the company is piling up quite a lot of capital. Pretty soon, you are going to have to consider investing most of this excess money."

Kellogg quickly replied: "I know how to invest my money. I'll invest it in people."

During the ensuing conversation, it was evident that the prospering manufacturer had long been considering the best possible use of his accumulating fortune. As he explained to Shaw:

"I never had a taste for high living. I never cared to own a yacht. I have never desired to become extremely rich although

W. K. Kellogg

I have had a natural wish to make enough money to live comfortably and to provide well for my family. But that's about as far as my ambition for wealth has ever gone."

Kellogg further emphasized that he was opposed, as a matter of oft-stated principle, to the leaving of a great fortune to his children. Nevertheless, once they started, the millions poured in and there was only one thing for him to do: to consider himself as but a steward for the money and to give it away as wisely as possible.

"I want to help those with little or no income," he continued. "I want to establish a foundation that will help handicapped children everywhere to face the future with confidence, with health, and with a strong-rooted security in their trust of this country and its institutions."

Of course, every man has a dream for his children, that they will grow up to have a richer, happier life than he has had. However, only a few have projected this paternal feeling to embrace the children of a nation and, eventually, of three continents. A feature writer of the *Detroit Times* saw great significance in the unfolding dream of W. K. Kellogg and posed these questions:

"Is one man's dream for contributing to the welfare of children to point the way out of a world dilemma? Is it to be a way of proving that the authoritarian state is not the only alternative to a welfare program by representative government? Is this philanthropic program a dramatic reawakening of the pioneer American spirit?"

There was something in the sweet trusting nature of little children that melted the stern W. K. Kellogg, and in their presence he was an altogether different person from his usual role of business Titan. An old friend recalled an incident of many years ago when Mr. Kellogg took the neighboring Barnes family for an automobile ride. Along on the ride was four-year-old Junior who, as youngsters will do, had created an imaginary playmate by the name of "Joey."

[304]

As the car rolled along W. K. asked Junior if he had brought Joey with him. The little fellow said "No." Thereupon Mr. Kellogg stopped the car, opened the door and, speaking to the imaginary playmate along the roadside, said, "Get in, Joey." Then this adult closed the door, moved over to make room for "Joey" and the ride was continued.

A remembrance of the tragic fall of his infant grandson Kenneth was an overtone to Mr. Kellogg's natural love for children, and he recalled in a letter to Dr. A. R. Dickson of Battle Creek:

"The establishing of the Foundation was due in part to the fact that although I was amply able to pay the medical and surgical bills for Kenneth, I found it almost impossible to obtain adequate treatment for him during the first ten or twelve years of his life. This caused me to wonder what difficulties were in the paths of needy parents who seek help for their children when catastrophe strikes, and I resolved to lend what aid I could to such children."

During the administration of President Herbert Hoover, the chief executive called together leaders from many walks of life to a White House Conference on Child Health and Protection. This assembly of leaders was but part of the evidence that adults of the world were becoming greatly concerned with child welfare—a dramatic demonstration of the growth of the human conscience since the days of ancient Rome when physically and mentally defective children were thrown into the Tiber.

Knowing of Mr. Kellogg's interest in children, Mr. Hoover asked him to be a delegate to this conference. The "Nineteen Points" of the Children's Charter enunciated at the meeting had a definite influence in Mr. Kellogg's plans for reshaping his philanthropies to provide greater and more flexible funds for the health, happiness, and well-being of children.

Once again, he was to be a builder—this time to build broader horizons for children—and Kellogg's love for efficiency played a part in his desire to have a professionally supervised vehicle for the stewardship of his money. While he had admiration for the altruism which had prompted his brother, Dr. John Harvey Kellogg, to set up many charities, the loosely organized and spasmodic character of these charities had displeased the more efficient younger brother. W. K. Kellogg believed that the routing of waste through precision planning, as followed in his company, could well be paralleled in his new venture of giving away money wisely.

In June of 1930 there was organized the W. K. Kellogg Child Welfare Foundation. This was quickly reorganized and broadened as to purpose within two months of its founding. The purpose of the renamed W. K. Kellogg Foundation as then defined was "receiving and administering funds for the promotion of the welfare, comfort, health, care, education, feeding, clothing, sheltering, and safeguarding of children and youth, directly or indirectly, without regard to sex, race, creed or nationality, in whatever manner the Board of Trustees may decide."

Kellogg had a particular desire to lighten the burdens of children, to set their feet on surer paths to health and happiness. However, along with the trustees of the Foundation, he gained an appreciation of the fact that in many instances the problems of youth are so involved with those of adults it is only through programs with adults that youth can best be served. Later, therefore, Mr. Kellogg suggested that the purpose of the Foundation be restated by the insertion of the word "mankind." Then the ruling premise of the Foundation became "the promotion of the health, education and welfare of mankind, but principally of children and youth. . . ."

On December 8, 1930, *Time* magazine took note of the promising young Foundation by commenting that "Will Keith Kellogg . . . again belied the general impression that he is a dour money-maker. He created the W. K. Kellogg Foundation, gave it $1,000,000 for immediate use and promised for it a total of $50,000,000 if and when needed. . . . The public knows practically nothing about him. Employees of the Kellogg Company have stern orders against exploiting him. Servants of the Kellogg Inn at Battle Creek, his legal residence, dare not talk. . . . Nor is there much small talk about him at Pomona, California, where he is breeding the largest registered herd of Arabian horses in the United States. Hence his public reputation for dourness."

"Dour" was not an apt adjective for the W. K. Kellogg who received such an obvious pleasure from the good deeds being done by those whom he had selected to run the Foundation. From then on he had an abiding interest in the philanthropic programs, causing one observer to remark that "If the Kellogg Company is the flesh of W. K., then the Foundation is his soul."

As there gradually unfolded the manifold activities of the W. K. Kellogg Foundation in the fields of health, education and the general welfare, a thirty-year mantle of frustration dropped from the shoulders of its founder. Now he was able to do something for those anxious faces which had crowded in upon him during the interminable afternoon interviews with people who couldn't afford the sanitarium rates for treatment. The faces of the crippled, the blind and the deaf—those faces which seemed to think he had the answer when he was only a glorified handyman at the San—no longer would they haunt him, for the one dream of his life, to make money and then to use it for the well-being of others, had come true. As his Foundation spread the influence of its beneficence from Michigan . . . to the forty-eight states . . . to Latin America . . . to the United Kingdom, he became the more convinced that the greatest investment he had ever made was in this investment in people.

Great as was Mr. Kellogg's interest in Foundation activities, more outwardly manifested was his innate characteristic of self-effacement. He would come to the meetings of the trustees, stay a short while and then excuse himself, often via a rather artificial device of pulling out his watch and saying, "Well, gentlemen, you will pardon me. It is a quarter to twelve, and I think I had better be going." Always willing to "bet on the man," he had complete trust in his staff and his trustees and, if left entirely to his own choice, probably would not have wanted to be a trustee of the Foundation.

"There was nothing dictatorial in his attitude toward the Foundation," recalls a long-time trustee. "We would go to him with ideas as a matter of courtesy and to seek his valued counsel, but he had not asked for this consultation and was not interested in the details. He had told the head of the Foundation, 'I don't want to restrict you in any way. Use the money as you please so long as it promotes the health, happiness and well-being of children. I want to see what you fellows are going to do with this fund while I'm alive.'"

Kellogg strenuously avoided any publicity in connection with his private benefactions and desired none for the Foundation. He felt that he was sufficiently before the public in connection with the industrial enterprise he headed. The occurrence of his name upon certain schools and other institutions to the construction of which the Foundation had contributed must be regarded more as testimony to the gratitude of the recipients of the aid than as any indication of his wishes. Indeed, the practicability of removing his name from these edifices was a topic that he could be counted upon to raise at least annually with the administration of the Foundation.

As late as the year of his death, he was urging upon his advisors the desirability of eliminating his name from the title of the Foundation itself. When convinced that the institution should carry the Kellogg name, he modified his argument to suggest the elimination from the name of his initials, thus making the label less personal. "The only way I could stave off this suggestion," recalls the institution's president, "was to tell Mr. Kellogg that to take the initials from the name of the Foundation would be to leave the public in wonderment as to which Kellogg (W. K. or John Harvey) was back of the Foundation."

Increasingly Mr. Kellogg was happy over his choices of the men who ran the Foundation during his lifetime. He appreciated that the course of the activities was in line with the original purposes. Only now and then, when some of the modern methods of implementing the programs conflicted with his ideas of thrift, would he venture a mild query or statement —"Why is it necessary to use the long distance telephone to give away money?" . . . "That certainly was a high telephone and telegraph bill for the month of May."

Kellogg's personal philanthropies, which he continued, sometimes caused complications within the accounting system of the institution. In several instances, he made gifts to the Foundation and later, forgetting that he had made such gifts, turned around and gave all or part to some other organization. As an illustration, the Dunedin, Florida, estate was given by him to his philanthropic organization. Later, the president of the Foundation learned that Mr. Kellogg had made a gift of the pipe organ from this estate to a Battle Creek hospital and, hurriedly, he had to get in touch with the donor to explain that the organ was listed on the Foundation books as an asset and that foundation assets are strictly accounted for to the public and to various governmental agencies. Kellogg took out his pen and his checkbook when he was told, "I'm afraid you will have to pay us for that organ."

Another time the industrialist-philanthropist made gifts of some fine Arabian horses (worth several thousand dollars each) to three of his friends in Battle Creek. Since these horses had become the property of the United States Army through a transaction earlier described, there were complications galore and once again Mr. Kellogg was in the position of having to write a check to cover his gift of something to which he thought he had clear title. He made no comment as he wrote this latter check, but in his only partly hidden irritation was likely some chagrin at his failure to remember that he had previously given the horses away.

Although Kellogg held aloof from the day-to-day work of the Foundation, his general conception of what a philanthropic enterprise should be and how one ought to function unquestionably made itself felt. As much as anyone, he was responsible for the circumstance that, although the formative years of the Foundation coincided with the Great Depression of the '30s, when the need for charity was acute, the organization has sought to achieve its aims primarily through educational means rather than through direct-service functions.

As the founder reasoned, direct relief was becoming primarily a function of government, and already in existence were funds in a wide variety of fields to promote research. Therefore, he believed that his Foundation could best serve its purposes by trying to develop practical and democratic ways in which to *apply* the knowledge that already had been gained through research in public health, education, sanitation and other fields. To him it was practical that the educational approach was being emphasized by his organization:

"Relief, raiment and shelter are necessary for destitute children, but the greatest good for the greatest number can come only through the education of the child, the parent, the teacher, the family physician, the dentist, and the community in general. Education offers the greatest opportunity for really improving one generation over another."

His interest was in children and particularly those who came from the less privileged rural areas. In his own particular background, he had fought at odds and regardless of the advantages that other contemporaries had enjoyed. This had led him to believe that paternalism in philanthropy was not necessary, that it would be a mistake to hand out money promiscuously, but rather that he should encourage individual initiative and group action by helping people to help themselves. There was no thought in the mind of W. K. Kellogg or his Foundation of dictating to any group how it should take action but rather to engender a spirit and desire on the part of people to reshape their own lives. Thus the resources of a community were increased through intelligent leadership and the aid to and persuasion of a latent group of community leaders to come forward to carry on their own shoulders health, educational and cultural programs.

Kellogg did not believe in indiscriminate charity as a means of abating the evils of poverty. Alleviation of distress by gift or dole, he believed, tended to defeat the effort to confer permanent betterment. The answer to the problem of mitigating misery was to equip potential victims with the means intelligently to combat it . . . education and enlightenment imparted humanely, comprehensively and in a kindly spirit and manner. W. K. Kellogg had an idea that his conception could be worked out in practical form. It would be a colossal task, but it could be done.

2.

At the age of seventy when most men are ready to call it quits and totter feebly into inactivity, W. K. Kellogg began a "third life," twenty-one years in which he was to see his Foundation strive to bring "the greatest good to the greatest number." He was to aid in attacking a problem that called for greater and more constant effort and a higher concentration of faculties than anything which had previously confronted him. Could a demonstrable example of the enjoyment and productiveness of a better-ordered design for living find popular acceptance, where precept alone probably would fail? If people observe that teamwork for better communities results in tangible and understandable advantages, will they follow their own leaders to evolve a plan distinctive and practical for their community?

Perhaps it was the magnitude of the idea which caused this "man in a hurry" to be content that his new Foundation was taking its time in evolving plans for the optimum use of its funds. During its first two years, the Foundation concentrated on a study of the activities of other large foundations and endowments. In the first twelve months, Mr. Kellogg's mail contained pleas for aid of various kinds which would have meant

an expenditure of more than $37,000,000. Most of these re-
quests were courteously declined, for the trustees and Mr.
Kellogg were studying a basic question: In what direction
should it invest its time, its money and its talents? Gradually
their study confirmed an earlier belief that the Foundation's
initial major efforts should be to assist certain nearby communities to become a laboratory in applied social welfare. Then
any sound methods developed could be taken over by other
groups and put to work in other communities, perhaps all over
the world.

In their two-year study of practical philanthropy, these
trustee-students came to agreement with a prevailing premise
that "Funds committed to a foundation's stewardship are part
of the risk capital of society. Foundations can well be risk-
takers on man's cultural and intellectual and humanitarian
frontiers." They respected the belief of a leading foundation
that:

"Foundations are always on the alert for leadership—men
and women (or communities) a step or two ahead in their
comprehension of the complexities of the contemporary scene.
Many of these people, through fertile mind and ideas, do not
always have access to the means for their accomplishments.
Such people seldom double as their own business managers.
A foundation can serve as the catalytic agent to assist these
people in their great work."

The study by the trustees confirmed the view of Kellogg
that the role of the philanthropic foundation in our free society was not as a source of funds for traditional charitable
purposes. The Foundation should be an instrument of social
progress rather than of social amelioration and with its "risk
capital" or "seed money" should assume the risks of pioneer
enterprises which, because of their experimental character,
might prove an unwarranted burden upon the regular administrative budgets of sponsoring institutions or communities. Thus
foundations can be in a position to make vital contributions

to the advancement of education, the arts, and many other aspects of human culture and welfare.

With the practical W. K. Kellogg as counsel, it seemed a logical conclusion that his Foundation would highlight practicality—not synopses of ideas which would bind beautifully and then be put upon a shelf to gather dust, but assistance to community leaders who would get ideas into action, who would seek the application of known and evolving ideas. W. K. wanted action and building, steamshovels working, the construction of clinics, schoolhouses, hospitals. In more abstract areas, he approved the premium placed by the trustees on assistance which would inspire people to seek more education, technological aids, and the advice of authorities so that their communities might become models of what the average man can do to enrich his own life and that of his fellow-townsmen. If communities could work out solutions to some of their own problems, then in that process, patterns and techniques doubtless would be developed to assist other people and communities.

The Foundation, as an expression of the ultimate practicality of its founder, confined its operations during the first twelve years of its existence to programs largely local or regional within the State of Michigan.

By 1935, a novel, dynamic and practical idea was evolving for the betterment of many communities of southwestern Michigan, an idea which, aided by direct action and Foundation financial assistance, was eventually to affect the lives of people in seven counties. Mr. Kellogg was pleased by this prospect and he expressed his pleasure in a breathtaking personal action. Up until this year, he had not made his major assets available to the Foundation. Instead he had requested the trustees to make recommendations and then provided sufficient funds to support the approved projects. However, he now believed his philanthropic organization was definitely on the right track. Therefore, betting on the men who were implementing his stewardship, he dissolved many of his previous trusts to

create a master trust, the W. K. Kellogg Foundation Trust,
No. 5315.

Through this new trust, Mr. Kellogg initially gave the Foundation a large portion of his holdings in the Kellogg Company.
Almost simultaneously he conveyed to the Foundation other
assets held by him. He added to this fund in later years until,
eventually of Mr. Kellogg's 60 per cent interest in the Kellogg
Company, he retained only 2½ per cent and the Foundation
the remaining 57½ per cent. Today, under this trust, the W. K.
Kellogg Foundation owns 51 per cent of the common stock of
the Kellogg Company and each year it is the intent of the
Foundation to disburse for philanthropic purposes all of its
income. This means that, through the Foundation, the Kellogg
Company is one of the few major American industries with
more than half the stock dividends paid going to charitable
activities.

The Foundation, with irrevocable rights to the bulk of its
founder's assets, was "really set up in the business of giving."
The organization's assets in 1935 totaled $35,000,000 and were
later increased by supplemental gifts to $47,000,000. Largely
through the appreciation of its holdings of the company stock
but also through sagacious investments, the Foundation now
has assets totaling approximately $120,000,000 . . . this despite
the fact that since 1930 it has given away about $50,000,000 and
that in nine of the last fourteen years, the gifts of the Foundation have exceeded its income.

3.

When the Foundation trustees had finished their preliminary
review of the activities of other organizations in the philanthropic field, they were ready for an important next step.
Proceeding on the principle that problem solving should begin
at home, they then studied the rural area around Battle Creek.
This study pointed out in dramatic fashion the wide discrepancy existing between what was known and what was prac-

ticed in the fields of health, education, welfare and recreation.

They found in the Battle Creek area, seven counties of southwestern Michigan, typically rural communities which possessed a little better than average economic resources. Yet in this time of the early 1930's, health programs were practically nonexistent, many schools were neglected and inadequate, and community facilities, such as hospitals and libraries, were often either absent or of poor quality. "In these respects the situation was no different from that to be found in thousands of other communities throughout the United States. The dis-

A nucleus of intelligent leadership made possible the organization of many groups with the common purpose of community betterment.

tressing thing was that no better use was being made of the opportunities afforded by the American system to provide really adequate answers to these challenging community needs."

In these counties, which had agriculture as their basic economy, were many intelligent, hardworking citizens eager to make their communities better places in which to live. The towns had an average number of practicing physicians and dentists. There were in existence some medical societies, loosely organized associations of school leaders, here and there a civic club or small Chamber of Commerce. Could these become nuclei for the intelligent leadership to organize all groups within the community for the common purpose of community betterment? The Foundation was willing to back with several millions of dollars its conviction that local leadership could be stimulated to develop effective methods to advance the cause of child health, education and welfare over many fronts.

The area, with its population of two hundred and eighty thousand, was conceived of as a gigantic laboratory and a demonstration or teaching center and the experiment became known as the Michigan Community Health Project. Special instruction was made available not only for professional workers but for leaders of practically every economic and social stratum of the communities. Foundation funds, aggregating more than $8,000,000 in the decade of greatest activity, made possible the subsidization of county health departments, medical and dental services for children, the promotion of community organization, the development of local libraries, the improvement and construction of hospitals and schools. In the area, the Kellogg fortune built three camps for underprivileged children, participated in the construction of thirteen consolidated schools, health centers, swimming pools and park playgrounds.

As the *Detroit Times* reported on its observations of the experiment:

"Every service is designed to bring to the communities of the seven counties, through their leaders, the best of current thought in order that those directly concerned with the problems can work out their own answers. Out of the area flows a continuous stream of physicians, dentists, nurses, teachers and ministers to colleges and universities for intensive, short postgraduate courses, especially designed and subsidized by the Foundation to insure better service to children. Fellowships meeting the cost of travel and instruction are offered by the Foundation to all who apply.

"To Detroit, Chicago and other educational centers are sent by the Foundation such diverse groups as school directors, township supervisors, educators, social workers, country editors, laboratory technicians, veterinarians, school janitors, parents, chiefs of police, local health officers, food handlers and probate judges.

"Into the area each year the Foundation sends undergraduate and recently graduated college students specializing in rural health administration, nursing, engineering and education. Possessed of the theory as taught in various institutions of the nation, the youngsters are assigned to the agencies operating in the seven counties that they may obtain actual field experience."

With the major objective of education, the Michigan Community Health Project imbued this rural community of more than a quarter-million people with a determination to maintain county health units and a supplementary health program of preventive medicine and dentistry. The building of strategically located consolidated schools and aids to the improvement of rural education proved a stimulating precept to the region which, at the onset of the project, had approximately eight hundred one-room schools. Approximately $1,000,000, with the Foundation providing three-quarters and the school patrons one-quarter, was used to renovate and modernize these schools. Scholarships and fellowships improved the quality of instruction within the schools. Advances were made in the safeguarding of food, water and milk supplies, in the care of expectant mothers, in the control of communicable diseases, and in equally important areas such as mental hygiene, character training and organized recreation.

In small, sometimes spectacular ways, unspectacular men, women and children demonstrated the large truth that, when ancient jealousies are buried, old town lines ignored and people begin to work together, democracy is quickened, and a new and evolving design for living can be forged on the anvil of good will. The indications were as subtle as a community picnic, as recognizable as a consolidated school, as indirect as the buying of craft products from another township. Community and intercommunity programs were made possible by an effective combination of scientific knowledge and cooperative teamwork under the democratic system.

The acceptance of the program by citizens in the seven counties was demonstrated in 1938 when voters, in response to a poll taken by the Foundation, indicated by a vote of 65,329 to 863 their willingness to tax themselves toward the support of important phases of the program after the termination of the Foundation grants.

Looking back over its first eleven years, the Foundation reported in 1941 that "many of the projects aided by the Foundation have assisted the people of numerous localities in working out practical solutions for many community problems. In all of our work we have in mind the possibility of utilizing our experience as a means of assisting other communities throughout the country in their efforts at self-improvement."

Thus in this typical rural area, where a policy of patronage would inevitably have failed, a program based upon citizen participation and cooperation made marked changes in the life of the communities. The MCHP for more than a decade was a dynamic movement, novel for its time and perhaps even now. Many social benefits accrued and perhaps some of the experiments affected the evolution of health and educational ideas in the nation. Only a study akin to the Lynds' *Middletown* could assess the full value of the MCHP and the relative permanency of the improvements achieved, but this center of the Foundation's activity during its first twelve years undoubtedly was an exemplification of its founder's philosophy of helping people to help themselves. Too, it was an expression of the practicality of W. K. Kellogg, highlighting immediate

The Foundation's Clear Lake Camp School accommodated fifty children in winter and one hundred and sixty-five in cabins in the summer. Two additional camps were similar in capacity and purpose.

The dining hall at Clear Lake Camp. *(Photos by W. R. French.)*

action to hurdle obstacles and to make needed improvements.

To say that W. K. was intrigued by the MCHP would be an understatement. Since he maintained an office in the Foundation's headquarters at Battle Creek, he attended some of the many meetings with citizen leaders to evaluate past results and to plan future improvements. He had long believed that

[319]

the "forgotten child" of America was not exclusively in the slum areas of cities but also in the rural areas where sociological and technological improvements were slow to penetrate. Therefore, he took particular pleasure in the amplified medical and dental care made possible for all children of the counties,

The children involved in the camping program took a particular interest in crafts classes.

Even energy-full boys need an hour of relaxation in the course of a busy day at camp.

(Photos by W. R. French.)

and in the camps which were constructed on lakes not far from Battle Creek.

Starting as summer camps, they were made year-round in nature for the benefit of many children who had been affected by the slowly receding economic depression. The health departments of the counties were concerned with the diet of a number of the farm children. There were recommendations made by physicians and nurses that farm and town youngsters have the benefit of a three to nine months stay at the lakes. Soon there was a flow of children to the camps, girls and boys from the ages of seven to sixteen, largely but not altogether from lower economic strata. The only proviso of the Foundation was that the welfare department of each county help with the improvement of the home environment so that, after the advantages applied by the camp, the child would not return to a greatly lessened standard of living.

During their camping sojourns, the children partook of wholesome meals. There was attention given to the development of good leadership and educational programs. Medical care, the services of nutrition specialists, and even of a camp psychologist, were coupled with a recreational program to develop strong, healthy children. "When the youngsters went home, some of them were so changed their parents didn't recognize them. They were changed physically, thirty or forty pounds heavier."

The camping represented only a small part of the seven-county teamwork to improve community life but Kellogg enjoyed visiting the camps, partly because his grandson Kenneth stayed for quite some time at one of them. His delight in what has been termed "the start of outdoor education within the United States" far overshadowed the irritation of one visit when he observed several cartons of a competing brand of corn flakes at the kitchen door of one of the camps.

Mr. Kellogg was a host to ex-President Herbert Hoover and Dr. Ray Lyman Wilbur in 1936 when the two distinguished visitors made a tour of the seven-county MCHP area. Later the following letter was received from Mr. Hoover:

"I want to express my appreciation of the opportunity which you gave me to visit the work of the Kellogg Foundation. You have established one of the greatest agencies for good in the United States that we have seen in our history. The men whom you have brought around it are approaching the problem with intelligence and common sense, and it fills me with complete enthusiasm and hope."

4.

After World War II, during which the Foundation temporarily revised its program to direct a large part of its resources to the war effort, the organization shifted its subsequent operations from the direct action of the MCHP to assistance primarily financial in nature to institutions, communities and individuals. While there was this change in the character of the assistance, the underlying purpose of the aid remained constant.

In the community and its people lies the faith of the Foundation, not in programs or systems but in the fundamental

Library days throughout the seven-county MCHP area celebrated the collection of 900,000 outworn, dog-eared books. Foundation grants provided one new book to libraries for every five volumes turned in.

yearning of the human being for self-improvement. W. K. Kellogg truly believed that within the people rests the initiative to improve their everyday surroundings and their community resources so that children and adults can live in healthier, more enlightened communities. Through the years, the yardstick applied by the Foundation to any request for assistance has been: What will the project or program do for the people?

Within the community are resources that shape opportunities for the improvement of family and community life—the school, the hospital, the library, the university, the playground or summer camp—but local leaders must be developed to help to bring from these resources the greatest good to the people. In this struggle for self-improvement, to shape a better future, lies the ultimate interest of the Foundation. With time, the philanthropic operations expanded to the entire nation and then beyond national borders, yet the approach of the Foundation remained as before. This was a continuance of the effort to aid people to use existing resources within the community and to provide facilities for the development of local leadership so that from these resources can come optimum benefits. With his talent for the succinct, W. K. Kellogg expressed this philosophy in a single sentence: "We will help people to help themselves."

In a continued adherence to the educative approach, the Foundation sought to secure better medical care for the people and improved leadership within the public schools, through fellowships to individuals and through subsidies with an aim of improving the levels of professional education at the great centers of learning. Thus the physician, the dentist, the hospital administrator, the nurse, the school superintendent and teacher had opportunity to keep abreast of contemporary ideas and new developments in their particular fields. This enabled them to improve their services to adults and children.

W. K. Kellogg recalled stories related by his mother of the inadequate medical care for the family in the pioneer days.

He remembered the teacher who had mistaken his nearsightedness for "dim-wittedness." So this trend of Foundation assistance had his enthusiastic approval.

Throughout its first quarter-century, the Foundation has preferred to lend its assistance first to agencies which are gaining preliminary experience and doing testing at a local level. Then if the success of such testing is significant and there is need for further expansion, the institution entertains requests for assistance to programs on a larger scale. For example, the people of Kalamazoo County, Michigan, desired to take action to reduce the number of deaths and injuries occurring from accidents in their homes. After three years of experimentation, with assistance from the Foundation, the accomplishments appeared to be of real significance. Subsequently, similar grants were made to three other local health departments and currently the state departments of health in California, Georgia, Kansas, Kentucky, Massachusetts, Maryland, North Carolina, and Oregon are being assisted in an expansion of the experiment to make the home a safer place for people.

Assistance to the improvement of the administration of hospitals was also premised upon the idea of preliminary experience and testing done at the local level. During the Michigan Community Health Project, the validity of this premise was graphically demonstrated. The communities in the seven counties of southwestern Michigan had only limited resources. If they were to have hospitals and health centers, the administration of these institutions had to be excellent, for there were not sufficient local finances to pay deficits incurred through wastage or mismanagement. Additional education opportunities were given to the administrators placed over the hospitals and health centers in the counties. Later programs for education in hospital administration were expanded to a nationwide basis and placed under the auspices of several universities. To meet the ever-increasing need for trained hospital administrators, seventeen additional programs have been established,

Grants from the Foundation and the PWA aided the City of
Allegan, Michigan, to build a well-equipped 40-bed hospital.

of which the Foundation has assisted eight, including five in
the United States, one in Canada, and two in South America.

Better schools for the seven counties of the MCHP were
made possible through opportunities given public school administrators and teachers for advanced education and special
training. This idea, tested and found valid in the local area,
eventually was to find great amplification in a nationwide
Cooperative Program in Educational Administration. Leaders
in education conferred with the Foundation and for two years
studied the possibilities of a program to reach nearly every
school administrator in the forty-eight states. The CPEA was
launched in 1950 and since that time the Foundation has
appropriated approximately $5,250,000 to assist the better-
ment of the public schools through the improvement of school
administration. Subsequently, a similar program was assisted
in Canada.

W. K. Kellogg was in full accord with the idea of the testing
of "ventures in miniature" before their expansion to a greater
area. However, he who had been "Mr. Average Man" up to
age forty-six, was beginning to have some reservations which
he did not voice until a similar thought was expressed by
Dr. Emory W. Morris, President and General Director of the
Foundation. Dr. Morris told Mr. Kellogg that in his opinion
the Foundation was becoming too exclusively identified with
the professional fields. The General Director wondered why
programs for the education and betterment of the farmer, the

TENTATIVE PLANNING

EXPLORATORY TRIPS

IDENTIFICATION OF
MAJOR PROBLEMS

PLANNING CONFERENCES
• MAJOR PROBLEMS
• STUDY PLANS
• IDENTIFICATION AND
  USE OF RESOURCES

The purpose of the Cooperative Program in Educational Administration is to improve leadership in the public schools. Educators believe this can best be accomplished by analysis of school problems and evaluation of the educational needs of administrators, followed by a redesigning of preservice and inservice programs to meet these needs. Since this far-reaching movement started in 1950, forty-five state departments of public education and in excess of 140 colleges and universities are involving thousands of schools and administrators in this self-help educational endeavor

STUDY AND ACTION

DISTRICT ORGANIZATION · FINANCE · INSTRUCTION · SCHOOL BOARDS · CONSULTANT SERVICES · POLICY MAKING AND INTERPRETATION

DISSEMINATION OF FINDINGS AND ACTION

ADMINISTRATOR'S NOTE BOOK · CONFERENCES AND WORKSHOPS · REPORTS AND ARTICLES

IMPROVED PROGRAMS OF PREPARATION
IMPROVED IN-SERVICE EDUCATION PROGRAMS
IMPROVED CONDITIONS AFFECTING ADMINISTRATION

garageman, the man who owns a small store, could not be developed.

"That expresses exactly an idea which has been recurring to me," said W. K., and, subsequently, the Foundation granted nearly $1,500,000 for the construction of a center for continuing education on the campus of Michigan State University at East Lansing. The program, later given additional assistance, was premised on a belief that the desire and need of people to learn continues long after the ending of formal education in high school or college. W. K. Kellogg knew that he personally had held such a desire for additional education, and he now took particular pleasure that the new center provided short courses for the average man and would annually afford continuing education sessions for hundreds of professional, trade and agricultural groups. (In later years, the Foundation subsidized a similar center for continuing education at the University of Georgia and a college of practical and cultural education north of Dublin for the thousands of members of the Irish Countrywomen's Association.)

Until a few weeks before his death, W. K. Kellogg kept regular office hours at the Foundation during that part of each year when the rigorous Michigan winter did not induce him to seek a more hospitable climate. All who knew him in his later years had a vivid impression of the vigor of his mind, the clearness of his recollections, the wide range of his interests, and the readiness and cogency with which his judgment of men and things were formed.

Perhaps his world travels kept W. K. Kellogg from the provincial attitude toward which many of us incline. Much as he had always loved Michigan (and his largesse was great to his native state), he saw the eventual scope of the Foundation properly to be far beyond the state's borders. Therefore, he was glad when the Foundation's philanthropy began to take on a national pattern and, later, to be reflected in the provinces of Canada. After World War II, he applauded a decision of

(*Michigan picture by Department of Information Services, Michigan State University. Irish picture by G. A. Duncan, Dublin.*)

the trustees to expand the activities to include the entire Western Hemisphere. He agreed with his staff that the welfare of the entire hemisphere was extremely important to the security not only of our own nation but also that of the world.

Kellogg's international outlook found an expression in his Foundation's efforts to assist professional education in the health specialties within several nations of Latin America. Fellowships for study in the United States had been granted to nationals of other countries since 1937, but the years of the last decade have seen accelerated assistance for programs to further international professional education. During each year of the decade approximately one hundred Latin American fellows have been brought to the United States for medical, dental and nursing study. This phase of the assistance creates dividends of inter-American understanding in addition to the contribution toward the development of professional leaders in many countries.

Basic to much of this aid has been an objective to enable Latin American universities eventually to prepare their own personnel for educational and administrative positions, gradually lessening the need for staff members to go to the United States or elsewhere for preparation. Through the fellowships, funds for laboratory equipment and library facilities, subsidies for some salaries or other items of the operating budget in the more than thirty institutions being aided, Latin American professional leaders are obtaining additional education which will enable them to impart information to the generations of youth who will study in the professional schools of our neighbors to the south.

W. K. Kellogg believed that the self-help principle was the only valid means for improving the quantity and quality of

W. K. Kellogg believed that the desire and need of people to learn continue long after the ending of their formal education. He, therefore, took particular pleasure in the grant of his Foundation to establish the continuing education center at Michigan State University (top). Undoubtedly he would have gained equal joy from later grants made for a similar purpose at the University of Georgia and for the Irish Countrywomen's Association. The later centers are shown respectively at center and at bottom.

health services in Latin America. It is a safe supposition that he would have approved the same principle used by the Foundation to aid the agricultural development in the hemisphere. In 1953, two years after Mr. Kellogg's death, the Foundation created a new division to study and assist in the important area of agriculture. This seemed a logical extension of activities, for the problems of feeding the world were always of great interest to Will Kellogg. The raw materials for the products he manufactured, of course, come from agriculture. He

In the long-range development of any program in agriculture, it is essential that youth be involved. The Foundation's aid to European agriculture has, therefore, included commitments to expand the organizations and activities of young farmers in England, Scotland, Wales. Much like the American 4-H Clubs, these United Kingdom groups are large and very active. Here a group watches a demonstration of sheep-shearing.

(Photo by Thomas Photos, Oxford, England.)

realized the great responsibility on the shoulders of rural people for the proper nutrition of a rapidly increasing world population and, familiar with the limitation of rural resources as compared to those of urban areas, he often had discussed with Foundation officials ways in which agricultural programs and personnel might be aided.

The subsequent Foundation assistance to agriculture has centered around an educational approach to develop better farm practices and improved communications to reduce the present ten to fifteen year lag between agricultural research findings and their general application by farmers. A recent grant to two agricultural colleges of the Republic of Colombia represented the first geographical extension of the Foundation's aid to agriculture after initial activity in the United States and the United Kingdom.

"Why is the Foundation supporting activities in England, Scotland, Ireland rather than appropriating the bulk of its international gifts to aid underdeveloped nations such as Iraq, Iran, or India?" The answer to this oft-asked question lies in the Foundation's reflection of the ultimate practicality of W. K. Kellogg. Progress and development, whether technological, sociological or economical, are dependent upon the prior possession by a people of tools and resources. If a community or nation has made a promising start, say, in agriculture, then it has the nuclei of leadership, at least partially educated personnel, and some finances and accomplishments upon which to build. Contrariwise, a community or nation greatly underdeveloped lacks these factors and until a later stage must look for help primarily from developmental benefits which filter to it from the efforts of more aggressive and enlightened neighbors.

Not for W. K. Kellogg was there any narrow outlook as to the borders of his philanthropy. Nevertheless, he was a great patriot and thought increasingly in terms of the improvement of the mental and physical health of the American people, particularly the children of our land. Just the year before his death, he took an occasion to compliment his Foundation's trustees upon the aforementioned CPEA. A program of assistance for strengthening graduate and postgraduate courses in thirty-eight schools of medicine, dentistry and nursing in the United States and Canada, the subsidization of dentistry and public health courses at the University of Michigan, assistance to a practical nurse training program in the South—these are but a few of the focal points of Foundation assistance which have been in accord with the belief of the founder that "Education offers the greatest opportunity for really improving one generation over another."

Mr. Kellogg's vision was a concern to him and to his friends

Oregon public health nurses visit glaucoma patients to aid in understanding of the disease and the importance of continued medical treatment in the preservation of vision.

(Oregon State Board of Health.)

for many years and for the last decade of his life he was blind —as shall be related in the next and last chapter of this biography. W. K. seldom talked of his blindness and never complained of the affliction. Once, however, in the privacy of the office of a physician in Battle Creek, he voiced a longing which must have been ever with him. He said to the doctor, "I would give all my money just to see the sun and the green grass again."

In his search for relief from his progressively worsening visual difficulties, he characteristically thought of others similarly handicapped, and his personal contributions toward sightsaving and aid for the blind started as far back as 1927. He made many such contributions to the American Foundation for the Blind, American Printing House for the Blind, Path Finder Guide Dogs, Inc., Seeing Eye, Inc., the Braille Institute of America, Inc., and the National Society for the Prevention of Blindness. He was one of the original contributors to the "Talking Digest" project for the blind and, as previously related, financed a research into the causes of glaucoma.

This, of course, explains the Foundation's special interest in the problems of the blind and the partially sighted. The Foundation presently is aiding the state health departments of Oregon and Mississippi to determine their roles in sight conservation, is collaborating with other agencies in Braille printing projects in Brazil and Mexico, has established an endowment for glaucoma research at the Johns Hopkins University Hospital, and since 1948 has assisted the Franklin Institute of Philadelphia in the development of sensory aids for the blind.

Since the W. K. Kellogg Foundation was established in 1930, it has assisted more than 1,500 projects and programs on three continents of the world. Nearly $50,000,000 have been appropriated for these activities and in recent years the annual program expenditures have approximated $4,000,000. Currently Foundation grants are made through its seven divisions: Agriculture, Dentistry, Education, Hospitals, Medicine and Public Health, Nursing, and Latin American. Approximately a thousand requests for assistance are annually reviewed by the Foundation's staff which has general guidance through the judgments of national advisory committees made up of eminent figures in the respective fields.

With headquarters in Battle Creek's The Inn, an apartment house built by Mr. Kellogg and his legal address throughout his last quarter-century, a staff of approximately forty persons devotes full time to the Foundation's philanthropic activities. Many of the professional and administrative personnel knew Mr. Kellogg personally. These veterans freely testify to the inspiration that he gave to the work of the Foundation and to the philosophy derived from association with him during the twenty-one years that he survived to observe and guide the accomplishments of the organization.

The spirit underlying the Foundation may be judged by an observation of the writer at the time the manuscript of this biography was nearing completion. It was noted that celebration of the organization's twenty-fifth birthday in June of 1955 was chiefly observed by the "forward look" always advocated to his company and Foundation by W. K. Kellogg. Through a series of staff meetings, projected advisory committee sessions, and discussions of the staff with persons eminent in educational, health and agricultural fields, an earnest effort was being made to determine "Where should the Foundation go from here? What should be its main endeavors? In the organization's next quarter-century, what would constitute the truest stewardship of the money left by Mr. Kellogg for 'the promotion of the health, education and welfare of mankind'?"

The Foundation's observance of the first quarter-century of accomplishment by immediate steps to survey its future activities doubtless would have had the full approval of the forward-looking W. K. Kellogg.

5.

Once in a great while would be revealed the *alter ego* which underlay Mr. Kellogg's taciturnity. When the Foundation trustees decided to give to Michigan State University the funds to build its continuing education center, W. K. directed his driver to take him from this Board meeting to the experimental farm near Gull Lake. With steps as fast as his blindness would permit, he made his way along the sidewalk to the farm offices and greeted the farm superintendent with, "Mac, I can't tell you just what now, but we have just done an awful nice thing for your alma mater." He gave no amplification but was so obviously pleased with the appropriation that he wanted to tell Mr. McCrary before anyone else could, even though he could not ethically give any details of the decision.

Perhaps one seldom could glimpse such almost juvenile eagerness in W. K. Kellogg, but the fighter in him was readily evident. When a ruling by the Collector of Internal Revenue at Washington claimed that the Foundation did not qualify as a charitable organization, W. K. was right back of his attorneys who filed voluminous exhibits in the appeal from the Collector's ruling. He took a personal interest in the assembling of evidence which, even at an early stage in the Foundation's development, showed that the philanthropic enterprises were many and aggregated a considerable amount of money. And when the Treasury Department, after reviewing the evidence, completely upheld the Foundation, his was the exultation of a successful battler.

Another side of the man was revealed in a happening recently described by a trustee of the Foundation:

"I had been asked to give a talk to the Florida Public Health Association which was meeting in St. Petersburg. Knowing that Mr. and Mrs. Kellogg had rented a residence in that city, I dropped by to visit the couple. Telling Mr. Kellogg the main reason for my being in Florida, I found that I would have to exercise a great deal of persuasion if I were to get him to come to the meeting scheduled for that evening. He knew that my talk and a number of picture slides had some reference to the Kellogg Foundation and its activities and therefore he believed that he in modesty could not be present. I finally gained a compromise by promising him that he could sit in the very last row of the auditorium and that no mention would be made to anyone that he was in the audience. So my speech, which had considerable reference to W. K. and his Foundation, was made and no one in that audience ever knew that he was in Florida, let alone right there in the last row of the auditorium. The public health people would have been delighted to know that he was present, but his desire for anonymity prevailed."

W. K. Kellogg shunned the limelight and never would sit on a stage. Here a candid camera shot catches him—not in his usual rear seat in a meeting hall but, at least, comfortably lost in the crowd and out of the public gaze—during the ceremony dedicating the auditorium which he gave to the City of Battle Creek.

W. K. Kellogg

Although W. K. Kellogg forever was to know the anguish of a shy man in his contacts with the general public, there was a counterbalancing comfort in the knowledge that his chief interests, his investments in his company and in his Foundation, were on solid ground. The company and the Foundation, "his flesh and his soul," were two firm bulwarks to his peace of mind and both were sustaining comforts amid the adversities of ill health and old age.

It was in 1945, some six years before Mr. Kellogg's death, that an old friend sat with him before a radio. Somehow a radio network, the Mutual Broadcasting System, had finally persuaded the industrialist-philanthropist to allow them to broadcast a dramatized version of his life. As the story unfolded, the friend watched the countenance of this blind and aged man. The broadcast came to a climax with these words:

"Long hours of work had hurt his health . . . but his life is in the children he has made strong, healthy and happy again. He has a thousand eyes to see for him, eyes that were once doomed to darkness. He has a thousand strong, sturdy feet echoing in his ears, a thousand robust voices ringing with a laughter that was once choked up inside bodies of children malformed and afflicted. Thousands of people have taken their needed, rightful place in the world, because he helped them help themselves. . . . 'That man is great and he alone who serves a greatness not his own.' Sometimes in an old adage, we can find the meaning of a man."

The friend, closely watching, could not see much change in Kellogg's impassive countenance, but he did note a tear that coursed from the corner of one eye. And when this friend attempted to discuss the broadcast, Mr. Kellogg hurriedly changed the subject by saying, "Any success of the Foundation is due to the trustees and the staff. They had the vision. I only supplied the funds."

CHAPTER 14

"I'm Going to Keep
On Fighting"

In 1937, when Mr. Kellogg was seventy-seven years old, an examination at a Santa Barbara hospital disclosed that he had glaucoma, an increase of intraocular pressure which leads to a gradual impairment of sight and often results in blindness. It is possible that there was a hereditary cause for his eye troubles. His half-brothers, Merritt and Smith, became blind in their old age, although W. K. Kellogg was the only one who had glaucoma.

During late autumn of 1937, Kellogg wrote his friend Arch Shaw:

"I am conscious of the fact that my eyes will be worse before they are better. Probably before the operations I had in June and July, I had the beginnings of cataracts in both eyes. The operations seem to have exaggerated the condition of my right eye and with it the vision is decidedly 'off.' I am very thankful that the left eye affords me fairly good vision. I am able to read a little but not as much as formerly. Perhaps in due time corrective measures will materially improve my vision."

However, additional operations in 1940 and 1941 were of little avail and, by the end of the latter year, W. K. could barely distinguish the shapes of large objects and the rays of glaring lights. His letter of May 28, 1941, to friend Shaw advised of this condition and added:

"Please excuse this mournful report. I don't think I am licked yet. At any rate, I'm going to keep on fighting."

The years brought no decrease in the fighting spirit which W. K. Kellogg had always evidenced. Old age, the increasing losses of friends and relatives through death, augmented loneliness; these saddened but did not intimidate this man of courage. When ninety years old, he wrote a friend that "I do not feel as young as I did when I was eighteen, but I do not know that I feel any older than when I was eighty-five. I seldom take time to think about or discuss my age."

During the last nine or ten years of his life, Mr. Kellogg was totally blind. "However, I have compensation," he told his son John L., "for my general health and digestion are almost perfect, and when I get my sleep, I really feel quite well."

He adjusted remarkably to blindness. Recognizing that in his unusually long life he had possessed sight longer than most people, he was enough of a Stoic to accept the blow from fate without whimpering. Seldom did Mr. Kellogg refer to his blindness, only doing so upon occasions where people otherwise might think he was impolite or brusque. He was determined to be as independent as possible of his handicap and in a way resented any efforts to help him get about. His nurses would warn his friends, "Don't be too solicitous about him. That irritates him."

In the months just previous to the total darkness which beset him, he had practiced writing his signature with his eyes closed many, many times and, therefore, was able to sign letters and documents after blindness. A nurse recalls that "He could shave and bathe just like any unhandicapped person. All he would ask was that his shaving material be placed on the washbasin.

Famous physicist, Robert A. Millikan, a longtime friend of W. K. Kellogg, was a guest at the Palm Springs home in 1950. John L. Kellogg was also a guest when this photograph was taken.

For a man who could not see, he could get around wonderfully. In the house, he knew the walls, the hallway and the placement of the furniture. He would come outside where we would be sitting on the patio. He could dial a telephone by the touch system. The only article of clothing he could not put on was a necktie. . . . At night his German shepherd dog would take him around the living room and together they took walks around the lawn."

It will be remembered that Kellogg always had placed a premium on neatness of habit and person and, before he became totally blind, he often had said that he never would eat in public after blindness because he had seen so many blind people in the sanitarium making a spectacle of their eating. Yet W. K. Kellogg, wearing the black alpaca coat which he invariably donned for home dinners, was always a figure of immaculateness, exhibiting amazing table manners for a blind person.

In accordance with a high sense of propriety, Kellogg had decreed that his dog should not be fed at the table. However, affection conquered his conservatism and he was the most frequent violator of this rule, tossing this or that tidbit to the dog. "In fact," recalls a nurse, "almost half his food went to the dog." Of the three German shepherd dogs which Kellogg owned (discounting a fourth dog kept only a short time because he was too fast-paced for his new master) the last, Rinette, was the most affectionate. Taught to take the newspaper to her master, to lead him to his room or from this room to the dining or living room, she had only partial training as a "Seeing Eye" dog but Mr. Kellogg would not have traded her for any other.

As with most blind persons, Kellogg developed special or accentuated sensory powers. He gained a certain satisfaction in being able to guess very nearly the actual weight of his visitors from the feeling of a handshake with them and the approximation of the length of the arm extended for the handshake. Occasionally he would say to his nurse, "What time is it?" She might say, "About 6:30" and Kellogg would counter with a "No, it's 6:15." Uncannily this blind man was usually able to name the exact time of day.

A nephew recently related:

"The last time I visited my uncle was at his Gull Lake home. Elsie Hoatson, his nurse, and I went with him in his car over one of the old unimproved roads that he used to travel as a salesman many years ago. He was blind but interested in the road and still familiar with it, as he had been in former days. We marveled at the way he remembered and described the corner crossroads, the houses we passed, and the way he frequently told us exactly where we were on the road. His sense of distance was keen, his memory of scenes marvelous. Of course, his early horse and buggy trips on this road would have been of little help in judging distances in a motor car. That he must have learned on infrequent automobile trips over the road after he became blind."

Many persons particularly commented upon the fact that, in car rides between Kellogg's Gull Lake home and Battle Creek, he could quite accurately name the number of miles that had been covered at any given time during the journey.

The only long trips made by W. K. Kellogg after he was blind were the usual seasonal journeys by train between Michigan and California. He continued to enjoy automobile rides as well as the sense of motion and the breeze off the water in motorboat runs on Gull Lake.

In conversation, Mr. Kellogg had a habit of saying, "I saw Jim Smith today" and, as stated by a friend, "One would swear almost that he could see. His eyes were always open and quite expressive so that some people had the feeling that he could see even after he was totally blind."

A man long associated with W. K. Kellogg also marveled at his extrasensory capacities. He recalled a conference at which were present the Foundation head, the president and secretary of a nearby college, and himself. "Mr. Kellogg came into the room, shook hands all around, and visited with us for an hour. During that hour, he never talked to the college president unless he turned around so that he could 'see' him. He did likewise to the rest of us. How he could remember the position of the individuals in the room, I could not fathom. It is true that one who loses a sense early in life usually finds another sense or senses intensified, but he had not lost his sense of vision until late in life and the alertness that the incident portrays illustrated a quality that he had during all his years."

Upon an occasion of a later day in California, Kellogg astounded a Foundation official with his ability to sense what was going on. This official was seated with the blind and elderly man on the front seat of a car parked in front of the Palm Springs home. On the rear seat of the car sat the wife of the official. As the men talked, the woman quietly and without comment was extracting from her suit skirt the hairs shed by Kellogg's dog when it previously had sat on the same back seat. Mr. Kellogg paused in his conversation, turned his face toward the rear of the car and said, "Mary, my dog certainly is shedding, isn't it?"

Without bitterness, Mr. Kellogg took blindness as a companion for his trip into old age. He had his memories which permitted him to warm his hands at the fires of yesterday. The activities of the company and the Foundation continued to hold his interest, he wrote many letters to relatives and a few old friends, and "with the very helpful nurse, I am really getting along fairly well. I try not to look on the dark side and keep my mind occupied. A radio in the room and another by my bedside, and a talking book machine with records of standard books, I find very entertaining." Always an inveterate reader—particularly in history where his tastes ran the gamut from Gibbon's *Decline and Fall of the Roman Empire*, through the works of Arnold Toynbee and even to popularized history such as Wells' *Outline of History*—W. K. Kellogg continued to "read" via the voice of his nurse, and his comprehension of classic, as well as contemporary, events astounded his friends.

2.

To the loneliness that accompanies blindness was to be added that which resulted from the fact that Mr. Kellogg, save for his household employees, lived alone the last several years of his life. Mrs. Kellogg, after increasing high blood pressure, suffered several paralytic strokes and in this illness preferred to be at her old farm home near Fenwick, Michigan. She never entirely recovered from the strokes and died in February of 1948.

Sorrows do not often come singly, particularly to the old. A compensating joy to W. K. Kellogg for the adversities of old age was in the close father-son relationship between him and John L. Although John L. had left the company, their love for the departed John, Jr. was a bond to their renewed intimacy. W. K., as has been related, aided his son in business matters, and business and affection occasionally brought them together for visits in Chicago, Battle Creek or California.

The last month of John L. Kellogg's life was spent with his

father in California at Palm Springs. The elder had purchased an Arabian mare, Surra, as a gift for the son, and John L. spent considerable time in desert rides upon the horse. Seated in the sun on the patio of the house or around an evening fire in the living room, father and son had many talks during the month, reminiscences of company happenings or of family affairs.

Death came very suddenly to John L. Kellogg. He had gone to visit his brother Karl at Chula Vista, California, when there occurred a fatal cerebral hemorrhage. The news reached W. K. Kellogg, as a nurse was giving him a treatment. She recalls that he "just mastered himself, squared his chin and put on an armor which seemed to steel him against adversity. He quickly groped for the phone and made the necessary arrangements. If he could just have given way to his emotions, he would have been so much better off. As it was, he had no outlet. He stayed in his room all that day and the news just about killed him.

"Nevertheless, even at his advanced age, he was a master of himself and of the situation. He ordered this done, wired about that. . . . He could just take care of any complication with remarkable courage and aplomb. I never actually saw him in a weak moment."

Spartan that he always had been, W. K. Kellogg was able to hide most of the evidences of grief, but the inevitable toll of anguish was evident in an unguarded moment with a friend when he said:

"It's a pity I have lived to be so old and both John L. and John, Jr. had to go so young."

Every man can be altered by repeated blows from fate and Mr. Kellogg perceptibly aged from the moment that he learned, little more than a year later, of the death of his beloved sister, Mrs. Clara Butler. A friend recalls that day and the funeral service:

"There sat Mr. Kellogg in a wheelchair and, as always, it

was hard to tell from his expression his innermost thoughts. However, I knew that he had always carried a real love for his sister and I sensed the grievous and lonely thoughts that must be passing through the mind of a man of ninety who had just lost a most cherished relative. I walked over to Mr. Kellogg, took his hand and said to him, 'I'm sorry.' He said nothing, merely pressing my hand in recognition of my friendship and sympathy. Even in this moment of great stress, W. K. Kellogg had mastery over his emotions. No tears were flowing from his eyes and those who did not know him well might not have understood that his was a grief too deep for tears or for words."

One by one the friends of this nonagenarian had gone, and the deaths of two of his most treasured relatives had a definite psychological and physical effect upon Mr. Kellogg. Yet his iron will and his ever held belief in a just and forgiving God kept him going. In discussing the funeral sermon for his sister with the Congregationalist minister who conducted the rites, he suggested that the poem "It Was Night When the Lord Was Born" be read. The essence of the poem was that one should remember, no matter how dark and gloomy might be the present, that it was night when Jesus was born, and that succeeding days dawned more brightly. "Every man has his Gethsemane" and in his days of anguish, Will Kellogg took much solace from the philosophy of the poem.

His nurse recalls that, though he had read both the Old and New Testaments several times, often in these latter days he asked her to read to him certain favored passages from his well-worn Bible. A friend recalls Kellogg's particular admiration for that doughty fighter and Apostle, St. Paul, and particularly Paul's charge to Timothy in which he recounted that "I have fought a good fight, I have finished my course, I have kept the faith." Those stirring words had been criteria for W. K. Kellogg throughout most of his ninety years.

Likely he sensed that he had not long to live, yet he exhibited no fear of dying. Much as he loved life, he did not believe that death would bring permanent, personal annihilation. As far back as 1933, his orderly mind had caused him to face the possibility of death at any time, and in a memorandum to his associates he had given instructions for a very unpretentious obituary and, for the rites, to "Use the 23rd Psalm, the Lord's Prayer and no sermon." A supplementary memorandum stressed that "I do not want a public funeral. . . . I do not care to be written up in the paper in the manner in which Mr. ——— was. . . . I do not want any long drawn-out sermon or eulogy of any sort. . . . The expenses should not exceed $500. . . . No flowers . . . (and) . . . burial should take place at Oak Hill Cemetery after cremation."

There was loneliness in the last months of Mr. Kellogg's life. Only a few callers breached the tangible and intangible barriers at his California and Michigan homes. A Battle Creek civic leader recently recalled, "I really saw very little of Mr. Kellogg in the late years of his life and in this I know I made a mistake. I should have called upon him but I figured that he was very busy. Now I realize that he, too, was likely very lonely. The barrier that naturally arises between the wealthy and the rest of the populace had isolated him."

Mr. Kellogg's family had never felt free to drop in at his home, always first telephoning to see if their visits would be convenient. On several of his last Christmases, he was alone except for his household staff. His last Christmas evening, in 1950, was made happier by a visit from his daughter and his grandson Kenneth, two persons very precious to him.

Even though W. K. Kellogg was not able to escape the loneliness which usually accompanies old age, he did in a measure foil Father Time. His extremely well-ordered manner of living, his respect for the rules of health and the advice of his physician, preserved him remarkably. A friend, who is also an eminent doctor of medicine, recalls that "He did not look his age of ninety (although when I last saw him, a month or two before his death at ninety-one, it was apparent that he was

Rinette, Mr. Kellogg's dog-companion, helps her master celebrate his nine-tieth birthday, a day in which the local newspaper found Mr. Kellogg not looking backward but "preoccupied with the future."

(Photo by John H. Williamson, Arcadia, California.)

failing in health). Kellogg, organically, was not old even dur-ing his last sickness. He wore out from age. As an aged man, his physical equipment was better than his special senses, his eyes, of course, being the main obstacle to his pleasure in later life. His mind did not fail. There were always clarity and understanding. His personality was quite intact and consistent throughout his life. There was no period in which he failed to grasp situations. To the last, he never looked backward but was a man who looked into the future."

A West Coast company official remembers the alertness of W. K. Kellogg upon the occasion of a visit just before Mr. Kellogg left California the last time: "He was full of questions about my sales activities and had in his memory information about the number of cars of cereals shipped from the factories the previous month. For awhile he held our baby on his lap and he seemed very interested in all our children, questioning each one with regard to progress in school."

The newspaper of his home town also marveled at his alertness and forward look, for upon his ninetieth birthday, the Battle Creek *Enquirer and News* found him "preoccupied with the future" and called him the "dean of the postgraduate school of public service" in an editorial here reproduced:

ONE'S YEARS ARE MEASURED BY WHAT LIES BEFORE HIM

A man's later years, they say, are filled with memories of his earlier deeds. Life these days, therefore, must be very full for W. K. Kellogg who today has reached four score and ten years.

Ninety years of accomplishment are enough to fill even the facile mentality of the man who has made Battle Creek so much a part of the world at large. We suspect however that Mr. Kellogg has a great deal more on his mind. In fact, he would be out of character if he were not preoccupied with the future. Some men retire from the hurly-burly of the business community. Others graduate into a life of service. But Mr. Kellogg occupies a special niche in the skein of life. He is the dean of the postgraduate school of public service.

The occasion has more than a personal meaning to the community and to those who are familiar with the work of the W. K. Kellogg Foundation. This is a time for all to ponder over the way of life which has made such deeds possible. It is a time to measure living in terms of that which gives it real meaning, which makes living worthwhile and which enables a man to reach ninety years with a sense of accomplishment and keen interest in the future.

While Will Kellogg held many memories and loved, in reminiscence, once again to recreate battles of the past, he at age ninety was a warrior not willing to hang up his shield. Pausing

a moment to send a memorandum to General Manager Vanderploeg, "Thanks for sending me the old-time advertising copy;
it reminds me of the fighting days of forty years ago," he spent
most of his time thinking of the future of his Foundation and
his company. Only two weeks before his last and fatal illness,
Mr. Kellogg counseled a young executive of the company:

"Remember that in this business you have got to give it
room to grow. In developing the California plant, be sure that
you obtain enough land so the factory can expand."

During the years in which his sight was gradually worsening,
W. K. Kellogg had continued to visit the Battle Creek plant
periodically. Knowing that he resented a helping hand at his
elbow, company officials had white squares painted on each
step of the administration building so that he might negotiate
the rises more easily. After blindness overtook him, he arranged schedules for company executives to visit him at his
office in the Foundation headquarters. Thus he had continuing
and comprehensive information with regard to plant activities.
This arrangement did not wholly content him, however, and
occasionally he would visit the factory which he could not see.
To the last, the commotion of a busy office and the roar of
giant machinery were music to his ears.

Although he had attained great age, W. K. Kellogg was still
eager to try new things. Never satiated by life, his curiosity
and alert mind continued to make him a man of action, to give
him a forward look. He was not far from ninety when there
occurred the aforementioned crisis with the federal government when it threatened to dissolve the Arabian Horse Ranch
and to sell the horses. However, he leaped into action with the
energy of a much younger man and his many telephone calls
and letters to men of influence had much to do with saving
the ranch.

Only a year or two previously, he had opened his personal
purse to insure a more efficient government for his home town.
The Griffenhagen Survey, financed entirely by him, has been

credited with the solution of many vexing problems which had confronted the Battle Creek municipality.

A hand in the development of a rehabilitation center for veterans at Pine Lake . . . a substantial contribution to the work of the American Heritage Foundation . . . the financing of a film on the simple diagnostic symptoms of glaucoma so that people could recognize such symptoms and thus seek medical care . . . encouragement of his Foundation's aid to state departments of health in sight conservation programs . . . personal experimentation with tape recording, including recitations into the machine of long-remembered poems . . . these were but a few of the interests of his very late years into which he poured both money and seemingly bottomless energy.

The "What's new?" so often heard in contemporary conversations was a question voiced by W. K. Kellogg through the years. He occasionally could be sold on fads and hoaxes, so eager was he to explore the many facets of life. He was willing to gamble his personal funds on experiments that might affect the future of mankind. This was consistent with the attitude displayed by him in the previously recounted episode of aid to a cancer "cure." At that time, it will be recalled, he said, "I am not sure there is anything in this, but suppose there was and I had not supported it!"

Believing that the "black sands" of Redondo Beach, California, would make valuable pigment for paint, he spent several thousands of dollars to back his belief. That gamble proved a loss since the sands proved comparatively valueless for this purpose. Now and then, however, an apparent loss was actually only the losing of a skirmish rather than the main battle, as in the case of his exploration of the possibilities of solar heating.

Mr. Kellogg had become convinced that the harnessing of the heat of the sun, by the use of much glass on the southern exposures of residences, might effect real economies in the American heating bill. Expressing a wish that "I would like to have Frank Lloyd Wright build a modernistic house, with solar heating, on Goguac Lake for me," he never actually had the house built, but he did finance for a year or two some of the aspects of solar heating experimentation. When a practical solution appeared currently impossible, he personally reimbursed some of his friends who had invested in the project. Today, only a few years subsequent to his exploratory interest, solar heating looms as a practical possibility.

Whether it was his characteristic eagerness to try the latest of the household gadgets as they came on the market—a new thermostat which sensitively reacted to minute changes in room temperatures; the most recent development in barometers—or his stubbornly held belief that proper philanthropy was the temporary bolstering of self-help activities rather than traditional charities, these ventures were only a few of the evidences that right up to the last weeks of his life, this man of action was usually able to get things done.

Nor did he confine himself to the material side of life, for in his last winter in California he had several long discussions with Dr. Robert A. Millikan concerning the realm of the spiritual. And this manufacturer-philanthropist, who never permitted his mind to stagnate, found his ideas of the hereafter and man's eventual destiny much in accord with those of the famous physicist.

3.

On July 24, 1951, Mr. Kellogg became ill and was taken to a hospital in Battle Creek by ambulance. There for three days, he then was returned to his Gull Lake home. He had suffered considerable shock from blood transfusions but rallied and gained sufficient strength to come to his office at the Foundation headquarters during several days in August and early September. He was able to attend the funeral of his sister Clara in late August, but he was weakened by sorrow and his condition grew steadily worse in the early days of September.

Mr. C. M. McCrary, superintendent of the experimental farm which Mr. Kellogg established and later gave to Michigan State University, visited the latter in his home on Gull Lake in September:

"Though Mr. Kellogg showed signs of the illness which had kept him in the hospital up to just a few days previously, he seemed in good spirits. He was lying on a davenport in the living room and asked me to sit down. Then he told me about the blood transfusion that nearly killed him, saying, 'I thought sure I was going, Mac.' But then a wee trace of a smile came to his face and he said, 'You know, Mac, I think they gave me some Irish blood and it did not mix with my Scottish brand.' It was the only time he had ever mentioned my Irish heritage and he chuckled over his joke."

In mid-September it was necessary to return Mr. Kellogg to the hospital in Battle Creek and during the balance of this month and in early October—those fall days of Michigan which this native son thought more colorful than autumn anywhere else—he grew perceptibly weaker. W. K. Kellogg remained calm and composed during the last days of his life. Each night he would repeat the Lord's Prayer, sometimes alone, sometimes with his nurses. As he had met most of life's challenges, he faced the challenge of death with courage. Other than a quiet remark to Nurse Hoatson, "It won't be long now," he ignored the imminence of his departure from life.

At his bedside during the last hours were his daughter Beth, his nurse, and his chauffeur. Although he recognized his daughter and undoubtedly was comforted by her presence, he was too weak to talk. Very quietly, in midafternoon of October 6, 1951, Mr. Kellogg died.

Gone was this son of the Puritans, a fighter who would give no quarter, yet a man who overrode his own troubles to ease the lives of untold thousands in three continents of the world. Gone, too, was a clean redolence of the past, of a vanishing age in which the demands of conscience and unswerving rectitude were prized above all else. W. K. Kellogg's ashes were buried in Oak Hill Cemetery in his beloved home town. But his spirit remains, an inextricable part of the American tradition of self-reliance and its corollary, a helping hand to those who temporarily are in need of assistance.

The flags in Battle Creek were lowered to half-mast and hundreds of telegrams and messages of condolence were received at the offices of the company and the Foundation. They were messages from people of all walks of life and of all creeds and colors. Leaders throughout the nation, and humble persons who had known Mr. Kellogg's generosity and counsel, expressed their sorrow at his passing. Perhaps there was a summation of the thoughts of all who mourned him in the words of the minister who presided at the last rites:

"In looking around for a monument for Mr. Kellogg, some will see the many buildings that pay tribute to his name and genius: factories the world over, hospitals, schools and churches that he helped. Others will point to his Foundation and similar groups through which his beneficences were performed. But I would point to the numberless men and women, boys and girls, whose lives are enhanced by this man who made the most of his opportunity and, in turn, improved the opportunities for countless people."

In Grateful Acknowledgment

W<small>HEN IT WAS</small> made known that this biography of W. K. Kellogg was to be written, his friends and relatives from many parts of the world responded. Many sent in numerous pages of reminiscence written laboriously in longhand. Nearly a hundred granted a half-day to several days for interviews. Entries from old diaries were received as well as pictures from many sources. Along with the recollections of scores of persons who had been aided one way or another by Mr. Kellogg, there came expressions of affection and respect for the subject of this biography.

Fortunately for this book, Mr. Kellogg corroborated his traits of efficiency and orderliness by retaining in neat files much of the significant correspondence of his long life. Many letters and memoranda thus preserved were particularly valuable as source material. The fact that he had many portraits taken during his ninety years, a paradox when his innate modesty is considered, made easier and richer the illustration of the book.

All important facts and quotations used in the biography have been authenticated and complete documentation is in the possession of the author. Grateful acknowledgment is hereby made by the author to the several scores of persons who devoted many hours, much thought and labor, to the research which preceded the actual writing of the manuscript. A particular bow is due Mrs. Bessie Young, Mr. Kellogg's secretary. During the year consumed in the creation of this book, she was cooperative far beyond the call of duty, and her recollections and her counsel were bulwarks to the authenticity of the character portrayal. Valuable and continuing help was similarly received from Mrs. Norman Williamson, Sr. (the "Beth" of the biography and daughter of the subject), Mrs. Elsie Hoatson Elbon, nurse to Mr. Kellogg for many years, and from Mrs. W. Rupert French, Mr. Kellogg's niece who, in addition to her recollections, contributed many photographs taken by her late husband, a Battle Creek photographer.

The reminiscences of Mr. Arch Shaw were valuable not only in the delineation of Mr. Kellogg's business career but also in the shaping of those portions of the book relating to the activities of the biographical subject in the fields of philanthropy, economics, politics and governmental affairs. Dr. Emory W. Morris and Mr. W. H. Vanderploeg, heading respectively the W. K. Kellogg Foundation and the Kellogg Company, made available the pertinent files of the organizations and were able to contribute much to the biography because of their long and intimate associations with the subject. Another long-time associate, Dr. Rowland H. Harris, gave invaluable counsel throughout the writing of the story.

Professional and empathic aid was given to the writer by Mr. Gerald Carson, author of *Early Days in the Breakfast Food Industry* and *The Old Country Store*, and by Mr. Robert R. Updegraff, known for his writings in the business field and as a foods consultant. Grateful acknowledgment also is made for the courtesies extended by the Battle Creek Historical and Archaeological Society, the Willard Library of Battle Creek, the Kingman Museum of Natural History, the *Enquirer and News* of Battle Creek, the Battle Creek Sanitarium, the Kalamazoo Public Library and Museum, the Kellogg-Voorhis Campus of California State Polytechnic College, the Department of Information Service, Michigan State University, the Michigan Historical Commission, and the General Conference of the Seventh-day Adventists.

The author also wishes to acknowledge a broad obligation to two unpublished manuscripts, compiled for and owned by the Kellogg Company—a biographical sketch of Mr. Kellogg by Mr. Putney Haight, and a three-volume history of the Kellogg Company by Horton and Henry, Inc., of New York City.

Many hands helped to shape this book and any failure to acknowledge such assistance indicates an unsystematic but not ungrateful author. Of real importance to the work were interviews and corollary aid granted by the following persons: Miss Mary I. Barber, Miss Linnie Belden, Mrs. Harold Braford, Arthur H. Brown, Miss Leta Browning, Mrs. Kemper Campbell, Miss Margaret M. Canty, Omar Cook, Mrs. Frances S. Cooper, L. C. Coulston, Glenn A. Cross, Mrs. Byron V. Curry, Jr., Dr. Haven Emerson, Frank M. Folkmier, Mrs. Lucille Gardner, Mrs. Alta Hall, Burritt Hamilton, E. L. Harding, Dr. Warren G. Harding, II, Albert W. Harris, Mrs. Rowland H. Harris, Paul A. Herbert, Lewis Hoffman, Dr. W. B. Holden, Dr. B. G. Holtom, ex-President Herbert Hoover, Oliver S. Hott, Otis A. Hudson, Elliott S. Humphrey, Mrs. E. C. Innis, Henry F. Johnson, Dr. Florence Keller, Burton Kellogg, Mrs. John L. Kellogg, Dr. Richard M. Kellogg, W. Keith Kellogg, II, Mr. and Mrs. Wilfred C. Kellogg, Will L. Kellogg, Miss Ruth V. Kelsey, Miss Anita Kritschgau, E. M. Leaver, Mrs. Marvin Lincoln, Mrs. Stanley T. Lowe, C. M. McCrary, Eugene H. McKay, George C. McKay, W. James McQuiston, Glen F. Merriam, A. L. Miller, the Rev. Carleton Brooks Miller, Mr. and Mrs. Clyde H. Miller, E. J. Muss, Dr. Leonora Nash, Mrs. Andrew Ness, R. P. Olmstead, A. B. Olsen, E. O. Orchard, William P. Penty, Charles Peterson, Elder A. K. Phillips, R. S. Poole, Miss Katherine Powell, Miss Lorraine Priest, Edwin Pumala, H. H. Reese, Dr. H. M. S. Richards, Leon V. Roberson, L. C. Roll, Wayne Rosenbaum, Andrew Ross, Dr. William S. Sadler, H. E. Sanders, Mrs. Wesley K. Sayre, Mrs. Kenneth E. Scott, Fred Sherriff, Charles Smith, Walter E. Sooy, B. W. Steinweg of Tabernacle Book Store, Miss Marguerite Swallen,

W. K. Kellogg

E. T. Swan, A. E. Udell, Mrs. Nellie K. Van Schaick, Dr. Henry F. Vaughan, Mrs. Genevieve White Wall, Mrs. Clara Way, Dr. Fred H. Weber, Leonard L. White, John H. Williamson, Kenneth S. Williamson, Norman Williamson, Sr. and Norman Williamson, Jr.

HORACE B. POWELL

Battle Creek, Michigan
August 1, 1955